THROUGH CO

Deleen Wills delights in working from home as a travel coordinator organizing adventures for groups, family and friends. Living with her husband in Oregon after retiring from her work as an administrator in nonprofit education, she volunteers for several nonprofit organizations.

Her passions are globetrotting and writing. She strives to write stories that entertain, enlighten and educate, hopefully encouraging others to realize how easy and enjoyable it is to embrace new friends and gain new insights while exploring our world.

"Travel Opens Your Eyes and Your Heart."
Deleen Wills

Other books by Deleen Wills
BEHIND COLORFUL DOORS
BECAUSE OF COLORFUL DOORS
Available on Amazon

Through Colorful Doors

A trilogy of a globetrotter's
adventures through
Ireland, Ecuador and Peru.

Deleen Wills

This book is a trio of nonfiction
travelogues.

iii

Copyright © 2020 Life of Riley Publishing

Printed by KDP/Amazon

ISBN-13: 9798696999906

First Edition

If you have any comments or questions, please contact Deleen through Facebook at Colorful Doors Adventure Books or deleenwills@gmail.com.

Cover Photo by Deleen Wills, taken in Ireland in 1998.

Back Cover Photo by Sisterchick, Sue Christopherson, taken in Ireland in 2018.

IN MEMORIAM AND DEDICATION:

In memory of my Riley Clan: My darlin' dad, Del Riley, and his sisters, my aunties Patti, Joyce and Colleen, and oldest cousin, Sheri Del.

Dedicated to my cousins: Bill, Brian, Jeff, Patti, John, Jason and Michael, and brothers, Mark and Bruce, all with Irish blood coursing through our veins.

To my extraordinary traveling companion and dear friend Joyce Gleason: For over two decades we've laughed ourselves silly first as roommates chaperoning high school students charging through three countries in twelve days. That was the beginning of more journeys mostly gallivanting throughout Europe. Especially remarkable were our two Iceland treks, and traipsing around and helping me find my roots in bonny Scotland. I will cherish those memories always. Thank you for sharing the adventures with me.

SINCERE THANKS TO:

Beth E. Pitcher	Copy Editor
Jessica Spurrier	Cover Design
NiCole Anderson	Interior Design
Joyce Gleason	Story Consultant

HONORABLE MENTION:

Beth Meredith and April Smith, Collette tour guides extraordinaire, who made Peru and Ireland even more special and educational.

v

ACKNOWLEDGEMENTS

Through Colorful Doors is a collaborative effort and my deepest appreciation goes out to my patient and loving family and friends who encouraged me to continue writing and sharing more travel escapades.

They include but are not limited to:

- Beth E. Pitcher, for expertly and patiently copyediting the stories and allowing me to bounce all kinds of thoughts by her. A dear friend who I would never know if we hadn't met in an elevator in Quito, Ecuador before our Galápagos expedition—serendipity at its finest.
- Jon D. Pitcher, for his expertise in British-isms and English grammar.
- NiCole Anderson, for her talent with technology, crafting the interior design, and for being such a loyal and trusted friend.
- Jessica Spurrier, jacket designer, photographer, graphic designer, artist and friend. See her work at GreengateImages.Etsy.com.
- Sue Christopherson, the sister I never had, who continues to encourage, support and love me as a true Sisterchick does.
- To my cheerleaders for their continued encouragement: Annette, Beth, Carol, Cathy, Davette, Doug, Heather, Jeannie, Joanie, Joyce, Linda, Michelle, Nancy, Peggy, Suzanne, Russ, Kate, Martha and many readers of *Behind Colorful Doors* and *Because of Colorful Doors*.
- Mark Wills, for his ongoing exceptional patience helping with technology issues.

This book was written in 2020 during COVID-19. Hopefully something good comes from the time you spent sequestered safely in your home.

Contents

Contents

The Green Door

Ireland & Northern Ireland with a dab of England

September 2018

My heart thumped an extra beat or two as I told myself to take a slow deep breath. Calm down. Breathe. I re-read the parchment sheet placed in front of me about the history of Cabra Castle. We were in the final night of a two-week Republic of Ireland and Northern Ireland tour in autumn 2018 and we were dining with friends in one of the ornate rooms of the hotel castle. Two lines jumped off the page like they were underlined, in bold and italics, size twenty font and meant to catch my attention: "The Original Cabra Castle, the ruins of which still stand on high ground in Dun Na Rí Forest Park. The Castle and the land surrounding it belonged to the O'Reilly Family until it was confiscated in the mid 17th century by Cromwell's orders and given to Colonel Thomas Cooch." What in the world? I am an O'Reilly.

I'd read in *The Irish Times* newspaper that this castle is the second scariest in the world. I hoped my O'Reilly clan was haunting it, preferably starting with the nasty Englishman Oliver Cromwell and the Cooch family.

Really? Okay, I settled down but needed some time to process this news. I knew my great-great grandparents on my father's side had come from somewhere around the Dublin area. My family name is Riley. What if? I couldn't wait to tell Dad this cool news. He had been the instigator over the years for my curiosity about our Irish roots. Every year for decades he sent me a St. Patrick's Day card addressed to his "Darlin' Daughter" signed by him. Mom usually wrote in a corner in small print, "and me, too." Of course, I knew she picked out the cards but made it seem like it had come from my darlin' Dad.

Excusing myself, I explained needing some time to myself. They understood because my ninety-three-year-old darlin' Dad had passed three weeks earlier.

Wandering out to the gardens of the castle, now turned into a quaint yet modern-day hotel, gray clouds hung low and a gentle drizzle misted the air. The light mist affected the end-of-the-summer flowers and bushes to create a silver shimmery glaze.

"What if?" "What if, what?" I said aloud then looked around to make sure no one stood too close to hear me talking to myself. As I walked around the grounds it felt like I wasn't there but instead outside of my body, actually like a shadow—you know, slightly off-kilter. I had a similar feeling when taking too much cold and flu medicine. Dazed, crazed or serendipity? Maybe all. Looking toward the ruins of the original castle, I saw movement in the distance. In the green field, I saw a person and assumed it was a woman because of the medium length brown hair and her flowing skirt or dress, but I couldn't tell her age.

Closing my eyes, I tipped my face upward feeling the soft mist on my skin. With my eyes still closed, I peeked once to make sure I hadn't been transported somewhere back in time like in the book *Outlander*. No way did I want that to happen.

I imagined seeing a young woman with reddish-brown long hair standing overlooking the sea or had I suddenly been teleported back to the mid-1800s? She watched and felt the breeze blow inland off the water as the waves rose and fell with their white peaks reaching to heaven. The waves crashed against the rocks leaving a white foam that bubbled as the water rolled out. Several seagulls on the beach were squawking noisily. Their bright yellow beaks were accentuated in color due to their head, neck and undercarriage looking pure white, blending into a soft gray body. Two had black backs. Each tail seemed the most remarkable part to me because the feathers looked like they had been dipped in black and white striped paint.

Could this woman be my great-great grandmother Maggie? Two quiet, giant gray wolfhounds romped around her. How did she get

3

there, some twenty miles from what was possibly her husband's family home?

The mist turned to heavier raindrops, maybe trying to wake me up. Shaking my head attempting to snap out of the trance-like state, I retreated wearing no headgear or overcoat to protect me from getting drenched. I was concerned about my mental state at this point, wondering where all this hallucinating about my great-great grandmother and Irish Wolfhounds had come from.

Protected from the rain under an original stately arch in the hotel garden, I glanced around the exterior of the current castle and visualized my O'Reilly ancestors. While hopeful, I knew it was highly unlikely that this could be my ancestors' home, the family castle. I wondered how it might have looked—regal, noble, majestic, stately, or did it resemble the bones of a relic gradually crumbling and deteriorating? Did ivy and weeds tug on the remaining walkway and creep in through the broken empty windows and up staircases stretching its vines to claim every last pillar and rock? Visions of my Mom's family castle, now ruins, in Sanquhar, Scotland, came to mind.

Some information I found in a history book explains that the O'Reillys and Reillys are the descendants of the Gaelic Irish sect, the O'Raghailligh of Breffny whose influence extended to many counties. The O'Reillys were such a powerful influence that at one stage in their reign of power they issued their own coinage. The O'Reillys throughout the centuries have produced churchmen and the long list would bore you. At the time of the Old Gaelic Order in the 17th and 18th centuries, the name was established on the continent of Europe, where the O'Reillys joined the armed services of France, Spain, Italy, Russia, Prussia and Austria. The name was also established in America, where many with the name became prominent. There was Henry O'Reilly (1806-1886) of Carrickmacross in County Monaghan who was a pioneer in telecommunications; Alexander O'Reilly (1845-1912) of Philadelphia was personal physician to President Cleveland; John Boyle O'Reilly (1844-1890) was a poet and newspaperman. There is Dr. A.J.F. O'Reilly or, as his friends called him, Tony, born in Dublin in 1936, who was an international rugby player for Ireland, solicitor and industrialist. He became president of the Heinz Corporation in 1979 and was an initiator of the Irish-American Association.

The O'Reilly motto is: "With Fortitude and Prudence" and the name means "Brave."

Ireland. Mysterious, wild and deeply beautiful—my homeland—well, one of several homelands anyway.

Twenty Years Earlier - August 1998

Taking off from London Heathrow I relaxed in my seat for a short flight to Dublin where our two-week Ireland exploration would begin. Shaking my head, I couldn't believe what we did to ourselves when we arrived one week earlier. After the fifteen hours of travel plus gaining a day, enduring customs, luggage pickup and shuttling to a rental car lot, we got in the red, medium-size manual transmission rental car and drove two hundred seventy miles south on the opposite side of the motorway (like our six-lane freeway), around and around the roundabouts. For some reason I figured we'd be fine with less than adequate sleep. I had pages of paper with the printed MapQuest directions including how to get out of the airport parking lot which was the first challenge of that early morning.

Cornwall would be our final destination as Part One of our adventure because we were fascinated by it since watching a 1970s British historical drama series shown on Masterpiece Theater on PBS. Poldark, the name of the series and central character, depicted the tough tin and copper mine industry during the late 1700s.

I'd done research in seeking accommodations on the water, and found the Don & Shirley Pengilly Bed & Breakfast, boasting beautiful sea views over St. Michael's Mount. The address sounded as cute as I imagined the lodging would be: Castle Nook, Turnpike Road, Marazion, Cornwall, population one thousand, two hundred eight. The Pengilly's children had grown and the parents converted one bedroom and added a tiny bathroom for rent. The adequate room had a double bed, dresser and a chair and was, as promised, on the waterfront. Right outside the bedroom window was St. Michael's Mount surrounded by water looking almost like an island. After dropping our luggage, we walked across the street for traditional fish and chips at The Tudor Chippy and around the cute coastal town. We went to bed before dark and fell into and sunk down in a small bed for an okay night's sleep.

After breakfast, Shirley suggested we walk over to the Mount with the tide being low. The Mount wasn't an island after all but an elevated walkway across the beach and rocks with the water parted on both sides. She told us to be mindful of the incoming tide or we'd be wading back waist high in water, or we could just take a boat ride which would be easiest and safest.

The granite crag rises from the waters of Mount's Bay and has perched on its top an embattled castle, originally a Benedictine Priory built in the 12th century. From 1660 until the present, it is the home of the St. Aubyn family. Inside the hall are the living quarters of the Captain of the Mount. A private sitting room of the owner and The Armoury contain sporting weapons and military trophies from various wars. The Library, formerly the breakfast room, is the oldest part of the castle. There were many more rooms, passages, staircases and a church we were welcome to visit. From the North Terrace, there are views of Marazion and the beaches. The South Terrace has a small walled garden containing subtropical plants not often found in England.

Just as Shirley said, the tide came in and we watched the brave (or stupid) ones on the walkway knee-high in sea water. We took the boat taxi back and walked around our cute little town lined with palm trees, orchids, hot pink hydrangeas, stone buildings, colorful doors and other tourists in shorts and tee-shirts enjoying the south coast of England.

That afternoon we drove to Penzance on Mount's Bay, the most westerly town in Cornwall and then to Merry Maidens, a Bronze Age stone circle where nineteen girls turned into stone for dancing on a Sunday. Down the road is Minack Theatre, an ancient Greek-style theater with the blue sea as a backdrop. Looking down below at the beach, we saw sunbathers enjoying the warmth, surfers trying with little wave-action, and palm trees and colorful plants littering the edges of the beach. I certainly didn't picture palm trees in England. Palms grow here due to the warming influence of the Gulf Stream with waters from the tropics. The coastline looked perilously rugged just like I'd seen in Poldark. We poked around an old tin mine. Many low-lying stone walls separated properties.

Standing at a sign, "Land's End, Penn-an-wlas," we gazed at the seafoam and aqua ocean below dotted with islands. After dinner, we actually stayed up long enough to see the colors created by the sunset reflected on the bay.

Thanking the Pengillys and leaving them a small token of appreciation, we bid farewell to them and this beautiful coastline region. Staying off the zippy motorway, driving the calmer and more interesting back roads, about four hours later we arrived in Winchester. We found the Best Western Royal Hotel without any problems by following pages six through nine in my MapQuest volume. For some reason they gave us the Millner Suite with three separate rooms and a lovely view of the city. In the early evening, we spotted a hot air balloon floating in the distance. If we'd had more energy we would have chased it down as we also had a hot air balloon. We were in for the night.

Since we were in Winchester, after picking up pastries and hot coffee and tea for breakfast we thought it only appropriate to see Winchester Cathedral, stunning on its own and probably made more popular by the Beatles song with the same name. Jane Austen and Izaak Walton are buried here. Students relaxed reading books, children romped in the grass and people strolled through the gardens.

At three o'clock we arrived at the home of dear friends Pearl and Howard who lived in Abingdon, a small town not far from Oxford, where Pearl worked at Mansfield College at Oxford University. I'd met Pearl through our mutual work at educational institutions and her college had hosted my alumni travel groups for several years.

We excitedly got up and around the next morning because they were taking us on a road trip and both worked hard trying to dream up special things for us to see and do. We drove through the ritzy Somerset district toward our overnight accommodations. Giving us no hints, we were stunned as we drove down the streets of Banwell, pulling into a castle and checking in at the hotel. The gothic revival castle, built in the late 1800s, surrounded a medieval house. It sits on twenty-one acres of grounds and gardens and is furnished in a Victorian style. We were booked into the Master Suite with a four-poster bed and canopy with curtains in a pastel floral design surrounding the entire double bed. Double doors opened onto our veranda overlooking the gardens.

We sat outside in the sunshine watching chickens, turkeys and peacocks roaming the gardens with an occasional romping red squirrel and lots of birds entertaining us while we sipped tea, ate crustless sandwiches and devoured sweet treats.

That afternoon we drove to the Wookey Hole Showcaves and Papermill where we saw how paper had been painstakingly made during Shakespeare's day. We also went into the Great Caves, famous since the Roman times. Carved out by the River Axe, the Cathedral Cave is brought to life by an atmospheric light and sound show.

Dinner reservations had been made that evening at the castle and we were about the only ones there except for a group having a birthday party for one of the adults in the family. They were eating and drinking and having a merry, very merry, time.

We had a delicious dinner in the softly lit dining room, each of us ordering something different from the menu to share small bites with each other. About the time we were finished with dessert, I'd picked up my purse and placed it on my lap as I thought we were leaving. One of the men in the party group came over to apologize for their noisy frivolity and offered us each an after-dinner drink of brandy. A large glass (much larger than a wine glass) with about a half-inch of brown liquid appeared and I was instructed only to sip it. This would be my first (and last) sip of brandy. I sniffed it first which made my eyes water and I sneezed really hard. Everyone laughed except me because I thought a contact lens from my right eye popped out. I wore hard contacts and this, although rare, could happen. Before I overreacted, I carefully ran my hands over my blouse hoping to catch it there. I informed the others what I thought had happened and before I knew it we were each on all fours gently feeling the carpet under the table. Yuck. I felt other things but not my contact.

I excused myself to go to the restroom thinking maybe it had slipped down into the lower lid. Those who have ever worn hard contact lenses would know exactly what I am referring to. In the dimly lit restroom, I couldn't see a thing. I returned knowing I'd just have to see out of my left eye or wear my pop-bottle thick glasses for the upcoming two weeks. I alerted the dining room staff of my predicament.

When we returned to our suite, I poked around my poor eyeball looking underneath my upper eyelid, down in the white part at the bottom of my eye, all in a dimly lit bathroom. I used our mini-Maglite, holding a flashlight in one hand while trying to pull down my eyelid with the other hand. My red eye hurt like heck. I went to sleep and tried not to obsess about it. In twenty years of wearing contact lenses I'd never, ever lost one. And I didn't have an extra pair with me because they were expensive. No more thinking about my lost contact, I'd just deal with it. But it still hurt.

The next morning while we were having a delicious breakfast, the staff reported that they carefully had cleaned up and did not find my lens. How kind of them for trying. The breakfast at Banwell, fit for a queen and king with tea and lots of food, appeared on china with matching placemats in a blue and white design.

Howard told Mark he'd set up a unique adventure for themselves and we were heading there next. The narrow gorge we drove through has a rock outcropping that looks like a huge lion. In a short time, we arrived at Cheddar and the home of Cheddar Showcaves & Gorge. The immense gorge splits the Mendip Hills from top to bottom. And some say it is the origin of cheddar cheese.

My poor husband had no clue that what was about to happen to him would scar him for the rest of his life. But what a story he would have to share. We learned "showcaves" in England means a place to see caves.

Howard had booked an adventure caving expedition for him and Mark without consulting Mark. Normally this would have been about the last thing my husband would ever do. Climbing around in caves tied to lines in the pitch dark with only a helmet light, up and down and across bottomless ravines, would be illegal in the USA. Howard thought it sounded marvelous and like great fun.

While waiting for their check-in time we had a few minutes for a cold beverage sitting outside at a café. Howard had a bit of a headache and asked me if I had any tablets; we call it a pill. I knew I had a few ibuprofen pills in my small makeup bag in my purse and I saw three loose ones that had sunk to the bottom of my small clear clutch. One looked weird being a strange color. I gently pulled it out and there, adhered like glue to the brick-colored pill, was my blue contact lens. When it popped out of my eye the night before it dropped into my purse that I had placed on my lap. Safe and sound. All four of us were astonished and laughing hysterically as Howard said, "Well, you certainly live the Life of Riley." Then I had to tell him my maiden name is Riley.

Our men, one reluctant and the other giddy, disappeared getting ready for the expedition. Mark had dressed in khakis and a polo shirt that he'd also be wearing for the next couple of weeks. We learned to mix and match clothing and pack light from our travel guru Rick Steves.

Pearl and I on the other hand, took a walk through a cave and saw some stalactites and stalagmites but we were far more interested in the glassmaking demonstration, heritage center, crafts and engravings, cheese and cider depot and spending some money.

We were to meet our husbands at a designated time and place a few hours later. Pearl and I had a marvelous time and knew our time had come to an end so walked to the exit area of the cave experience. Out walked my husband as pale as I'd ever seen him, clothes filthy even though they had coveralls on, and a bit unsteady on his feet. Then we heard the entire story. To this day, when he repeats the harrowing adventure, it's as if no time has passed.

The Timeless Cheddar Cave brochure was full of information but here is what is says about Adventure Caving: "Cheddar Caves provides a helmet, lamp and boilersuit (our coveralls) and groups of up to ten persons are taken into these wild areas by an expert caver. Four chambers are visited: Sandy Chamber, Mushroom Chamber and then down a forty-foot ladder to Boulder Chamber before climbing into Far Rift, the fourth and last chamber. Exiting via April Fool Squeeze, a small passage blasted out on April 1, 1982, and around the Wire Traverse Ledge. There are a few formations in this part of the cave but the spirit of the exploration takes over everyone who struggles through the environment of total darkness. When standing on the site of Lafferty's camp, one can appreciate the enormity of his achievement. The expedition is designed to be as much like a normal caving trip as possible. It is a dangerous sport and just because it is taking place at the rear of the showcave makes it no less so. Participant's safety is therefore of paramount importance. By the end of the trip the full significance of the motto is realized: It's hard, It's dirty but it's Fun!"

My husband would say two out of three are correct. And nobody exiting smiled the way they were showing in the color promotional materials.

That night we returned to Pearl and Howard's bungalow in Abingdon and after playing the best two out of three games of crazy golf, our mini golf, we had a delicious dinner of assorted Chinese dishes at one of their favorite restaurants.

We went to bed with Mark taking some ibuprofen on spec. We washed his clothes three times then threw them away when the Cheddar cave dirt didn't come out and certainly was not a souvenir he wished to keep. Now down one pair of pants and shirt for the next two weeks, his luggage became lighter.

The next morning, we dropped Pearl off at Mansfield College and with hugs and tears said farewell until they would come to visit us the following year. Pearl was like the sister I never had. We drove back to Heathrow, returned the snazzy red car miraculously unscratched and boarded our flight. I chuckled pretty much the entire flight to Dublin especially recalling the caving incident.

My Celtic roots were tingling, jumping and dancing a jig as we were about to touch ground for the first time in the homeland of my paternal grandfather's family. Peering out the window of our airplane, several thousand feet below lay a plaid quilt of various shades of green. I spotted green tones of basil, lime, celadon, fern, mint and pine in the miles-wide circle before flying over a city with spires looking historic and gray. We landed in Dublin.

As a Riley, I was heading to my fatherland, so to speak. I grew up hearing some but not a lot about my Irish roots, honestly, because we knew almost nothing. We mainly understood that we had Irish blood coursing through our veins; therefore, we were highly susceptible to alcoholism, so we were never to drink anything with alcohol—ever.

We only knew that my father's great grandparents, Michael O'Reilly and Mary Margaret McGinnes, called Maggie, lived somewhere around Dublin but left by ship from County Cork. They fled because of the Great Famine hoping for a better life.

They had choices of where to start anew. Undoubtedly, many of their young friends and some family were also going, if they were still alive. Should it be to America, Australia or to Canada? Had they remained they could have been in the statistics of the one million who perished. Then I wouldn't be here.

I fantasized that Maggie was riding her brown horse carrying a pouch full of soda bread, potato scones and cheese to share with her red-headed, blue-eyed love, Michael. Did they plan a clandestine rendezvous away from the glaring sad eyes?

Definitely into the drama of Irish history, the truth is that most of my family roots were not factual; we just didn't know for sure. I don't know how much my great grandparents suffered until they left for America. Did they leave earlier than other friends and family? Did they wait so long only to see many friends and family die from starvation, suffering totally unnecessary deaths because no one from other countries would help, not even England?

When did they learn the devastating news that much of their crops of oats and rye were being shipped to the continent not even feeding their own people? Did they try to overtake a squad of dragoons, attired in red vests and long breeches, with wagons loaded with bags of their oats and other foodstuffs, headed to a port? The laws regarding exports wouldn't be changed in time to make a difference. Or would they be among those who did fight back?

They, like other tenants, needed to make money to pay their rents to their English landlords. And they could only do that by selling the food they grew. My thoughts turned dark as I pictured sad ghosts in their dirty worn clothes, huddled along the side of a road, many clutching one bag of belongings. Sunken faces and eyes, starving people with nowhere to go. Proud people turned into beggars. How could the government let this happen, I incredulously asked myself? Over two hundred years later, certainly we would all learn from history and never allow something like that to happen ever again, anywhere in the world.

I had read dozens of historical fiction and nonfiction tearjerkers which didn't help my emotional state at all. It was disturbing and heartbreaking to read descriptions of how Irish properties were taken by Englishmen who were clueless about Irish traditions, then turning Irish property owners into tenants, having to work and pay to live on what had been originally their property. Most English landowners didn't even spend time at their estates and hired an agent, usually someone originally living there, to oversee the land while they continued to reside in England. And most inherited their estate through English lineage. I felt pretty sorry for my Irish ancestors.

I recalled my Scottish roots and my mother's family's similar situation where my great-great grandfather was the caretaker or agent of a castle owned by an English lord. I was fortunate to have visited this small village in the borderland region of "bonnie Scotland" the year before.

Most Irish tenants lived in sod houses on the estate acreage that had been divided and then subdivided to accommodate the growing tenant populations. I saw photos of fields that were split by rectangular walls constructed of brush and stone. The tenant farmers lived on these plots of land. Fertile potato ridges, abundant with green leaves, cut across their tracts.

At some point, my Irish great-great grandparents learned of the rot and decay that quickly spread through their potato crops. Most women were taught only how to prepare food and meals made of potatoes. Did Maggie's mother ponder what to cook when potatoes were no longer available?

Most farmers had crops of oats and rye in some other parcels. As more lush potato ridges turned dark, their leaves crinkled and blackened quickly; some called it The Plague. There were comments that the summer of 1845 had been mild and wet, excellent for growing potatoes. Some would say the curse came from the rain and wind, others blamed insects, and some feared there were those who would claim it came from God. More positive souls would say not to worry about such things, luck would provide. I can only imagine my family discussing these issues, realizing the crop was ruined and they'd have to start over for the spring. How would they pay the rent if they would have to eat oats and rye that they normally sold? Without potatoes there would be nothing to eat. These questions went around and around, apparently with no answers.

The Great Famine, or the Irish Potato Famine, was a horrible time of disease, mass starvation and emigration between the years 1845 to 1849. The population fell by about twenty-five percent due to both emigration and death, and it's estimated that about one million people died and a million more left Ireland for a better life. The greatest areas affected were to the south and west of Ireland. Their widely spoken Gaelic language lost a great number of its speakers to death and emigration due to poverty.

My family, Michael O'Reilly and Mary McGinnes, from somewhere around Dublin, selected the United States of America. I have no accurate details of their journey. I can only speculate from the multitude of historical readings I've perused. It's safe to say it wasn't a pleasant journey. Many were seasick the entire time.

The first thing that happened coming through Ellis Island would be the change of the spelling to Riley. It became commonplace that immigrants changed the spelling of their original names or changed them completely to sound less ethnic and more American. Sometimes an immigration officer shortened or wrote the name as he heard it. We assume they could only afford steerage, so had to undergo inspection at Ellis Island. First- and second-class passengers received a quick inspection while on board ship based on the notion that "if people could afford to purchase a first- or second-class ticket, they were less likely to become a public charge in America due to medical or legal reasons," says the Statue of Liberty-Ellis Island Foundation.

The five hundred or so employees at the station had to work quickly during those first waves of immigration, processing each immigrant in a matter of four to seven hours. The inspectors interviewed four to five hundred people in a day, processing a million a year during the peak of the flow.

In the mid-1800s Irish immigration was not a new event. It had been increasing since the 1820s right along with dramatic increases in the Irish population itself. Data show that the largest numbers of immigrants coming into the United States as a result of the potato famine settled in two states—Massachusetts and New York. Most were encouraged to bring enough money to move west where land and jobs were greater and not stay in Boston and New York City. Most could not as the emigration from Ireland took their entire fortune.

Port cities like Boston, New York, Philadelphia and New Orleans became overwhelmed with the new arrivals from Ireland and the disease and poverty that came with them.

Michael and Maggie are recorded in the first records I can find and are on page thirty-nine of the United States census in 1865 in Carroll, New York. Records show sons John and Daniel were both born in New Jersey. I know the family moved to western New York State and lived there for a while. They are listed again in 1870 living in the same area. We know that they had four children born in the United States but read somewhere that they had two in Ireland. Well, maybe. Did they leave them with family until they got established somewhere in America? Their first, John, was born in 1845, the first official year of the potato famine, followed by Daniel, Kathryn and James. James, born in 1852, is recorded in Trenton, New Jersey. He is my great grandfather. So, for sure, they arrived before 1845 hopefully before the potato famine, causing hundreds to die daily.

Great grandfather James married Lina Ingrabretson who was born outside of Oslo, Norway. However, it was spelled "Engelbretsen" in Norway. She passed October 4, 1946 in Chinook, Montana. James and Lina had four daughters and seven sons, one being my grandfather, William McKinley Riley, born 1901 and died in 1979.

I did learn more of the recent Riley family history about my great grandfather James and great grandmother Lina. Now I want to explore Norway one day. This definitely wasn't a happily-ever-after story.

After James and Lina married, they moved to North Dakota where Lina's brother John lived. Then they moved to Montana because land was given to those who would be farmers. Great grandpa James had a large farm outside of Hingham, Montana.

I'd heard off and on over the years when the Riley history came up that great grandpa James shot himself with his rifle in his barn. As a child, this led me to questions but all we knew is that he had a severe illness for several years which caused much pain and he couldn't deal with it any longer. Today we call it stomach cancer. His obituary from the *Hingham Review*, March 7, 1913 read:

Last Wednesday this community was shocked and saddened to learn that James Riley, a responsible farmer living seven miles south of town, had committed suicide. He shot himself in the right temple with a rifle. Mr. Riley had been in poor health for the past year and during several weeks prior to his death had been confined to his bed most of the time. He had never said anything that would lead anyone to think he intended suicide, and was kind and cheerful to his family to the last. On Wednesday afternoon he walked out in the yard with the rifle concealed under his fur overcoat and committed the terrible deed, which is thought it have been the result of a temporary derangement of the mind. Everyone has unbounded sympathy for his family and especially for his good wife, who is considered a blessing to the community in the way of caring for sick people. The Rileys are held in high esteem by their neighbors.

Then a follow-up article on March 14, 1913 read:

James Riley's Funeral

Last Sunday afternoon a large concourse of people gathered at Kimpel's Opera House to pay their last respects to James Riley, deceased. Mr. Riley was 61 years of age and leaves a wife, three daughters, and seven sons to mourn his loss. One son, J.E. Riley, arrived from Mobridge, SD, to be in attendance at his father's funeral.

The deceased had suffered much during the past five years from an ailment of the stomach, from which there seemed to be no relief. He was considered a good man by those who knew him. The family have the profound sympathy of everyone in the community.

Trying to keep some of my family history in mind, even though I had no proof of exactly where they were from (I'd heard County Cork and around Dublin), I was there to soak in whatever history vibes I could.

Embarking on a two-week tour using *Europe Through the Backdoor* for its expertise, and with sixteen of our favorite travel buddies, we arrived and began our tour in Dublin staying in the historic district at the Harding Hotel where Dublin's oldest medieval street, Copper Alley, actually runs through the hotel's reception area. Our modest room, situated directly above the bar, had a large window with side panels that opened for fresh air. Out our window stood the majestic Christ Church, with lovely quarterly bells, except in the middle of the night. Nigel Murray, originally from Kilkenny now living in Dublin, would be our experienced motorcoach driver for the two weeks. Our guide Roy hailed from Somerset in merry old England.

That night we ate our first Irish dinner at The Shack Restaurant, right in the heart of the renowned Temple Bar district. Walking in felt like a step back in time with wide plank hardwood floors, walls adorned with pictures and photographs of scenery and still life fruit and vegetables. Doing a complete three sixty of this charming eating establishment, the wooden walls blended with blocked gray stone walls and more artwork. Light poured in from the only window, and a section of the wall displayed colorful patterned Irish plates on wall racks.

Temple Bar has the reputation as a cultural area in the heart of Dublin. Covering just a few blocks on the south bank of the River Liffey, the area contains everything from the best restaurants and lively bars, to theaters and art galleries situated on charming cobblestone alleyways with street performers galore. Kelly green, dazzling white and blaze orange pennants waved in the gentle breezes on many buildings and across alleys.

Appetizers are called Starters and that's what we had, beginning with oak-smoked Irish salmon with homemade brown bread for me, and garlic mussels in their shell, tossed in a pan with garlic butter and white wine, for my husband. For the main entrée I selected the traditional fare of Bacon and Cabbage. The loin of bacon is traditionally cooked and served with buttered cabbage and parsley sauce. It tasted flavorful and hearty. My husband had Irish stew made with lamb, carrots and potatoes. This would be just the beginning of eating potatoes prepared in dozens of different ways.

We woke up to sunny skies, a perfect way to begin our day of exploring historic Dublin. Our first stop would be Trinity College and the famous *The Book of Kells*. What are these books exactly? Roy explained they contain a Latin text of the four gospels copied and beautifully decorated by Irish monks around 800 AD and contains six hundred eighty pages. Since the 1660s, it has been safely stored at Trinity College Dublin and exhibited in the college library since the mid-19th century. Other medieval copies of the gospels ranging from the 5th to 15th centuries are on display, showing that in the Middle Ages, copies of the gospels needed to be made in large quantities, all by hand.

Viewed by looking down at the open pages protected under thick glass, the printing of the letters and numbers was straight and narrow. The ink colors were vibrant and amazingly well-preserved. Display after display showed the artisans' painstaking work of this transcription. One life-size display stated that most of the text pages were written in iron gall ink made from oak galls (or oak apples), mixed with iron sulphate and wine or vinegar. Some lines of writing were in yellow, purple or red.

Another display was labeled "Pigments." It explained that pigments were made from a variety of mineral and organic sources in early medieval Ireland. The yellow came from the mineral orpiment and yellow arsenic sulfide, known as a gold pigment. Purple was created from a dye from an orchid lichen. This was mixed with white to create pink. Different pigments were displayed in photographs of a dog-looking creature, a cross, a person and script writing. Reading all of this certainly gave me an appreciation of what creative scientists they had hundreds of years ago. I couldn't even imagine how long it took to find and then experiment with these plants, minerals and other things in order to get these colors that withstood the sands of time.

We sauntered to the Long Room, really the main chamber of the Old Library, over two hundred feet long. The dark wood columns flanking each alcove of precious materials seemed to stretch forever. It houses around two hundred thousand of the library's oldest books. It is kept a bit dark to protect precious history and smelled like old books—musty. When built, it had a flat plaster ceiling with shelves for all the books on the lower level. By the 1850s the shelves were bursting at the seams. In 1860, the roof was raised to allow the construction of the present barrel-vaulted ceiling and gallery bookcases.

The Pantheon in the library displays busts of famous and important men such as scientists, statesmen, writers, philosophers and thinkers from history (not a woman in sight), and lines both sides of the Long Room. The farther away, the smaller the statues appeared, becoming white dots instead of a man's head. This collection began in 1743 and supposedly a committee drew up names of the "greats" they wanted included. A variety of artists were commissioned. I spotted Aristotle, who seemed impressed with himself looking lofty or even haughty. Also included are Homer, Isaac Newton, Plato and then William Shakespeare wearing a collared jacket, just as we've seen pictures of him with wavy hair, mustache and beard. Many had curly hair and frilly collars; some were clean-shaven and some not. There is an Irishman, writer Jonathan Swift, author of Gulliver's Travels, with a full head of wavy hair and wearing a scarf around his neck tucked under his jacket. But they all had one thing in common—they were carved of white marble.

Walking a bit farther I came upon The Harp. It is the oldest to survive from Ireland and probably dates from the 15th century, they say. It is constructed from oak and willow with brass strings. I always appreciated harp music and now had even higher esteem for the musicians who mastered such an instrument.

We also got a glimpse at a copy of the 1916 Proclamation of the Irish Republic. This signaled the start of the Easter Rising when read aloud outside the General Post Office on April 24, 1916.

This college library is one of the world's great research libraries holding thousands of large collections of manuscripts and printed books in Ireland. Working at a university, I appreciated this library and the valuable resource it is for students who are privileged to study here. I can see how one could get lost in history for days and days.

We stopped at the café for cranberry bread and a bottle of pink lemonade made in Ireland by D.P. Connelly & Sons, Merchant Family. I always try to support local businesses when traveling and this brew did not disappoint. In the library shop, I purchased a pencil, as I did at any university I visited around the world. Another memento was The Book of Kells made into a bookmark calendar, every month showing different scenes from the Kells.

Strolling down O'Connell Street we stood at the base of a well-preserved statue of the man himself, Daniel O'Connell, the liberator and elected Member of Parliament for County Clare in 1828. Below him, flanking the base of the monument were four winged angels that represent virtues attributed to O'Connell: courage, fidelity, patriotism and eloquence. It is large and impressive. I read that he is known as the liberator and a major Irish political leader at the beginning of the 19th century, best known for campaigning for Catholic emancipation and for arguing for the repeal of the Act of Union 1800, which tied Great Britain and Ireland into one "United Kingdom." Throughout his life he never supported the use of violence but rather believed the Irish should instead assert themselves politically. Being Catholic, this prevented him from reaching the uppermost circles of his profession.

There were more castles in Ireland than I could count. Our first, Dublin Castle, made of brown stone on the bottom with reddish on the top half, has a six-sided clock with a pistachio green top that displayed almost noon. I read in my guidebook that this castle is one of the most important buildings in Irish history. From 1204 until 1922 it was the seat of English, then later British, rule. During that time, it served principally as a residence for the British monarch's Irish representative, the Viceroy of Ireland, and as a ceremonial and administrative center. The castle was originally developed as a medieval fortress under the orders of King John of England. Constructed on elevated ground once occupied by an early Viking settlement, the old castle stood approximately on the site of the present Upper Castle Yard. It remained largely intact until April 1684, when a major fire caused severe damage to much of the building. Despite the extent of the fire, parts of the medieval and Viking structures survived and are still available for visitors, lucky us. Viking history is all over Ireland, much like Scotland, I found. And I have Norwegian and Swedish DNA coursing through me so it made perfect sense to feel such a kinship and empathy for these people and countries.

Following the fire, a campaign of rebuilding in the late 17th and 18th centuries saw the castle transformed from the medieval bastion into a Georgian palace. The new building includes a suite of grand reception rooms known as the State Apartments. These palatial spaces accommodated the Viceroy for state occasions. In the early 19th century the castle was enhanced by the addition of the Chapel Royal in the Lower Castle Yard. It remains one of the architectural highlights of Georgian Dublin today. This explained the influence of the many Georgian-style colorful doors we would see.

On January 16, 1922, the last Viceroy of Ireland handed Dublin Castle over to Michael Collins and the government of the newly independent Irish state. The end of the British presence had come about in the wake of the Easter Rising of 1916 and the Irish War of Independence. These momentous events paved the way for the creation of the Republic of Ireland and were closely associated with the history of Dublin Castle. Irish governments have continued to use it for important national events, such as state dinners and commemorations.

Over the centuries, those entertained at Dublin Castle have included Benjamin Franklin in 1771, the Duke of Wellington in 1807, Daniel O'Connell in 1841, Queen Victoria four times between 1849 to 1900, Charles Dickens in 1864, Princess Grace of Monaco in 1961, John F. Kennedy in 1963, Nelson Mandela in 1990 and Queen Elizabeth in 2011. Somewhat fascinated by the British royal family, I hoped to see the regal and stately Queen Elizabeth, who is the exact age of my mother. Several years later I would serendipitously encounter Queen Elizabeth in Victoria, British Columbia, and Nelson Mandela in Oxford, England. You can read about these exploits in *Because of Colorful Doors*.

I had no idea of the captivating history surrounding this castle. Inside, the tour started with the medieval undercroft and the mini-Dublin history lesson referenced above. The medieval undercroft is basically the ruins of the original castle that are under the administration building. They created a nice stairway and walkways so you can get close to the history without damaging it. You can even view a bit of the city walls and the River Poddle that flows under the city.

Next, we visited the Chapel Royal, which opened in 1814 replacing an earlier church on this site. There is ornate and elaborate woodwork inside the chapel. Downstairs, it felt cooler and darker in the crypt of the Chapel Royal, and there is the Revenue Museum which offers insights into the history of taxes in Ireland.

We were guided into the opulent State Apartments appearing exactly as you'd expect the inside of some magnificent castle to look. The walls in each room were painted a different color with plenty of gold and shiny impressive chandeliers with hundreds of glistening crystals in the shape of raindrops. The tapestries adorning the walls, the carpets on the floors, plus a splendid staircase, communicated stately magnificence. This was no ordinary majestic staircase; it was, in fact, a Grand Staircase, and the first of its type in Dublin. Its architectural form created a suitably regal first impression of the State Apartments. During the social season, debutantes and members of the aristocracy ascended this staircase in grand attire on their way to attend balls, dinners and presentation ceremonies given by the Viceroy. Since 1938, it has been part of the main ceremonial route used during the inauguration of the President of Ireland in the State Apartments. I pictured our famous American Princess Grace of Monaco on the grand staircase, gracefully descending, gliding, almost floating down, just like in the movies.

The Wedgwood Room used the blue and white color scheme that mimics the colors of Wedgwood pottery. Completed in 1777 in the neoclassical design, it later became the castle's billiard room. Lit only from above by a small glass-domed roof, it was a favorite place in the 19th century for the creation of temporary indoor gardens filled with exotic birds, trees and water fountains.

The Portrait Gallery has two walls filling almost every inch with paintings of important people and a dining room where state dinners were held in the early 18th century. This room continues to be used for state receptions by the Irish government. The elegant dining table is laid with Waterford crystal and the Irish State dinner service, which features the national emblem—the gold harp.

The Throne Room, created in 1788, has an audience chamber in which the Viceroy received guests on behalf of the British monarch. The throne was made for the visits to Ireland by King George IV in 1821. Later, Queen Victoria and King Edward VII used it during their visits to the castle.

The State Drawing Room is chock-full of marble-carved busts, gold-framed portraits, full-size sculptures of whomever, all against red walls. There is an ornate tapestry carpet with a pinkish sofa across from a grouping of uncomfortable-looking chairs, with vases, clocks, candlestick holders, and three large crystal chandeliers overhead.

We entered the Connelly Room that is named after James Connelly who led the Easter Rising in 1916. Not only one of the signers of the Proclamation of the Irish Republic, he was held here as a wounded prisoner. The Easter Rising being unsuccessful, Connelly was executed. This did not sit well with the Irish people and therefore increased their quest for Irish independence. The round plaque on the wall reads "In this room, James Connolly signatory to the proclamation of the Irish Republic lay a wounded prisoner prior to his execution by the British Military forces at Kilmainham Jail and his interment at Arbour Hill 12th May 1916."

We ended the tour in St. Patrick's Hall, the largest room in the State Apartments. Parliament used to meet in this room but now it is used for inaugurations and other stately functions. You can sense the importance of this room by the magnificent paintings, the royal blue carpet with columns of gold, and mammoth sparkling chandeliers. Square tapestry flags flanked each side of many mirrors.

Walking through the Temple Bar district located in an area on the south bank of the River Liffey in central Dublin, our guide mentioned there were over six hundred pubs in Dublin. Temple Bar is crammed not only with taverns but shops, restaurants, attorneys' and doctors' offices.

Not far away sits the creepy and sad former Kilmainham Gaol, commonly known as Dublin Jail. It opened in 1796 as the county jail for Dublin. The doors closed in 1924. Today it is a museum symbolizing the tradition of militant and constitutional nationalism from the Rebellion of 1798 to the Irish Civil War of 1922-23. On wall plaques I read that leaders of the rebellions of 1798, 1803, 1848, 1867 and 1916 were detained and in some cases executed here. Many members of the Irish Republican movement during the Anglo-Irish

War (1919-21) were also detained in this jail, guarded by British troops. Not only were notables housed here but it held thousands of ordinary men, women and children. Their crimes ranged from petty offenses such as stealing food to more serious crimes such as murder or rape. Convicts from many parts of Ireland were held here for long periods waiting to be transported to Australia. The New Jail, built as a response to the poor conditions of prisons in the 18th century, soon had many of same problems of the old jail, mainly as a result of overcrowding. Until the 1860s, overcrowding led to disease, poor health and hygiene and no full separation of adult and child or male and female prisoners. The prison reform movement, led by John Howard, protested this atmosphere and encouraged a move to single cells, and facilities for hygiene and health.

Many Irish revolutionaries, including leaders of the 1916 Easter Rising, were imprisoned and executed in the prison by the British. Not only notables but many were there for stealing a slice of bread to feed their family, or for throwing a stone breaking a window. A plaque outside prison cells reads "John Shaw (32) Shoemaker. Breaking a window and stealing bread thereout. Sentence: One Month."

The exterior of one door had been painted orange at one point, then black. Blotches of orange bled through the black, like a bright personality trying to escape darkness. On the back wall of another cell hung an oval painting of Mary holding baby Jesus. There were scribbled names etched in walls. Spiral staircases led to the second and third floors as a way for a quick ascent if the main staircase wasn't fast enough. Three stories of rooms in a circular fashion are lined up directly above the next. As I walked into a cell and closed the heavy solid wooden door with only a small hole for identification, communication or light, I felt a chill of dread and thankful my relatives didn't end up here but instead left for a new life in America.

Back outside we meandered up a street lined with colorful Georgian doors. They seemed out of place, newer than the rest of the area. An emerald door and a ruby door surrounded by ivy, adorned the side-by-side homes. Sometimes called the Doors of Dublin, Merrion Square is one of the most intact Georgian Squares and where Oscar Wilde lived. Lower Baggot Street is near Merrion Square and has many beautiful doors along both sides. Fitzwilliam Square is the smallest of Dublin's great Georgian squares and one of the last Georgian squares built in Dublin. Many of the buildings are covered in ivy.

I really wanted to peek inside of one of those colorful doors. I had become obsessed with colorful doors the year before on our trip to Scotland. Sometimes things happened to me because of colorful doors. I have a special word, "graviosity," a combination I made up. But sometimes it happens, gravity and curiosity blend to cause a pleasant surprise around or behind or through a colorful door. Maybe it would happen on this adventure, maybe not. But I felt a tug to the green door that was slightly ajar; did I dare?

In a row doors are crimson, cherry red, sunshine yellow and slate blue with a white H in the ornate scrollwork in the fanlight. Two black doors are side-by-side with one surrounded in beige and the other in white woodwork and fanlights. A fuchsia door is right next to a periwinkle, purplish blue door, both without as much fanlight flare as the others. Two doors were almost identical shades of sunshine yellow except for the mail slots and door knockers.

Our guide told us that these doors can be traced back to the 1700s, when the old medieval city began growing and becoming quite prosperous. Fast expansion led to remodeling of the city's streets and squares and a need to develop outside the city center, especially to create residential areas. Strict codes were enforced for structural designs which created restrictions for buildings. The resulting style and time period had come to be known as Georgian Dublin, named for four kings that ruled during that period. To show some individuality and set themselves apart, the former residents of Georgian Dublin painted their front doors whatever color they fancied. Breaking from the strict architectural uniformity, residents started adding their own touches to set their houses apart from others. These flairs of personality or maybe independence included fancy knockers, intricate designs or fanlights above the door and most striking, front doors painted in a variety of colors. Today, most of the houses have their original fanlights, some still with box-shaped glass recesses in which a lamp would have been placed.

Christ Church stands guard above the River Liffey. On the borders of the lawn surrounding the church were orange geraniums with bushes of delicate yellow flowers filling in the corners. Light and darker gray blocks of stone, lengthy and tall stained glass windows and lots of arches were my first impressions. When approaching the church, it looks like it is protecting its neighborhood from evil. And it is ancient, built in 1172 to 1220.

Our guide explained that over the centuries, Christ Church accommodated many significant events including the crowning of Edward VI in 1487. Today, it houses the important Treasures of Christ Church which features manuscripts and ancient artifacts as well as a spectacular exhibition of original 16th century costumes.

Constructed in the early 12th century, and still the oldest structure still in use in Dublin, the creepy crypt is home to a mummified cat and rat. According to cathedral lore, the cat chased the rat into the pipe of the organ and both became stuck. There are hundreds of relics among the collection. Looking skyward, stained glass windows are plentiful along with the medieval floor tiles in every shade of brown to gold, fading into orange with different designs on each tile. There are thousands of them. In one section there is a perfect square of four rust-colored tiles; next were black and white in a triangle pattern with brown and gold flower patterns in the middle. Each section around the cathedral had different tile patterns and colors.

There are many magnificent stained glass windows, some narrow and long, some in a flower pattern, some typical with arched top, one even in the shape of an eye with an eyeball. Some were crests, individuals, groups and designs but what is special about these is that between each picture you will find an interesting fact from the cathedral's history. The wording alongside the eyeball reads, "The church bells range in weight from a quarter of a ton to two and a quarter tons." Under a red crest, two large gold keys cross over each other and beside them a plaque reads "Christ Church Cathedral was founded in 1028".

After plenty of walking that afternoon, we rode one of the most useful modes of transportation for any tourist in a city for the first time—the Dublin City Hop On-Hop Off bus. Fortunately, the prerecorded in-depth tour was in an easy-to-understand Irish accent. The big news today was that my eye felt fine so I could now wear the infamous contact lens. The first sighting of St. Patrick's Cathedral bathed in sunlight took my breath away as it stands on the oldest Christian site in Dublin. St. Patrick is said to have baptized converts to the Christian faith in a well which once existed north of the tower in the present park.

At one time a river flowed around the cathedral but now it's a culvert. I thought at first it was a cool moat but no, just a culvert. Because of its sacred association with St. Patrick, a church had stood here since the 5th century. In 1191 the Normans built another church in stone on this site. Rebuilt in the 13th century, it is the same building today. The first university in Ireland, founded in 1320, continued for nearly two hundred years.

As we strolled into the cathedral the grand tall arches were purposely designed to raise one's eyes upward to God. There are colors and memorials of old Irish regiments and a Roll of Honor containing names of fifty thousand Irishmen who fell in the Great War of 1914-15. An intricately carved spiral staircase leads to the organ.

The great organ, the largest and most powerful in Ireland, sits in an interior gallery of sorts and upper part of a choir loft. The Cathedral Choir took part in the first performance of Handel's Messiah in 1742. I recalled the many times I had sung the Hallelujah Chorus in choir while in high school and in many Christmas cantatas in my younger years. That first audience must have been totally wowed.

The cathedral is full of statues, tombs, windows, and memorial tablets, each with its own story. To me, St. Patrick's is more special than any other building we'd seen. The cathedral represents the history and heritage of the Irish people from the earliest times to the present day. But I really appreciate how it's open to anyone who wants to worship their God.

For dinner that evening we experienced Indian Tandoori, boasting authentic Indian cuisine. I don't know how authentic but it was delicious. I knew only one other Indian restaurant with which we had to compare it from the year before in Oxford. After dinner we walked and stepped over cables through a well-staged movie set with laundry carefully hung on two lines between buildings. Pants, shirts, blankets, sheets and bloomers were carefully placed.

We wrapped up our time in the city, packed up and boarded our motorcoach that would escort us for the next ten days around the Irish countryside. Our driver Nigel, a curious fellow indeed, asked us many questions about where we lived, our livelihoods, our families and what we did for hobbies, similar questions that we asked him. He also seemed interested in what we thought of our president, William Clinton. The president, involved in a salacious scandal with a young intern named Monica Lewinsky, had denied any involvement. Some in our group didn't believe it and that it had been made up by conspirators from the opposing political party. Others in the group did believe it because unfortunately the president had a track record of extramarital affairs. I felt glad to be away from home and the bombardment of this sordid, embarrassing-for-our-nation news coverage. The Irish revered our president because he had helped pen the peace accord in 1995 in Belfast. Out of character, I chose to stay quiet.

The Wicklow Mountain range is just south of Dublin growing thick deciduous trees, with mostly lush scenery covering over fifty thousand acres. It is littered with bogs and heath blanketing the hillside, slopes and peaks. Fast-flowing streams and sometimes short waterfalls dumped into deep lakes of blue. These mountains weren't like the Cascade Range in Oregon but lower and more meandering with many shades of green depending on which type of vegetation grows there.

The sky with white puffy clouds moved quickly overhead. Purple heather clumps dotted some areas but weren't in full bloom quite yet; probably another two weeks and the entire countryside would look like a royal purple carpet. Nigel mentioned that the mountain range is the largest continuous upland area in the Republic of Ireland and the mountains stretch into County Dublin so are sometimes called the Dublin Mountains. The highest peak, Lugnaquilla, is about three thousand feet. The mountains are mostly composed of granite but there are much older rocks of quartzite. Copper and lead have been the main metals mined and a brief gold rush in the 18th century. Several rivers have their source in the mountains including the Liffey which we'd just seen in Dublin. Powerscourt Waterfall is the tallest in Ireland at three hundred ninety-seven feet.

On a hilltop I stood gazing out at a mountain that dropped off sharply into a flat area covered in grass with hundreds of fluffy sheep, like large slow-moving cotton balls. The grassy area flowed into a white sandy beach then blue ocean. I saw a light bluish-gray-backed bird with white underparts and a dark head, about the size of a large crow, flying rapidly. Later when checking my bird book, I discovered it to be a peregrine falcon.

Glendalough, scattered with ponds and lakes, probably because it is a glacial valley, is well-known for an early medieval monastic settlement founded in the 6th century. The clouds created shadows on a calm lake. We walked through a low stone arch that led to the site of an early Irish monastery built between the 10th and 12th centuries complete with round towers over one hundred feet high. I had shivers while meandering through stone ruins once sturdy and sacred.

Across a creek, we strolled through St. Kevin's Cemetery, just a short distance from the village of Laragh. The cemetery is part of the monastic site we'd just explored. Celtic crosses in all shapes and sizes adorned family plots where many headstones were crafted with lots of different looks, some standing straight but most tilting one way or another due to centuries of erosion. But most were in surprisingly good condition. It is an old cemetery still in use. I walked for a while hoping to scribble names and dates in my journal but after a quick walk up and down the rows, I didn't discover even one O'Reilly in the bunch.

The size of this cemetery was modest yet quietly haunting and I found it hard not be to be moved by the dozens of headstones. A few people, not part of our group, were milling about, clutching bunches of flowers and I assumed looking for some familiar family name. At one end of the cemetery sat an elderly woman resting her hand on the corner of a stone. I felt a strong pull toward her. I couldn't see what was written on the gray, weathered headstone but I said hello softly not to startle her and when she looked up, I saw she had tears in her soft blue, aging eyes. Then I did, too.

I walked through the old church and peered out a long window. It overlooked a portion of the cemetery with the tallest Celtic cross tipping slightly to the right. It is set in the foreground of shrubby trees, a stream, grasses of different shades and rolling hills. I could see the appeal that St. Kevin saw. Going outside, there were several beautiful horses in a nearby field and a small, red hand-painted sign that read "DANGER" in capital letters and "Keep Away From Horses, Please." One horse came trotting up, clearly expecting a carrot or treat of which I had none. He seemed friendly enough and not at all menacing or dangerous as the sign would imply.

Drizzle and gray clouds matched the same color of Kilkenny castle and church. Kilkenny means "Church of Cainneach" and sits in southeast Ireland built up on both sides of the River Nore. We explored this small medieval town and its castle. Like other towns, the castle was built and walls were added to protect their good residents from the bad invaders. They had their share of rebellions and conquests.

Standing behind a plot of ground only consisting of deep red roses, a portion of Kilkenny Castle loomed across the grassy acreage. This portion of the castle looked like it was being held up by gray stones and seamlessly constructed into a gigantic round container of Quaker Oats, perfectly round and tall. The middle section with four chimneys poking out the side looked like a soda cracker box tipped on end. It stands grand and stately but not terribly pretty. However, few buildings in Ireland can boast a longer history of nonstop occupation than this castle. Founded soon after the Norman conquest of Ireland, the castle has been rebuilt, extended and adapted to fit changing situations and uses over a period of eight hundred years.

The town's coat of arms is the castle flanked by two columns beside which are two soldiers with a bow and arrow, pointed outward. Below in green grass is a bright red lion, smiling; not a growl but a smile with a blue tongue that matches his blue claws. Everything has meaning but this one wasn't clear to me.

Kilkenny is a historic old city and celebrated its three hundred ninetieth year in 1998. Its foundation began in the early 6th century with a church built in honor of St. Canice, now St. Canice's Cathedral, also known as Kilkenny Cathedral. The tower and the church are about the same height.

Touring the inside of the church we certainly appreciated the hand-carved wood highlighting the details and workmanship. I noticed dogs at the feet of some of the tombs. Dogs represent loyalty. I felt the hairs on my arms stand up not because it was scary but rather from its formidable history within the walls of this architectural marvel. Worship has taken place at this site for over eight hundred years. The remarkable stained glass windows and The See Chair of the Bishop of Ossory dating back to 1120 are equally impressive.

The Round Tower is the oldest standing structure in Kilkenny City and only two people at a time can climb. No, we didn't climb the narrow, steep wooden ladder of one hundred twenty-one steps.

Leaving the charming town of Kilkenny, we soon came upon the Rock of Cashel. Also known as the Cashel of the Kings and St. Patrick's Rock, it is a historic site located in County Tipperary. Legend says the Rock of Cashel originated in the Devil's Bit, a mountain twenty miles north of Cashel, when St.

Patrick banished Satan from a cave, resulting in the Rock's landing in Cashel. The limestone outcrops rise two hundred feet above the surrounding plain. In 1001, the King of Munster donated his fortress on the Rock to the church. Outside I spotted the 12th century Irish High Cross at the Rock of Cashel, a perfect Celtic cross made of sandstone.

Cormac's chapel, the chapel of King Cormac on the hill of Cashel, is the jewel in the crown of Irish Romanesque architecture with construction in 1127. It has opposing doors on the north and south sides, twin square towers, steeply pitched stone roof, an altar bay and arched windows all done in white, beige, yellow and brown bricked-shaped stones. Looking through the bars in the castle windows, Ireland was aglow in goldenrod weeds or broom as it's called in Scotland. Farther out were acres of greens divided by uneven rows of bushes and rocks. The oldest and tallest of the buildings is a well-preserved round tower about ninety feet high, dating from 1100. They used the dry-stone method when building the tower. I'd seen this in Scotland the year before and recalled being told that it's a method by which structures were constructed from stones without any mortar to hold them together. This technique was used frequently in building stone walls, traditionally for boundaries in fields and churchyards or as retaining walls for terracing. But dry-stone sculptures like this tower, buildings, bridges and other structures also still exist.

When entering the chapel's south door under vaulted ceilings and wide arches I felt a warmth maybe from all the sunbeams pouring through windows. Frescoes have survived after somebody discovered they were whitewashed then magnificently restored in the 1980s. At the north door are five arches supported by five columns and above the doorway is a centaur shooting at a lion.

But it's all about the views from this vantage point. There are extraordinary views inside and out. Wandering outside I spotted old grave sites and the abbey below.

Stopping for lunch this day wasn't anywhere outstanding. Some days were like that because of where we were driving. Some gas stations in the UK and Europe have a restaurant and full grocery store. We had an hour here for lunch. In the market I read their version of ABCs: A-Apple juice, B-Beef, C-Cheese, D-Duckling, E-Eggs, F-Fresh salmon, G-Green beans, H-Handmade chocolates (I LOVE Ireland), I-Ice cream, J-Jams, K-Kippers, L-Lagers, M-Mushrooms, N-Nibbles, O-Ostrich, P-Prepared meals, Q-Quality, P-Pork, R-Rashers, S-Stout, T-Truffles, U-Unsalted butter, V-Venison, W-Whiskey, X-Xtra Large Pizza, Y-Yoghurt and finally Z-Zucchini.

Roy always did a "Buddy Check" before departing which meant you had eyeball-to-eyeball contact with your buddy no matter where the person might be sitting on the bus. As we were rolling down the ramp to the motorway, from the

back of the bus Ann shouted, "We're missing Dan."
Looking back toward the station, we could see Dan
trotting toward us as Nigel carefully and slowly
backed up the bus. Before Dan boarded there were
already ripples of laughter. He was apologetic,
mumbling something about the queue at the loo.
Ripples turn into a wave of laughs. Dan had been a
local news anchor in Portland, Oregon, for years and
had a deep, reassuring distinctive voice, much like
Walter Cronkite's familiar voice.

Detouring a few miles off the main road to
Cork, we drove into the village of Mitchelstown,
population three thousand. The River Gradoge runs
by the town into River Funshion and it is best known
as a center for cheese production. We were stopping
to give a hearty hello to one of our fellow traveler's
grandparents. John's grandparents opened their
green door and gave us a big wave and welcomed us
warmly. I would love to have gone into their home
but didn't dare ask. John would be having dinner
with them that evening in Cork. Their squared-off
door was bordered by a white stone-carved arch and
surrounded by ivy. I took a picture.

We stayed overnight in the city of Cork and
watched the sunset light up the sky in amber, pinks
and oranges that reflected off the ripple-free River
Lee.

The next day were we looking forward to spending
time at the well-known Blarney Castle in County
Cork. It seems we all know about the infamous

limestone block called the Blarney Stone that is built into the battlements of the castle. And that kissing the stone endows the kisser with the gift of gab or nicer maybe, the gift of eloquence or skill at flattery. The stone had been set into a tower of the castle in 1446. All I could think about were the millions of germs on the rock.

There is a lot more to see and do than kiss that dirty stone where you lay down on a boardwalk, hang upside down and bend backwards dropping your head down with some man holding you so you don't slip down several stories. Nope, not for me, but I did walk by and touch it. We were able to hike all around the medieval fortress and the tower house that was built between the 15th and 17th centuries. Beautiful flowers of all colors and types adorned the well-kept gardens complete with interesting rock formations known as Wishing Steps, Witch's Cave and Rock Close. The Bog Garden shows off two waterfalls where we walked on a raised wooden walkway, then through a willow tunnel before passing through large groups of giant rhubarb plants which look like a prehistoric landscape, something you'd see in "Jurassic Park."

The oldest trees at Blarney Castle are found here. One humongous tree had limbs that could have been individual trees, dozens of them. A group of three yews are clumped together on an island and supposedly have been there for up to six hundred years. This entire area evoked a feeling of calm. I couldn't really explain it so decided I'd keep my self-awareness hidden. We had some yummy homemade refreshments at a café that had originally been the stables.

I intended to find just the right gift for my Irish Dad and figured Blarney Castle would be appropriate because he sure had the gift of gab and told a story like none other. And I'd found it—a green plaid tie with matching pocket scarf. I knew he'd wear it every March 17 from then on. He dressed in a suit every day for work as Linn County Clerk in Oregon. He oversaw the county elections, licensing including marriage, was the keeper of many records and had a stellar reputation within the state. He had been elected by the citizens for many terms. I called him from a red-colored British phone booth knowing he was extremely busy working to pass a bill in the Oregon Legislature that would allow all voters in Oregon to vote by mail. We'd already been using absentee ballots for years and even though this would be similar it was also new since it would be statewide. Linn County, the pilot county for this procedure, had already completed several successful elections. He was convinced that it would save money, and be much more secure than the traditionally used methods. It would be up for a statewide vote November 3. He worked tirelessly hand-in-hand with the Secretary of State and several other county clerks who had already successfully followed Del Riley's lead. I knew he would wear this tie set even if he didn't really care for it, just for me.

He loved it. Years later on one St. Patrick's Day I took a picture of him wearing the biggest smile ever.

As we left the area, heather bloomed brighter and hillsides gave off a purple radiance. Decrepit or maybe well-used churches and buildings sprinkled the countryside. One lone blackface sheep stood in the doorway of a tumbledown stone structure, peering out as if asking, "Do you have a goodie for me or are you just another bothersome tourist who wants to take my picture because I'm so cute?"

We stopped at a small market and selected lunch items for an upcoming picnic. There was assorted yogurt in containers with graphics and pictures much different than ours, fresh fruits and vegetables, breads, several types of smelly cheese, sticks of cured salami and peppered beef, large juicy red strawberries, apples and grapes. We sat overlooking the lake munching on our proper Irish picnic marveling that we were actually there having lunch on a lake at a mansion—Muckross Mansion in Killarney, mind you. A squatty jar held some chocolate spread called Nutella. At first bite I became hooked on this new dippable, spreadable, delectable, chocolate delight. We dipped apples, celery, carrots, bread and about anything else (even our fingers) into this milky hazelnut chocolate heaven. It was a new day—out with peanut butter and in with Nutella. It would be the first thing I would look for on returning home. One year later it appeared on store shelves in Oregon. Excitedly opening the jar at home and submerging a chunk of banana, that first bite didn't quite taste the same as sitting on the lakeside in Ireland.

Muckross Mansion, even in late summer, was covered in red ivy that wound up the walls and chimneys, giving it a DayGlo Rocket Red gleam. There were two Irish Wolfhounds in the distance and we learned that this is an ancient Irish breed of dog and also famous for being the world's tallest dog dating all the way back to Roman times. They were once used to hunt wolves, elk and wild boar. Interestingly, their characteristics are their sweet temperament, intelligence and patience. Sadly, the average lifespan is only seven years. As we sat on a bench overlooking Killarney National Park and the lake with Aghadoe Heights in the distance, it looked like another idyllic place to live.

Often I'd see "Céad Míle Fáilte" or "A Hundred Thousand Welcomes." I did feel welcome.

Touring on our luxury motorcoach, not just a bus, one sits higher than in a passenger car and most times I was at eye level with anything on a second floor. As we drove through little villages, I'd see lace curtains in second-story windows with wooden boxes and wire baskets covered in moss and chock full of colorful flowers, usually trailing down over doorways and first-story windows. If the curtains were open, I had a fleeting opportunity to peek into someone's life. I began to use the words "charming" and "quaint" frequently or even "old-world" or "picturesque."

Still driving in southwest Ireland and on the northern side of the neck of the Dingle Peninsula before reaching our next stop, Kerry Kingdom Museum, there was something quite out of the ordinary. There is a town called Tralee, with around fifteen thousand people. Had I been magically transported to The Netherlands? There on the side of the shore sat a white Dutch-looking working windmill with a one-story yellow building, maybe even a homestead, and a white three-bay shop or garage. The closed door had been painted shamrock green. The sun created a duplicate scene in the still water. It is still a postcard in my mind.

The topography between Tralee and Dingle flattened out as we drove along the west side of Ireland's coast. The patchwork quilt effect from green pastures and fields separated by shrubbery was frequent and I never got tired of looking at the landscape. Sometimes the patch was dotted with white sheep. And sometimes the green quilt slipped off the side of the hill into the blue sea.

In a field, men with shovels were harvesting peat known as turf. Roy explained peat has been an invaluable source of heat and energy throughout Irish history. It is basically an accumulation of partially decayed vegetation and called peatlands, bogs, mires, moors or muskegs. He said peat moss is the most common component in peat, although many other plants can contribute. Peat is harvested as an important source of fuel in certain parts of the world. He said it has been harvested for centuries by a method known as "cutting." It was found to be a useful alternative to firewood for cooking and heating throughout Ireland and other parts of the European continent. Roy showed us historical photos of men and women with flat blade shovels. Peat is the forgotten fuel and while oil, coal and natural gas are exported around the world, few people outside Northern Europe are aware of this energy source. Peat is thick, muddy and when harvested, looks like dark earthen bricks. These sods were cut and stacked on one another in a formation that allowed the dry summer air to pass through. After drying for a week or two the bricks were carried from the bog in baskets or nets. To save labor, donkeys and small horses were used to carry the turf back to the farm where they were stored in a nearby shed to keep them from getting wet. This fuel creates a thick smoke.

Our smallish room at Bambury Guest House on the Dingle Peninsula contained two twin beds, with a small table and a lamp separating the beds. The plaid curtains in several shades of blue perfectly matched the bedspreads plus the shade on the small lamp.

That evening after dinner we took a walk toward town. We passed black, old world street lamps, Murphy's Pub painted in eggplant purple, John Benny's Pub done in royal blue with two orange doors with matching window trim, and on a corner was An Droichend Beag, a gold building trimmed in Celtic green. As we walked we heard music coming down Bridge Street.

The lively sounds emanated from a flagstone building with the front door painted crimson and windows outlined in the same color. A little plaque read "Headquarters of the Dingle Fife and Drum Band, the Green and Gold Wrenboys and a place where the history of Dingle Gaelic Athletic Association is revered." This hallowed ground sums up the central role the pub has played. We were at the famous O'Flaherty's Pub, where farmers and fishermen plus plenty of tourists were squeezed in having a pint, and tapping their feet and trying to discuss whatever was happening around them, but drowned out by the energetic band. A guy played his harmonica, another strummed a banjo, another plucked a big base, another blew a flute-thing that didn't really look like a flute, and others had a fiddle and a small accordion. The fellow on the harmonica really rocked as they played a jig that made you want to move but by now there was standing room only. They took a short break to introduce themselves as Kilian, Fergus, Flynn, Niall, Rourke and Caelan.

A man named Fergus told us O'Flaherty's came to be in 1957 after his father, who had been a fisherman, broke his leg and had to give up fishing. Fergus turned out to be the current owner.

Pictures hung on the walls, and the pole in the middle of the bar was covered with stapled flyers and announcements promoting whatever they wanted. After the delightful hour of Irish tunes, we strolled back to our hotel as a sundown of coral and amber danced on the water.

The next morning, prowling around the far western tip of the Dingle Peninsula, a local guide named Mark met up with us to escort us into Dunbeg Fort. It butts up against, and overlooks, the Atlantic Ocean and is in the middle of an open field with homes and farms some acres away. We walked the well-worn stone path and he shared some basic history that the Iron Age followed the Bronze Age and lasted about one thousand years. The Iron Age in Ireland was from about 500 BC to 500 AD. The most significant relics found from this area are the promontory and hill forts. These are usually monuments with a large stone wall enclosing a large area of hilltop or cliff ledge. On the whole, they were defensive structures, but often a refuge of last resort. There are few promontory forts left and we were at the steps of one of them called Dunbeg Fort.

The wall surrounding the fort is made of flat, layered gray stones and a narrow doorway gives access to the interior. Then similar walls are the remains of a roundhouse inside the fort. The interior of the house has a floor of gravel but my guess is that once it had been a sod floor of this home. Looking down out a low window I could see from this side of the house how disconcertingly close it is to the cliff's edge. We discovered a small chamber probably used originally for storage. The roof had deteriorated over the centuries. Grass and weeds with white flowers covered berms. A tall square tower remained and we peeked through slits in the sides of the structure that warriors, when inside, could shoot arrows through to protect their fort. It is rather small but darn impressive located on a sheer cliff which projects south into Dingle Bay at the base of Mount Eagle. We had plenty of time to prowl around this somewhat eerily ancient site.

One lone enormous tree, maybe a fort of its own for a number of different types of birds, stood guard. Several birds obviously were from the finch family but different in color than ours in the Pacific Northwest. Their goldfinch had red around its orange beak that bled down its chest and up toward the crest of his head. One lime-colored bird, guide Mark said, was a Greenfinch, which made perfect sense. Another had a scarlet underbody with black and white feathers down its back and a solid black head. Mark said it was a Bullfinch. The sparrows also looked similar but different because of the coloring.

We continued to mill around and I heard some musical notes floating along with the breeze and wondered where they were coming from. Turned out Mark, also a musician, sat on a pile of rocks blowing into his penny whistle. He said it was cold and it helped to blow warm breaths into it before playing. It looked like a thin white flute and he explained that the penny whistle is commonly called a tin whistle and is a woodwind instrument often heard in Irish music. Ah, that's what I saw the night before in the pub. This small instrument has six holes plus a mouthpiece and is played by blowing air into it and using your fingers to cover different holes to produce different sounds. He serenaded us with an Irish jig followed by a slower somber song which evoked a melancholy feeling in my soul.

Mark shared more insights about the central causeway that provided access to the interior, only about half the length recorded in 1854, because much of the western half had already fallen into the sea. He said that with the absence of dateable finds, this creates difficulties in coming up with a chronology for the site. A radiocarbon date of around 800 AD from the base of the inner fosse suggests it was in existence in the 8th or 9th century AD and dates of around 900 AD from the occupation layers in the beehive suggest it was inhabited in the 10th or 11th century AD. That's old. As he shared his Irish history and wisdom he entertained us by playing a few more light, cheery tunes on his penny whistle. The melodies seemed to be carried off the rugged coastline reaching who knows where. The coastline reminded me of the coastline in my home state of Oregon where the hillside drops quickly into the gray ocean. White waves beat the shoreline as gulls soared overhead, probably watching to make sure we weren't getting too close to their nests.

Off in the distance were the Blasket Islands with one larger than the others. Mark pointed out the image of a man lying face up. I could easily see why he is named the Sleeping Giant. There are several legends of how this giant came to his final resting place in the ocean. One is that some druid put him to sleep and another is that he resembles a reposing Finn McCool, another Irish tale of its own.

We strolled to Gallarus Oratory in County Kerry, down a lane covered with blooming wild fuchsia bushes about six feet high which overlooks Smerwick Harbour. Gallarus means either "rocky headland or house" or "shelter for foreigners." Completely encircled by a low two-foot walkway, built between the 6th and 9th centuries, it's an early Christian stone church. Like Dunbeg Fort, the gray flat stones were layered one on top of the other creating a slightly bulging pyramid. We all fit inside and peered through windows in feet-thick stone. It's one of the best preserved and most iconic early Christian churches. Over one thousand years old, this small building was constructed entirely from dry stone masonry and is the archeological and architectural highlight of the Slea Head Drive. We saw the Three Sisters and Mount Brandon farther out in Smerwick Harbour. A rock standing about four feet high had early Celtic writing etched in it.

As we drove a bit longer we came to Kilmalkedar Church, a Romanesque, early Christian, and later medieval site and is spread over about ten acres. It is associated with St. Brendan and thought to be founded by St. Maolcethair, a local saint. Even though deteriorated with no roof, it seemed to be in pretty good shape. It consists of a nave and chancel.

Outside on the northern side of the pathway that leads to the church, there is a remarkable holed ogham stone that stands six feet tall and three feet wide at the base. There is an inscription made by slash marks that all mean something. This stone may have been a standing stone with the ogham writing added during the early Christian period. There are a number of other standing stones with holes and some without.

The Chancellor's house is a rectangular building built on top of a boulder foundation and situated on sloping ground with an incredible view of the Three Sisters and Smerwick Bay. We prowled around and followed a path and steps that led us to a kitchen area. Outside of the house were above-ground stones which were vessels or tubs used in cooking. They looked perfect as a rainwater collector for birdbaths now. Christmassy green ferns and small bushes popped through any gap they could find, stretching for sunbeams.

Our next stop in Ogham had even more ancient stones from about 300 AD and some of the earliest Irish script. On a tall rock were dozens of straight slash marks which were from the Ogham alphabet. I found the alphabet in a bookstore and could almost decipher the words. Well, not really but hoped I could.

That evening, like the previous night, we went to O'Flaherty's for Irish jigs and music. The room was crowded, so many stood at the bar listening to the traditional Irish music. More people piled in to listen. I couldn't get enough of it but my husband did and passed on this evening's Irish entertainment.

Friday morning before others were up, I walked alone in the bright sunshine along the shoreline as Scotch Broom with its goldish-yellow flowers, really weeds and full of pollen, caused my eyes to feel like little bark twigs had suddenly appeared. In the distance, the water was calm and I could see where we'd walk later that day, toward the Dingle Tower.

Several hours later when the tide was out far enough, we walked in the damp harbor sand which wasn't easygoing. The sand touched the sea and we kept watching for a popular water attraction, a Bottlenose Dolphin named Fungie. As we reached the tower, I gazed back toward Dingle with the blue water and emerald collage countryside taking my breath away. I wondered if my relatives had been in this beautiful area. As we strolled back on the path through a cow pasture, friendly black cows thought we should be sharing some treats with them. We'd not brought anything so they turned away and resumed munching on boring grass. The only thing we had to watch for were their gifts of cow pies. As we got closer to Dingle, there were dozens of large chartreuse fishing nets piled with orange weights tied in various spots. A young man slept soundly stretched out in the sun probably exhausted from hours of fishing, or hours at O'Flaherty's. And sure enough, like pressing the ON button, Fungie jumped out of the water, did an acrobatic dolphin flip and smoothly glided back into the blue bay. He or she is a friendly dolphin and swims playfully alongside boats. I don't know if this was Fungie II, III or VIII but she or he has been around for decades.

Still not tired of Irish music, we returned for one final evening of entertainment at O'Flaherty's for song and dance. We politely pushed our way in and eight of us crammed around a table for two.

We visited the well-preserved 15th century Bunratty Castle and Folk Park in County Clare the next day. This folk park is a living reconstruction of the homes and their environment a century ago.

The main street has typical 19th century urban Irish buildings like the doctor's house where the parlor was used as a dispensary and for surgeries. The pub in the center of the village would have been used by well-known customers. Irish linens, poplin and woolens are still famous. Sean O'Farrell's Drapery displayed cloths in the family's rooms upstairs.

Each typical small town printed pamphlets, handbills, notices and newspapers in the print workshop with all typesetting done by hand. Cuala Press prints, established by the Yeats family, are still produced on the premises. Yes, the famous Yeats. The grocery store held all foodstuff as well as imported goods, then McInerney & Sons Hardware Factory made tools and utensils. Lastly, on Main Street is the post office. Different types of farmhouses dotted the area from a one-room dwelling of a poor laborer to the home of a farmer rich from the lands complete with stables and a corn barn. Piles of peat logs were loosely stacked against most buildings.

After absorbing this seemingly first-hand history lesson by stepping back in time, I could smell baking pastries somewhere. Our noses led us to the Tea Room where we feasted on refreshing tea complete with milk and sugar, and hot buttered scones with freshly made fruit jams. We needed plenty of refreshments to increase our strength for our own invasion of Bunratty Castle, built around 1425. During the 16th and 17th centuries it was an important stronghold of the O'Briens, kings and earls. It is furnished with mainly 15th and 16th century furnishings in the style of the period of the Great Earl. The main building has three floors, each consisting of a single great room or hall. The four towers have six stories each. We entered the castle across a drawbridge to the Main Guard. A small gate leads to a dungeon that looked too creepy to me.

In the Public Chapel are finely decorated 16th century stucco ceilings and several precious artifacts including a 15th century Swabian altarpiece. Swabian you ask? Me, too. It is one of the dialect groups of Alemannic German that belongs to the High German dialect continuum. It is mainly spoken in Swabia which is located in central and southeastern Baden-Württemberg (including its capital Stuttgart). Once the guide mentioned Stuttgart, I knew exactly where he was talking about.

The Great Hall, appropriately named, is the original banquet hall and where the earl would give judgments sitting in his Chair of Estate. French, Brussels and Flemish tapestries hang on every wall. There is an oak cupboard dated to 1570. The prominent coat of arms of the reigning family was conspicuously displayed. There are private apartments in the South and North Solar. The South Solar ceiling is partially a replica in Tudor style. The North Solar apartment housed the earl and his family. The oak paneling dates to 1500 and the table is said to have been salvaged from the wreck of a Spanish ship. The earl's bedroom includes a magnificent carved bed draped on the top by fabric. A lady's dress lay on the bed. Food was prepared in the earl's kitchen and large turtle shells were used as dishes and covers. And it had its own garbage chute. It is an impressive compound.

Later that afternoon on the N67 highway toward Galway, we navigated a brightly adorned roundabout with circles of pink begonias and red chrysanthemums. We pulled into Galway, a city of around fifty thousand people. Some of us stayed at the Graduate Bed & Breakfast, an interesting name for accommodations. Some stayed at a hostel downtown. I don't know why we got the B&B, on a busy street and not anywhere close to the city center.

Galway became a royal town in 1232 and was first recorded in 1124 when a fort was built there. The Great Famine had a catastrophic effect on the population in this town and region.

That night after dinner we listened and moved to live music. One couldn't help but move some body part, tap a finger or foot or get up and dance. I noticed one man playing a penny whistle. We went to bed that night hearing the international news from the United States that our president Bill Clinton was in a political and personal predicament as a young female intern accused him of a sexual encounter, and even though at first denying it, he had fessed up as she now had proof.

I heard a few people speaking in low voices about something that had happened mid-afternoon in a smaller town in Northern Ireland about one hundred miles from us.

After the musical extravaganza, we returned tired to our small B&B and climbed in our twin beds. I woke up sweating and discovered a plastic cover under the sheets. It also made plenty of crunching noise when I moved.

Before departing for our day of touring the countryside, we picked up other members of our group who stayed at the hostel downtown. They were gaunt and exhausted, awake all night because of people in the streets expressing their anger and sadness and most in the hostel crying and protesting over a horrific bombing the afternoon before. In protest, students staying at the hostel opened and slammed doors all night. Rebecca and her dear mother Marty told me about the night and being frightened themselves not understanding the goings on. Half of us were clueless what our travel mates had endured.

Then our guide Roy and driver Nigel told us the devastating news that at 3:10 p.m. the day before, a horrific five hundred-pound bomb packed in a car had been detonated with a remote trigger in a town called Omagh about three hours away in County Tyrone, Northern Ireland. Reports said they only knew it occurred in a busy marketplace and dozens had been killed. Shop fronts on both sides of Market Street, not even the marketplace, were blown back on top of customers inside. Glass, bricks and metal tore through the crowd on the street as a fireball swept out from the epicenter. Twenty-one people were killed instantly, some of them were never found, because of the force of the blast. A water main under the road ruptured. Gallons of water gushed out. Some of the dead and badly injured were washed down the hill. More than three hundred people were injured. It took hours to hear accurate news but these early reports were grim and heartbreaking.

Subdued, nervous and maybe even a bit scared, Nigel, skilled beyond belief driving down small lanes, tried to divert our attention and drove us to a Fairy Circle. I tried my hardest to find one of the little shadows, or people or whatever, with no luck. The luck of the Irish wasn't with me that day. What a somber day. I didn't understand how something like this could happen in such a civilized, beautiful country. Wild ferns, purple thistles and bluebells popped out where they could around rocks and mounds reaching for sunlight without a care in the world.

We stopped at The Burren, a limestone plateau and wandered around this rugged rocky area of Dolmen or Portal Tombs, megalithic tombs from 2000 BC. More old stuff. It didn't surprise me to learn Burren means "great rock." The different landscape began not as rock but as limy mud at the bottom of a tropical sea. What the heck? Tropical sea? Yes, three hundred fifty million years ago. Just the opposite from lush, multiple green fields just a few acres away, to stark flat gray rocks and dirt.

My first impressions were wrong. First, it wasn't really flat especially once you started walking on the pockmarked surface. Ankle-twisting holes were just ready to nab you. These were initiated by the erosion and collapse of the limestone in preglacial times. Two million years ago the Ice Age had a major part in shaping this area. I learned a lot about glacial retreat, moraine in the form of rounded boulders, meltwater flow and much more.

Another thing that is so cool about this rocky phenomenon is that four hundred or so ringforts date from the first millennium AD. The majority are stone built and contain elaborate underground passages used for storage and hiding. There are oodles of rock freestyle "tee" like an American Indian Teepee, and then some with sides and a flat top. One particularly large rock tent has a flat surface for a roof with rock pillars holding it up, probably six feet tall and about as wide. Everywhere I looked there were rock legacies made in cairns of numerous sizes and shapes, having served a purpose at one time.

A closer look revealed that it provides grasslands, limestone heath, bogs, lakes, wet grasslands and many types of wildflowers. A bright red flower poked its blooms between two flat stones. A dainty purple orchid stood out among the grasses and a little white daisy-like flower called Mountain Avens dotted the brown twig foliage. There were many more arctic-alpine and mediterranean basin plants side-by-side due to the unusual environment. I never would have noticed if Roy hadn't pointed out these various rare flowers.

A golden butterfly, with wings as if dipped in black paint and with black polka dots, flitted past. It is called a Pearl-Bordered Fritillary. I appreciated my trifold bird, butterfly and insect guide I had along for reference. A camouflaged lime moth clung to grass and I never would have noticed it if it hadn't flown away. This region overflowed with smaller animals and we spotted a family of foxes and had been warned to watch out for nasty badgers and herds of feral goats. Overhead the gulls were active and noisy. Offshore were guillemots, with solid black bodies and heads, and all-white wings with bright reddish-orange legs and feet. There were several other shorebirds that I couldn't identify and there wasn't a puffin anywhere. This is an amazing piece of geology and history all rolled into about one hundred square miles.

As we proceeded, the tragic news about victims at Omagh filtered in throughout the day, becoming even worse with each report. Roy explained that books of condolences were in churches and it is the custom to write words of sorrow and encouragement. At each church we entered, we signed our names with condolences.

I just couldn't grasp how this violence could continue decade after decade in such a seemingly civilized country. They looked just like me, not monsters. They drove modern cars, lived in homes, went to church, shopped in modern stores and got groceries. How were they so different from me? How could some harbor such hatred for people they didn't even know? How could they commit such an unspeakable act?

Coming down from my condemnatory pedestal, I recalled how an anti-government militant and his co-conspirator bombed a federal building in Oklahoma City three years earlier killing one hundred sixty-eight people including nineteen children and injuring about seven hundred others. Also, I couldn't comprehend how a person could take a gun and kill bystanders, people with whom they have no connection who were in cafeterias, office buildings, a high school, restaurants, post office buildings and workplaces. Tragically, this was an increasing mental illness epidemic in America.

In 1994, from his autobiography *Long Walk to Freedom*, Nelson Mandela said, "No one is born hating another person because of the color of his skin, or his background, or his religion. People must learn to hate, and if they can learn to hate, they can be taught to love, for love comes more naturally to the human heart than its opposite." I hope that is true.

We were to head to Northern Ireland for the next part of our trip. Would we dare go?

The next morning, we stopped at Kilfenora, a village of about one hundred people in County Clare, situated south of the limestone region The Burren, to see an ancient building and cemetery. What caught my attention were the dozens of well-preserved stone Celtic crosses, some inscriptions and designs still visible. I could see how it became known as the "City of Crosses" for its five high crosses. A tall Celtic cross stood in front of the ruins of the original church like a soldier protecting its captain.

We stopped at the famous Cliffs of Moher. Rising six hundred fifty feet from the sea and about five miles long, the cliffs were shrouded in mist. There were no fences and barriers that we would certainly have at home warning or protecting those daredevils who just had to get as close as possible to the edge. And of course, some daring young man did just that. I couldn't watch for fear of what might happen to him especially with winds gusting around forty miles per hour. The heavy mist pelted my face like sand when walking along the shoreline. Standing at the O'Brien's Tower, one could see up and down the coastline. Seagulls and other seabirds were tucked away safely between rocks on the cliffs. They weren't as stupid as some tourists.

On our way back to Galway for another overnight stay we stopped at the well-preserved Dunguaire Castle, a 16th century tower house overlooking Galway Bay. The tower is seventy-five feet high. It wasn't the largest castle we'd seen but certainly unspoiled. The now child-friendly footpath led to the arched entrance but I imagined it differently hundreds of years ago caked with mud and maybe a few rocks. We'd return to this same castle in a few hours for a medieval dinner and entertainment.

In the tradition of the medieval King Guaire, we were welcomed to savor a delicious four-course dinner. Seated next to a couple on our tour, we dodged a bullet when they were selected to be the official king and queen of the evening and were moved to a high table at the front where all could view them, every bite they took. A harpist played during the meal while locals dressed in period attire served us authentic mead, Irish oak-smoked salmon with traditional soda bread, customary leek and potato soup and supreme of chicken served with a creamy mushroom sauce accompanied by fresh seasonal vegetables and potatoes. Dessert was a favorite for Americans—apple pie and cream. I hoped for Sticky Toffee Pudding. The evening included fine wines, stories and excerpts selected to lift our souls and lighten the heart. I was especially grateful there were actual forks and knives because I'd heard that for some of these medieval banquets you used your hands.

As we drove to Connemara, yet another day in stunning countryside, we were still a subdued group. We stopped at Cong and another Celtic cemetery. I stood overlooking a perfect river curving through grassy banks jam-packed with shrubs and trees and a well-worn red boat just waiting for someone to use it for fly fishing. Where were they?

With wide open range where cattle and sheep roamed without fences, we stopped at Abhainn Oirimh in Gaelic or Errif River, where a low waterfall, like two steps, had brown water flowing over it, not sparkling blue like we'd seen elsewhere. I'd never seen brown water like this, almost a root beer color. Workers were harvesting peat not far away. The dark peat influenced the color of the river, like glacial melt would do in Alaska or Canada.

We drove by house after house that used thatch instead of shingles on their roofs. One white home had a bright red front door with matching red window trim, flower boxes with red geraniums and a neatly trimmed thatched roof.

While in County Sligo we stopped at Drumcliffe—Yeats country! We visited the protestant church where William Butler Yeats likely would have attended. He had been a pillar of the Irish literary establishment and was not only a famous poet, he helped found a theater and also served as a senator of the Irish Free State. We found his gravesite in another quaint churchyard. On the flowerless, plain square stone these words were engraved: "Cast a cold Eye On Life, on Death, Horseman pass by W.B. Yeats." Once again, well-worn from centuries of weather, Celtic crosses of various shapes and sizes stood reverently at the head of plots.

By now our conversations were about whether we were going to stay in the Republic of Ireland or head into Northern Ireland. Roy had been in contact with our tour company in the United States, Europe Through the Backdoor, and owner Rick Steves said he'd leave the decision up to us. Even though the momentous peace accord had been signed in April, obviously there was still plenty of unrest with the bombing three days earlier. As we sat on our charter bus on a bright sunny day watching Ireland's Department of Transportation clear heavy equipment from the roadway, we talked about it once more. We were getting all sorts of information, true or not. And we were all wondering, do we continue our tour plans to visit Northern Ireland? Do we or don't we? Unanimously we decided to go.

As we crossed into Northern Ireland no one at the official border crossing stopped us where several months earlier, everyone was stopped. We were heading for what had been called Londonderry for years and shortened to Derry, a modern town on the banks of the River Derry. On the side of a building were the words "YOU ARE NOW ENTERING FREE DERRY." As we drove by the Craigavon Bridge, there is a statue with two men reaching toward each other almost touching hands, and the inscription reads "Hands Across the Divide." The meaningful, striking bronze sculpture of two men, one Protestant and the other Catholic, arms outstretched to each other yet not touching symbolizes the spirit of reconciliation and hope for the future. It was unveiled in 1992, twenty years after Bloody Sunday. Basically, one side wishes to form a united Ireland and the other side wants Northern Ireland to remain in the United Kingdom. This has been the main conflict behind the Troubles, or the Northern Ireland conflict that started in the 1960s.

Northern Ireland just felt different to me. At first glance, I saw red, white and blue painted curbs, identifying political parties. And the flag at half-staff for Omagh victims. Guard stations which used to hold men carrying guns were now empty, just a remembrance. As we walked the Derry wall, just recently opened, our local guide explained as much as he could about the history, politics and feelings of both sides of people living there.

We toured City Hall and went into a church where we lined up with quiet, somber locals to sign books of condolence for the Omagh fatalities.

Still along the North Coast, later that day we checked into Bushtown House Hotel and Country Club. The hotel is set in mature woodlands on the outskirts of Coleraine. Standing closest to the receptionist desk, I smiled at a grumpy middle-aged man because we were the first to check in. He did not smile back. I quickly thought there could be dozens of reasons he seemed abrupt and unwelcoming. Not shy, I said "Hello, I am happy to be here." He replied in a curt Irish accent, "Are you brave or stupid?" I said, "How about curious and naive?" Then he warmed up for whatever reason, smiled and said, "I thank you for not canceling your reservation and plans to visit my country. We are not all like those who have created such a bad reputation for us." We would hear many people during the next week thanking us for coming.

That evening we had dinner at The Stable Restaurant, originally the Bushtown House horse stable. The original stone walls with arches, furniture and antique knickknacks still remain, giving the feel of its true, traditional character and farm-feel charm. The dark wood beams against the white ceiling showed off the crystal chandeliers nicely. Historical painted plates lined the plate rail at the top of the walls displaying different scenes, a stag and flowers. They are well known for using fresh local produce, dry aged beef and fresh fish caught daily from the waters of the Atlantic. The green beans tasted as if they'd just been plucked from the garden; beef tasted flavorful and cooked just right; different grains were used in making the dense bread; and ice cream tasted like it had been hand-cranked ten minutes earlier using an old-fashioned ice cream maker.

The following morning we drove through countryside of purple blooming heather, perfectly squared lots bordered by dark pine-colored shrubs, and in one plot something bright yellow was blooming.

We drove the rugged coastline to Carrick-a-rede and a few walked across the flimsy, unsteady-looking rope bridge, some eighty feet above the sea. I didn't like it at all being not crazy about heights, so I didn't do it.

Just a short distance beyond was a destination I'd seen in many pictures, The Giant's Causeway in County Antrim. I couldn't wait to get off the bus and start exploring. The rocks are stepping stones of all different dimensions that look like they could have easily reached Scotland and Iceland. Ancient lava flows have eroded to reveal columns of unnatural regularity.

Roy explained that Finn MacCool (or McCool) is supposedly the giant who built The Giant's Causeway. He then told us the legend of the popular character Finn. His real name was Fionn MacCumhaill who was the greatest leader of Fianna, the ancient warrior band of old Ireland.

Finn is credited with creating The Giant's Causeway as stepping stones from the North of Ireland to Scotland. The second version tells how he threw a large piece of the land into the sea at an enemy, that piece of land becoming the Isle of Man. The hole left behind by the clump of land he threw became Lough Neagh.

Another one of the stories claims Finn loved a giant woman living on Staffa and he needed the Causeway to bring her back to Ireland.

The death of Finn is a mystery. One legend suggests that he is not dead but merely sleeping in a cave under Dublin, ready to strike back against Ireland's enemies. The stories and legends of Finn have never been forgotten and he remains one of the most powerful figures in Irish mythology.

We easily climbed stepping from stone to stone for some time. I sat on the rocks overlooking the sea and wondered whether my relatives had explored this area or stayed in their small area around Dublin all their lives; my guess is the latter.

In a gift shop I spotted something I had to have, a clear glass paperweight. I even got a certificate that reads "Maralyn O'Keefe, who designs glass art based on The Giant's Causeway exclusively for The National Trust will not be designing or making any paperweights to the specifications of the limited edition of forty-three at any time in the future." It is dated 1st August 1998 with a gold seal and her signature on the bottom. What a treasure.

It is six-sided, three inches tall and one-inch thick clear glass, not perfectly smooth but with some ridges, bubbles and swirls. And she etched "MOKeefe with 8/43" on one edge in tiny print. I have used it for years as a paperweight but now it is safely displayed with other special Irish Belleek and Waterford mementos in a china hutch in my office. As I write, I have picked it up and felt the unevenness and marveled at my fortune to come across it within a week of her delivering these special pieces to the shop.

We enjoyed the marvelous adventure hiking around the Causeway. I laughed when we took a break sitting on a bench looking down at a woman's shoes that were open-toed, white sandals and certainly not suited or safe for climbing the Causeway.

In County Antrim, we stopped at the Old Bushmills Distillery. The distillery uses water drawn from St. Columba's Rill, which is a tributary of the River Bush. It is well- known for centuries of producing the finest Irish whiskey and founded in 1608, which is proudly printed on the label. I found it to be stinky and stuffy and hot inside the building. Several in our group volunteered to be tasters but I declined.

Back in the fresh air our next stop was the ruins of Dunluce Castle. The round towers are in pretty good condition. One wall with several open windows still stands where other walls had already crumbled. This 13th century ruin is balanced on a cliff overlooking the sea. Ivy climbed its decrepit sides likely holding the castle together. There were many types of birds catching the wind drafts above the castle and blue ocean below.

Down the road we came into the pleasant town of Portrush. Homes are built along the roadway, the only thing that separates them from the sea. It's all about the ocean in this village where businesses provide fishing, water sports and seafood restaurants. Most homes are painted coastal white with shutters accented in different colors to give them some extra zing and personality. I could see why it boasted being the most popular seaside resort in Northern Ireland.

That afternoon, we drove into Belfast which would be our home port for several days. A jovial local man joined us as our special guide of this historically troubled city. He thanked us for coming to Belfast and mentioned the economy appreciated our contributions, too. Belfast's coat of arms is prominently displayed in many locations. In the 17th century, Belfast started out as a typical small village.

Then came the industries such as linen, rope-making, shipbuilding, engineering and tobacco. The population grew rapidly to over three hundred thousand. The citizens built the magnificent City Hall whose work started in 1898 and was completed in 1906, built in the Classical Renaissance style in Portland stone. It's rectangular in shape enclosing a quadrangular courtyard. Sitting on top looking like a crown is the great dome, covered in copper so its aged green patina matches the rest of the emerald countryside, along with a stone lantern. The dome is one hundred seventy-three feet high and made for an easy landmark when we got turned around. Ornate lamps are situated at either side of the main gate. The lamps are adorned with cherubs and seahorses, symbolizing the industrial and manufacturing heritage of the city. Six similar but less intricate lamps are evenly placed on each side of the main gate.

Inside the hall are marble memorials and statues of famous Belfast-born people. The walls at the entrance are dramatic in black with white marble flooring. In the southeast part of the hall there are large stained glass window memorials to officers who died in two world wars.

The Grand Staircase, "Grand" being an understatement, is a magnificent dome with multiple types and colors of marble with elaborate plasterwork. When sunbeams shine just right through stained glass windows they cast rainbows around the area. Standing at attention is a bronze statue of the Earl of Belfast. On either side of the Grand Staircase are two more stunning stained glass windows illustrating the historic events of that period including the bombing of the City Hall during World War II.

We went into the Council Chamber with the entry bay having arches springing from piers seventeen feet high all stretching to the richly decorated dome. The galleries and oak-paneled walls are intricately carved as are the seats for members. There is an elaborately carved oak screen which forms a backdrop for the Lord Mayor's Chair, with smaller chairs for other important city staff. They didn't let visitors sit in the chair that looked much like a throne. But we did get to sit in the gallery as we listened to a City Hall guide give us the rundown of this particular room. Various large portraits adorn the spacious walls but I only recognized Queen Victoria.

The Great Hall on the east side of the building is covered with a vaulted ceiling rising to forty feet. The room was bright with sunlight streaming through the several stained glass windows, reflecting colors bouncing around the hall. This hall was almost totally destroyed by a German air raid in May 1941. Fortunately, in 1939 the unique windows had been removed for safekeeping in case of just such an eventuality and when the Great Hall was rebuilt the original windows were reinstalled.

And then there is the banqueting hall topped by a dome rising to thirty-six feet with plasterwork on the vaults and domed ceiling. The walls are paneled in carved oak to a height of nine feet and the windows are filled with stained glass showing the Royal Arms, The Coat of Arms of the City (vicious-looking seahorses with chains and snarling mouths), and two Lords.

Impressive is an understatement and not a sight to be missed on any visit to Belfast. In fact, if you visited nowhere else, you'd learn all the history in one place.

The outdoor gardens and grounds are equally as stunning with a marble statue of Queen Victoria with bronze side-figures symbolizing shipbuilding and spinning. There is a short stone column bearing the inscription "U.S.A.E.F. (United States of America Expeditionary Force) landed in this City 26th January, 1942" and many more memorials.

Now common, we saw more and more flowers and remembrances for the Omagh victims against fences, pillars, gates and church doorways. Many bouquets were also placed at the entrance to City Hall.

The next day we boarded a train for a scenic trip to Bangor, a coastal town. It sits on a pretty harbor with a clock tower and historic buildings. We stayed at the Royal Hotel on Quay Street. Our bright and airy room had a separate area with a large bed through an arched entrance and a sofa, table, television and desk in the living area.

There were boats of all colors and sizes from yachts to motorboats and fishing boats as we walked along the harbor wall. We returned to the hotel for traditional afternoon tea, coffee and snacks in the Library Lounge. Feeling a bit down, I knew this was our final night in Northern Ireland and close to the end of this amazing adventure.

That evening we had a delicious, hearty dinner of tasty beef, root vegetables and potatoes as the main course. The hotel's restaurant is called The Quays and many enjoyed their final Guinness of the trip or an Irish coffee.

The next morning there was Nigel with our motorcoach and we headed back toward Dublin. We stopped at the Boyne Valley at Newgrange, a UNSECO World Heritage Site, where perfectly round mounds with sprouting wild grasses made them appear even taller. Rocks surrounded each mound.

This is the oldest Neolithic burial site in Ireland. Dirt paths led us from one burial chamber to the next. The passage tomb, Si an Bhrú, is one of the most famous prehistoric monuments in Western Europe. Built over five thousand years ago, the burial chamber is entered through a long stone passage, with the whole thing covered by a huge mound.

One mound itself covers more than an acre and was constructed from over two hundred thousand tons of stone and earth. Standing about thirty-six feet high, its diameter is about two hundred sixty feet. It is bordered by a curb, made of ninety-seven uneven stones, many of which are decorated.

The passage alone is forty feet long and is lined on both sides by standing stones. It leads directly into the burial chamber. The magnificent corbelled roof, sort of a squared arch, which is twenty feet high, has remained intact and waterproof for more than five thousand years. We couldn't walk through the passage but could see down into the darkness.

Just one of Newgrange's notable phenomena is the small opening over the door. At dawn on the morning of the winter solstice, the shortest day of the year (December 21), and for a number of days before and after, a shaft of sunlight penetrates the passage, creeping slowly to the back of the chamber. To the Neolithic farmers, this may have been a sign of rebirth, with the New Year giving renewed life to crops and animals.

We were able to wander around this ancient site surrounded by a mammoth hedge, seeing the passage tombs, the medieval cemetery, Tower House and standing stone. I couldn't fathom how this was constructed five thousand years ago with no modern equipment, just strong backs and animals.

Back in Dublin our final accommodations were at the Harding Hotel, where our trip began. On Saturday we wandered the city not like tourists anymore but more like guests who knew a lot more than when we started.

In Dublin Harbor, Tall Ships were ending the Cutty Sark Tall Ships Race, an international race. You could sense the anticipation and excitement of each crew as they sprinted up poles and proudly unveiled their country's flag coming into the harbor. Poland's tall ship was called Barquentine, built in 1980. One hundred boats sailed into Dublin Harbor, many clean and white and all with colorful pennants and their countries' flags rippling in the breeze. One white ship had a red stripe around the entire hull and all the men were lined up in dark attire, wearing white hats.

They had been racing for six weeks leaving Falmouth via Lisbon and the Spanish port of Vigo. We learned that the Cutty Sark Tall Ships Races are among the world's most prestigious maritime events, and competition to host the finale is intense, with over thirty cities vying for the 1998 honor that Dublin won.

Dublin basically turned into one big street carnival from morning to night with parades, street theater and music of every type. That evening were extravagant fireworks and water displays that lit up the night sky. Nearly five thousand young crew members, mostly men, from over thirty countries throughout the world were visiting this city.

We wandered around the river stopping at the monument for the victims of the Irish Potato Famine, with skinny, sad and despair-filled faces. It meant more after learning the history of this horrible time.

Situated right next to Christ Church and linked by an elegant bridge is DVBLINIA, a medieval trust to recreate the formative period in the city's growth from the arrival of the Anglo-Normans in 1170 to the closure of monasteries in 1540. It was a journey of everyday life in medieval Dublin. There is a scale model of the city showing the original location of public buildings and street layouts. We enjoyed cold beverages while looking at original 18th century prints of Dublin. We climbed St. Michael's Tower for a unique panoramic view of Dublin's city and surrounding area. Of course, we concluded the tour at the gift shop, buying lace handkerchiefs and anything with a shamrock.

Here we were, at the end of our tour back in Dublin. We entered Christ Church Cathedral on Saturday, August 22 for a 3 p.m. memorial service honoring those lost in Omagh. The service began with a half-muffled peal of bells, traditionally used at times of mourning. We stood in silence as the choir entered. They sang Psalm 23 from the Scottish Psalter of 1650, with the melody by Jessie Seymour

Irvine written in 1836-1837. A minister read from Revelation 7. At 3:10 p.m. we observed one minute of silence in memory of those who perished in the bombing. The congregation quieted and honored those gone so quickly. Cars, taxis, buses and people all stopped. It felt like the world had stopped briefly but really only on the island of Ireland.

This terrorist attack was carried out by a group called the Real Irish Republican Army, a provisional Irish Republican Army (IRA) splinter group who opposed the IRA's ceasefire and the Good Friday agreement. This turned out to be the deadliest single incident of the Troubles in Northern Ireland.

This bombing caused outrage both locally and internationally. Spurred on by the Northern Ireland peace process, it dealt a severe blow to the dissident IRA campaign. The Real IRA denied that the bomb was intended to kill civilians and apologized; shortly after, the group declared a ceasefire. The victims included people of different backgrounds and ages: Protestants, Catholics, teenagers, young children, a mother pregnant with twins, two Spanish tourists and others on a day trip from the Republic of Ireland. Both unionists and Irish nationalists were killed and injured. As a result of the bombing, new anti-terrorism laws were swiftly instituted by both the UK and the Republic of Ireland. This began a turning point. Women stood strong and did the right thing by reporting the murderers, many within their own families. Relatives reported relatives, friends reported friends, and vowed it would not happen again.

Another minister read, "God be in my head and in my understanding; God be in mine eyes and in my looking; God be in my mouth and in my speaking; God be in my heart and in my thinking; God be in mine end, and at my departing," written by Henry Walford Davies (1869-1941). We sang the old hymn, "Be Thou My Vision," a traditional Irish song. The melodies lifted my spirits as tears rolled not only down my cheeks but those of almost everyone around me. Locals and tourists were united in solemn remembrance. The Archbishop closed the service with The Blessing.

We flew home on August 23. I couldn't wait to tell Dad all about our adventures and show him pictures from where his great grandparents had come. In fifteen hours we were home and I was a changed person. What was to be a tour exploring a new country and maybe discovering some family roots became much more. It turned into a trip of realization, enlightenment, sorrow and more understanding—and tolerance.

Little did I know August 23 would become a meaningful day in my life but that was way in the future. I knew I would return one day to further explore one of the countries of my heritage and prayed peace and healing could come to these small countries.

August 2018

I watched BBC news on August 15, 2018, as the news anchor reported the twentieth anniversary remembrance in Omagh, Northern Ireland of the horrific bombing at 3:10 p.m. in the center of their town, killing twenty-nine innocent lives. I felt transported back twenty years and cried, just as I had when we were there. An emotional wreck anyway because my dear ninety-three-year-old dad, who had fueled my fascination with this country because of his roots, was in quickly failing health from a recent finding of cancer.

My husband and I were scheduled to depart September 1 on our second trip to Ireland but I wouldn't be going since my father had been diagnosed as only having six months of life left. I would never miss out on two entire weeks with him by going to Ireland. He said I should go. I told him we'd wait and see. He passed on August 23 and two weeks later I did go to Ireland for a second time.

Cathartic? Maybe. Healing? Nope. Emotional? Absolutely.

My thoughts returned to home over five thousand miles away, as I recalled what my father had told me one month earlier, "Darlin' daughter, you have to go to Ireland; you can't miss this opportunity." My reply after the third or fourth conversation on this topic became "I will wait and see, darlin' dad."

The "darlin'" started during my childhood. Dad's father's grandparents came from the Dublin area, escaping the potato famine and poor working conditions. Michael O'Reilly married Maggie McGinnes and they left their family and friends for a new world called America. He changed his name to Riley when they arrived. So, I was his darlin' daughter; he my very darlin' dad. The next generations would call him darlin' grandpa and darlin' great grandpa.

My dad had been diagnosed with stage two (really four) lymphoma located in his spleen which is extremely uncommon. His oncologist explained it would be aggressive and was also found in his lower abdomen. We heard the numbers "four to six months" without treatment. Treatment meant chemotherapy which was not an option my father would select due to a chronic World War II injury that he dealt with daily from age eighteen. He was an Army 10th Mountain Division ski trooper, ascending Mt. Belvedere in the Po Valley of the Italian Alps fighting back the German army, when another soldier stepped on a land mine and my dad was seriously wounded.

No way would I waste two weeks in Ireland when I could spend that precious time with my darlin' dad. But he chose to do things his own way and passed ten days before the planned trip to my motherland, or in this case, fatherland. My mother reminded me that dad wanted me to go. My brothers and other family suggested I go. So, my husband and I joined our eight friends and went with Greg and Linda from Oregon, Bruce and Nancy from California, Chris and Jeanine and Dave and Sue from Washington. Sue and Jeanine are sisters. My secret hope, with their help, would be to return home renewed, refreshed and healed.

We began and ended our two-week tour in Dublin with Collette, a land-based tour company that we have travelled with around the globe. Arriving in the afternoon after about sixteen hours of travel, we dropped off our luggage in our spacious room at the Clayton Hotel Ballsbridge, a neighborhood of Dublin. As is our practice, we arrived a few days before the actual tour began to get over any travel issues and prowl around Dublin on our own at a relaxed pace.

We sat on the top level of the Dublin Hop On/Hop Off bus touring the city but mostly for the fresh air to help us stay awake. "No napping" had been our mantra. Greg and Linda sat toward the front of the top deck and as we went under a tree with branches too low, Greg got smacked in the face, fortunately not too hard. We all ducked thanks to Greg's leaf encounter. He was having some unexplained health issues and we'd be watching our friend carefully.

We returned to the hotel restaurant for a dinner of whitefish, broad plank potatoes (chips), mushy peas and dense white bread. I skipped the peas, whether mushy or not, absolutely not a favorite vegetable of mine. Turning on the faucet in one of the biggest bathtubs I have ever seen, and after about five minutes of filling it up complete with bubbles, I slipped in to soak away close to twenty-four hours of travel dust and aches, except for a few hours of sleep on the flight. I set the alarm on my phone clock, careful not to fall asleep in the tub because my knight in shining armor would be no help, already fast asleep.

We awoke bright-eyed and ready for our first full day in Dublin. Walking into the center of the city would take around a half hour through a lovely neighborhood of homes, small businesses and a few restaurants and pubs, scouting out where we would have dinner for two nights before the actual tour began.

At the Dublin Church, a plaque caught my eye as the last name sounded familiar. It read "Erected by the citizens of Dublin to the memory of John McNeill Boyd." We have dear friends at home, Tim and Heather, with the last name of Boyd so I hoped it could be some long lost relative of Tim's. I read a lengthy inscription, "John McNeill Boyd, R.N. captain H.M.S. Ajax born at Londonderry 1812 and lost off the rocks at Kingstown Feb. 9th 1861 in attempting to save the crew of the brig, Neptune. Safe from the rocks, whence swept thy manly form the tides white rush. The stepping of the storm, borne with a public pomp, by just decree heroic sailor! From that fatal sea, a city vows this marble unto thee, and here in this calm place, where never din of earths great waterfloods shall enter in: when to our human hearts two thoughts are given, one Christ's self-sacrifice, the other heaven: here is it meet for grief and love to crave the Christ-taught bravery that died to save, the life not lost, but found beneath the wave. All thy billows and thy waves passed over me: yet I will look again toward thy holy temple."

On a corner I spotted Reilly's pub decked out in black paint proudly displaying the gold Guinness sign and shamrock promoting the National Lottery Sold Here signage along the top, with wooden posts trimmed in Kelly green paint.

The cherry red-painted Queen of Tarts storefront had shelves lined with homemade delicacies, most topped with some type of berry.

It was unusual not to see a building decked out with flowers, flags and banners. Most buildings where white, gray or reddish rusty stone. Multiple hues of gray stones made up many churches and Celtic crosses. Walking by Bulmer's Fish and Chips, we paid twelve pounds for an authentic lunch.

Close to Trinity College we came upon a life-size Molly Malone statue erected in 1988 to commemorate the heroine of the famous song, "Cockles and Mussels," a popular song set in Dublin. Molly lived in the 17th century and was known as a hawker by day (seller of fish) and part-time prostitute by night. The statue sometimes is also called "The Tart with a Cart" or "The Trollop With the Scallops." Molly is wearing a low-cut blouse, barely covering her bustiness. On the cart sits three empty woven baskets depicting what, I don't know.

We toured the university's impressive and meaningful *Book of Kells*. It hadn't changed much in twenty years except for creating a more efficient flow for tourists to view the books.

Popping out of a crack in the stone wall at the cemetery grew a lone lush fern. Dozens of stone or cement Celtic crosses towered above other lower gravestones.

We returned twenty years later to the unchanged Kilmainham Gaol (the jail). This time the top floor displayed a historical tribute to Nelson Mandela who we'd seen in Oxford, England, twenty-one years earlier. It still felt as ominous, heartbreaking and depressing as our first visit.

After strolling all morning with hunger pains becoming sharper, we shared a Beef and Guinness, a thick, dark brown savory stew with two mounds of mashed potatoes on the top, each about the size of an ice cream scoop.

That clear warm afternoon we mostly wandered along the river looking at boats, memorials and people. For dinner we tried our hotel's vegetable soup with Irish soda bread. The soup, called Dublin Coddle, is made of Irish pork sausage pieces in a potato and herb broth. We shared a grilled chicken fillet with herb stuffing served with pepper sauce, and a baked fillet of salmon with Cajun sauce, sautéed leeks and brie cheese served with cranberry sauce in puff pastry. And here's a tip: We don't pronounce the "h" in herb but they do. So Herb could be a man's name or an herb (erb).

Dessert didn't look particularly traditional, just a typical chocolate brownie but the bonus of the Irish liqueur ice cream turned it into something lip-smacking for sure. A dollop of whipped cream decorated with raspberry drizzle made for a lovely show and delicious dessert.

The next morning our official Collette tour began. Twenty others now joined our already merry band of ten, along with our guide April, who is of Scottish origins, and driver Bill, who lived in the area. We headed to Merrion Square Park in one of Dublin's five historic Georgian squares. A local guide named Alexander, who looked like you might guess would be a typical Irishmen with a thick head of collar-length white hair that matched his bushy eyebrows and a pinkish glow to his skin. He wore a blue shirt with a snazzy blue and beige tie with a gold fleur-de-lis pattern and a gray sport coat with black slacks.

Alexander joined us for the morning and explained that this park memorializes the famous (and infamous) Oscar Wilde, author, playwright and poet and was born in 1854 at #1 Merrion Square, just across the road from where we stood. The memorial consists of three pieces—the stone sculpture of a reclining Oscar, a pillar with a bronze of his pregnant wife, and a pillar with a bronze male torso.

Our knowledgeable guide said the memorial's Irish sculpture, commissioned by the Guinness Ireland Group, was erected in 1997. He used polished colored stones and interesting textures to create a striking lifelike pose of Oscar relaxing, laying back on top of a thirty-five ton boulder of white quartz from the Wicklow Mountains. The artist wanted to depict Oscar's love of beautiful objects, including stones, as well as his colorful personality. Even his clothing is unique as Oscar wears a green smoking jacket with a pink collar, long pants and shiny black shoes. Alexander made sure we all carefully noticed Oscar's face that is most unusual because of having a two-sided expression, both sadness and joy. Black and white magpies dotted the grassy park. It reminded me of one of my favorite Oscar quotes, "With freedom, books, flowers, and the moon, who could not be happy?"

On the front of stones around a square were several of his quotes: "It seems to me we all look at nature too much and live with her too little." And another one: "There is only one thing worse in the world than being talked about, and that is NOT being talked about." My guess is that he might have been referring to politicians or himself.

Before this Irish adventure, I thought about what I wanted to learn and glean from my second time here and decided I would pay more attention to meaningful people not just charming historical architecture and gorgeous scenery.

St. Stephen's Green (or "park" as we would call it) is smack dab in the center of Dublin. There is an official national holiday on December 26 for the man who is believed to be the first Christian martyred sometime around 33 AD.

I felt an immediate calm overcome me even though traffic surrounds all sides of the square. The twenty-two acres are extraordinary with clean, well-maintained historical monuments, trees, oodles of different flowers in perfectly manicured beds, a large water fountain with a small girl sailing her little toy boat, and ponds with ducks, and children feeding them chunks of white bread.

It wasn't just the beauty and serenity of this gem but the history that is especially meaningful as it was one of the areas the Irish held during the 1916 Uprising that ultimately won them independence. There is an abundance of statues of lords, poets, a knight, a king and the famous Three Fates. Down a pathway through an arch of greenery is a stone sculpture garden and a sad, somber reminder of the Great Famine. The tallest person is headless; a scrawny dog is barely alive; another headless person is holding a pole in her left hand that touches the ground and her other hand reaching out to a person sitting on the ground. But it is part of history for this country. It deserves to be remembered. On a lighter note, it's the only place in Dublin where you can find an elephant and tiger if you have time to search.

Right across from the Green is the main shopping street, Grafton Street. Looking to the left is the Gaiety Theatre, Chester Beatty Library, City Hall and Dublin Castle. To our right stood the National Library of Ireland and the Royal Hibernian Academy. This particular academy was founded as a result of about thirty Irish painters, sculptors and architects who petitioned the government for a charter of incorporation in 1832.

Within a short distance down the street, cloaked in granite and storefronts, was an archway through which we came face to face with a life-size Pieta, then continued through large wooden doors entering a lovely, peaceful, small Catholic church called St. Teresa's Carmelite Church, founded in 1792. The altar area is breathtaking and the alcoves for quiet prayer are humbling as locals came and went for a brief time of prayer and reflection. A sunbeam worked its way through gorgeous stained glass windows that reflected a kaleidoscope of rainbow colors onto the tile floor.

There are exquisite statues with their own individual altar where you can light candles. Whether Catholic or otherwise, my advice is to light a candle and make a wish. Apparently, it's an Irish tradition here.

St. Teresa, born in 1515, was a prominent Spanish mystic, nun, author and theologian who led a contemplative life through what was called mental prayer. I asked Alexander about "mental prayer" and he said it meant nonverbal. Being a Carmelite, she lived, prayed and worked as a member of a united family in Christ. Carmelites serve God's people.

After all this walking it seemed time for a treat and we'd heard some reports about fudge, yes, Irish fudge. We went into an open-air market with stalls displaying pastries, meats, sandwiches and about anything else one could want. Sue spotted it first, the Man of Aran Fudge, with its promise of creamy, buttery fudge made especially for you, which meant me. The fudge creator, Tomás Póil, grew up on one of the three Aran Islands off the coast of Galway. Times were tough and his grandmother made a toffee mixture like no other. When he was sent away to school in Galway, he treasured the taste. Those sweet memories never left him, thus fudge for the masses. He makes the exact same original flavor today called Tiger Butter Fudge with plenty more types to sample. I selected Salted Caramel Fudge, Hot Irishman Fudge and Peppermint Chocolate Chip Fudge and requested that he cut them into small cubes to share with friends. All were delicious but I bought a separate piece of the salted caramel and didn't share.

At City Hall, Daniel O'Connell was a bigger than life man and has a bigger than life statue in his honor. Born in 1775 and died in 1847, he is known as the "liberator" and sought "Catholic Emancipation" to gain more rights for Catholics, concluding with the changes enacted in 1829 which removed the major remaining laws discriminating against Catholics. O'Connell gave his first ever speech in City Hall, then at the Royal Exchange. In 1841, he became the first Catholic Lord Mayor of Dublin since 1690.

As we stood under the stone arched gate, I read "Gates of Fortitude and Justice." Erected in 1750, this is a pair of massive inner arches which flank the Bedford Tower and provide symmetry to the north side of the courtyard. Large sculptures of Fortitude and Justice stand at the gates. Justice is the main ceremonial gateway into medieval Dublin Castle.

Ireland's most famous writer, James Joyce, stands on a marble block located right off O'Connell Street, near the Spire of Dublin monument. The novelist is leaning on a walking stick, his bespectacled eyes looking upward from under a hat as if in thought. He is dressed in a shirt with a tie, slacks and shoes with an overcoat that touches his knees.

The Spire, also called the Monument of Light, is a large, stainless steel straight-pin-like memorial completed in 2003. Almost four hundred feet tall and consisting of eight hollow cone sections, it really didn't seem to fit into the architectural correctness of this area but I know Ireland is a country of monuments for whatever the reason or cause.

Behind the castle we saw buildings painted in bright colors of yellow, red, lime and blue, and the yellow building had a royal blue front door. A short distance away is an oval plaque inscribed "#7 Hoey's Court (now demolished) about 100 feet NW of this spot reputed that Jonathan Swift dean of St Patrick's Cathedral was born on the 30th day of November 1667. He died on the 19 day of Oct 1745."

My fellow readers will recognize his name as the author of *Gulliver's Travels*. Swift was an Irish author, clergyman and satirist. His father died two months before he was born so Swift grew up under the care of his uncle. He received a bachelor's degree from Trinity College then worked as a statesman's assistant. He became dean of St. Patrick's Cathedral in Dublin. For some reason, most of his books were published under pseudonyms. I hung on every word and detail Alexander shared with us. Using a local guide provides insight that you might miss when wandering on your own, or with your head buried in a travel guide.

Walking down the street, we saw a third-story window to which was firmly attached what appeared to be a gigantic peeping-tom—a black and white peacock made of cloth and feathers. Alexander was clueless on this peculiarity. We strolled by Kennedy & McSharry, a well-known men's store where hats, caps and ties are available for purchase. I thought of my dad, a true tie man over the decades. He always dressed up for work. While an elderly salesman held a traditional tie showing it to an equally mature patron, I wondered if this shop would be around in twenty years.

Around another corner stood a brightly teal-painted building which houses the cheerful little Chorus Café in the Temple Bar. Special "Chef's Dishes" were posted on a stand-up menu board at the door: Mexican chicken wrap & chips, chicken burger & chips, BLT & fries, for about the same prices as at home. Across the square, Handel's Hotel is several stories high with an impressive statue of a man standing on a thin twenty-foot tall pedestal using both arms as he is conducting a choir. If you didn't look up, you'd miss him.

The historic Liffey Bridge (Ha'Penny Bridge) built in 1816, was commonly called Ha'Penny Bridge because a toll was charged on the bridge until March 1919. Its original name was Wellington Bridge and since 1836 has been officially called Liffey Bridge. It spans the Liffey River and is now a pedestrian-only bridge. Many photos are taken under the white-iron-scrolled archway with a lantern perched at the top, right at the crest of the bridge. We took plenty, too.

On this second visit, not only did I want to learn more about notables and people who had made a difference in Irish history, I didn't want to miss anything new that had been built in the past twenty years.

Ireland is a mecca for memorials, historical places and public sculptures but few are as haunting and somber as the Famine Memorial on the bank of the River Liffey at Custom House Quay at the city docklands. The collection of statues designed and crafted by Dublin sculptor Rowan Gillespie was given to the city of Dublin in 1997, one year before our first visit. I didn't recall this memorial from our first trip and wondered why.

This memorial is a permanent reminder of the many people who emigrated because of the Great Famine. It's built on the site of the Perseverance, one of the first famine ships to leave the area in 1846. The seventy-four-year-old ship's captain quit his office job to transport the starving people from Dublin to America. All of his passengers arrived safely and the Perseverance was one of the first of thousands of ships to make that epic crossing.

I wandered through the memorial of emaciated men and women trudging along the banks of the river, with their various facial expressions of sadness and anguish, yet determined to save their lives. The bronze sculpture also includes a starving dog walking behind his people.

The skeletal figures, four males and two females, are shabbily dressed and wearing nothing more than rags. The first couple figures are each clutching one bag tightly against their chests. The third person is a man carrying his belongings in one hand against his chest with his tattered hat in the other hand. The woman in the back isn't carry anything; her bony arms and thin hands are at her sides. Her face is pointed heavenward with a questioning look on her face. The last male has a smaller corpse wrapped around his shoulders, maybe his child. They are wearing no shoes.

I felt no joy or hope in these figures. Just a few steps away from the memorial is a tall ship moored in the water that is set up as a famine museum. The Jeanie Johnston is a replica famine boat. This memorial was here when we visited in 1998 but I brushed by it quickly, gladly allowing the tall ships from the Cutty Stark Tall Ships Race to divert my attention. Nothing distracted me this time.

Not far upriver, sparkling in the sunshine, is a white bridge. The design caught my attention because it looks much like a harp laid over on its side if one uses imagination. I asked our guide about this unusual expanse and he told me it is called the Harp Bridge by many but really it is the Samuel Beckett Bridge, which opened in 2009. Ah ha, something else new since we'd visited in 1998. Beckett was awarded the Nobel Prize in Literature in 1969. It is the second bridge designed by Calatrava, the first being the James Joyce Bridge farther up river. I smiled as we left this area of the river and Dublin.

The next day we departed the hustle and bustle of the city for our ten-day tour road-tripping around the Emerald Isle. Just before we arrived at our next stop, Kilkenny, I noticed dozens of black birds about the size of crows, on fences, rooftops and lampposts. Were they guarding their turf? I was wrong to assume crows. They are jackdaws, a bird similar to our crow and a frequent visitor to many places we would see on this trip. According to Kerry tradition, those of Kilgarvan could once talk. To escape the unwelcome attention of the crows, they asked if they could move into the towns. At first, due to the opposition of the chief druid, the king said no, but later, when a jackdaw found the king's missing ring, he relented. It is possible to teach a jackdaw to talk and this may have given rise to the story.

Stopping at our first charming town, Kilkenny on the River Nore, it would be our first of many "step back in time" feelings. We decided to do a city tour on a miniature train, more like a trolley pulling two cars, that would hold around ten tourists. Plus, walking in drizzle didn't sound too inviting. Around the first corner, one charming house had brightly painted yellow trimmed windows upstairs and down, and double doors trimmed in the same happy yellow. Window boxes overflowed with red geraniums and tiny delicate white flowers. As we continued following closely by the original rock wall, about ten feet tall with ivy trailing down from the top, I could touch the roughness of the rocks. Around another corner stood a sunshine yellow house next to a pink house which was right next to a teal house. Our transportation putted along and our guide told us all kinds of interesting lore. We drove by St. Canice's Cathedral, looking a bit bleak because of the gray weather. Two side-by-side houses attached by a brick wall showed off a bright red door and the other a soft yellow one.

While on board we received an education on spirits, fairies and leprechauns which I thought was important in order to keep them straight. Apparently, I'd forgotten the differences over twenty years.

—A Leprechaun is a solitary fairy, a shoemaker or tailor, resembling a small man of grumpy temperament. The leprechaun is said to have a pot of gold, which he must surrender to whomever catches him.

—A Banshee is a female fairy attached to a family who it warns of an approaching death by giving an eerie wail. I recalled hearing about the banshee in Scotland the year before as it is also prominent in Scottish lore.

—Fairies are either pint-size beings, or a little bigger like a leprechaun or someone of normal human stature and can be either female or male. They go around in troops. They have the gift of healing, which they can pass on to humans. Sometimes a mortal may be sought by a fairy lover. If he refuses her advances, he is her master; if he surrenders, she dominates him. Fairies live in mounds. I just wanted to see one, any one of them.

After our thirty-minute riding tour we stopped for ice cream at Murphy's. I mean, who doesn't love ice cream, rain or shine? The sign reads "Taste the Atlantic with our sea salt ice cream." It wasn't a surprise to find Dave and Sue in there already sampling the goods. A picture of a happy brown cow read "Creamy, creamy milk from the rare, indigenous Kerry cow breed" explained where its goodness came from. And when I read "One of the best ice cream shops in the world..." we were goners. Not only did all the publicity on the walls create high expectations, the handsome Irish guy serving up the delectable delights told us about certain favorites like Dingle Gin, Irish Brown Bread, Irish Coffee, Elderflower, Dingle Sea Salt—stop right there—I had to have sea salt. But wait, also Sticky Toffee Pudding, yep, another must try. He told us that the worst flavor they tried creating turned out to be the smoked salmon ice cream; he said it tasted horrible. The best weird flavor is blue cheese and caramelized shallot. The oddest customer request that they actually made into ice cream was green pea and mint, reportedly not great. He also told us in which towns we could find Murphy's and we'd be looking them up in Galway, and when we returned to Dublin.

Back in our spacious motorcoach, we headed to Waterford where I really looked forward to stopping since it would be our first time here. Enjoying the drive through multiple shades of mint, pear, lime, fern and moss, with short stone walls separating the farms, I didn't want to miss a thing. Lots of magpies that were hanging around the sheep are navy, really almost black with white, and they supposedly foretold the future. I thought, why not? In Ireland anything can happen. I have some Waterford collectibles at home and would be searching for a Christmas ornament. My husband had given me a few pieces, and after several years we finally had a complete set of a Waterford nativity scene that we brought out for the entire month of December. I already had a Celtic Cross and a thatched cottage.

We were staying in Waterford, home of the House of Waterford Crystal, with our hotel conveniently located just down the street. But before being released to support the local economy, we toured Christ Church Cathedral Square complete with several all-white houses lined up in a row. One had a bright red door with a cute ceramic birdhouse nailed to the upper right-hand side of the door casing and the next home had a bright blue door with a black #7.

This Georgian style cathedral with pillared portico, internal columns of varied styles and a spectacular delicate stucco plasterwork ceiling, is a must-see. Sparkling at me were two jaw-dropping, shimmering Waterford crystal chandeliers looking like an upside-down ice cream cone with the cone quite long. Prisms of light ricocheted off everything, bouncing colors all over. The white scrollwork on white columns and arches with the soft yellow ceiling radiated a cheery peaceful feeling. The internal walls are adorned with many elaborate memorial monuments and reliefs. There is a beautiful pulpit, baptismal font and magnificent organ. The tomb of James Rice dating back to 1482 is supposedly one of the finest cadaver tombs in the country. It felt cold and really creepy so I didn't stay long.

In the square is also a life-size Viking boat outside of Reginald's Tower, a Waterford landmark monument and Ireland's oldest civic building. The tower occupies the site of the earliest fort and built by the Vikings, led by Reginald, when they first settled in Waterford and founded the city in 914. The fort was built to guard the entrance to their harbor, the tidal marsh where St. John's River flowed into the River Suir in the area of the present-day city hall.

The ground and first floor date to King John's time. John visited Waterford twice, in 1185 as a young prince then again as king in 1210. The walls on the ground floor are over thirteen feet thick, impressive yet typical of towers of the period. The ground floor is tiled and upper floors are wood. Built into the wall of the tower is a staircase with steps that were deliberately designed to be of different heights and widths, making it difficult for attackers (and visitors) to climb. Steps like this are known as stumble steps. The spiral staircase was oriented to the right making it impossible for right-handed attackers to swing their swords properly as they climbed up. Smart Vikings.

Rebuilt by the Anglo-Normans in the 12th century, the top two floors were added in the 15th century to house a cannon. Until about 1700, the tower was the strongpoint of the medieval defensive walls that enclosed the city.

In the archways are numerous displays presenting a bird's-eye view of how the town would have looked around the year 1050, almost a century and a half after it was established. The modern streets of Waterford still follow the lines of the original streets set out over a thousand years ago.

In a display case is a Viking lead weight decorated with an enamel bearded human face. This lead weight, dating from about 850, is one of over two hundred found during archaeological excavations at the Viking site near Waterford. Before coins were used by the Vikings, for money they traded pieces of silver which were weighed using lead weights like this one.

There is a brooch called the Waterford Kite Brooch made about 1100 and is Ireland's finest example of personal jewelry from this time period. These kite-shaped brooches are basically cloak fasteners with elaborate heads worn by high-status women and men. This brooch would have been used to tie a cloak or a shawl. It is made of silver and decorated with extravagant gold foil and amethyst glass studs. This piece shows the wealth of Waterford's inhabitants at this time, as well as the exceptional talent and ability of its craftsmen.

There is a cannonball on the top floor of the tower but also one embedded in the outside tower wall. The cannonballs date from the siege of

Waterford by the army of Oliver Cromwell in the 1600s, when ships on The River Suir bombarded the city with cannon fire.

Even though a fairly small tower, it is packed with impressive history and treasures and truly a fine education for all of us.

After our walking tour I had the afternoon open to explore so I headed right for the Waterford Crystal store hoping to find the perfect remembrance. I knew I had to find just the right Christmas ornament as I love to collect something for my tree from any country we've visited. A terrific marketing piece propped up in the corner of the window of the store was a full-size harp adorned with thousands of shimmering crystals.

I stuck my hands in my coat pockets for fear of bumping or breaking something. To the right stood a door and not just any door but a door with an oval-shaped mirror. Surrounding the mirror was a myriad of distinctive crystals, row after row around the entire mirror. Impressive and extraordinary are understatements and only thirty-two thousand euros, not including delivery. A display case held the Reginald Tower engraved on an exquisite crystal vase. I looked to the left and there they were, several types of ornaments. It was hard to select just one but I did. It's a wreath of ivy complete with a bow at the bottom with 2018 engraved on it.

While walking back to the hotel to drop off my Waterford find for safekeeping I noticed a colorful poster promoting Kyle Riley & The Temper Tantrums, a folk and rock music and show for toddlers under eight. They would be performing the following week at the Theatre Royal.

Looking out our hotel window that evening reflecting on the day, I watched as the sunset changed the colors of the river. Light clouds turned apricot then pink against the amber sky. Lights were twinkling on each home lining the roadway across from the river. The homes and lights disappeared from my view as they wound around the corner.

From our open window somewhere in the distance I could hear a familiar sound that I loved. And sometimes I was the only one who seemed to be able to hear it. I knew there were bagpipers somewhere but my husband didn't hear them. He reminded me we were in Ireland not Scotland and he noted I had a tendency to hear bagpipes when no one else did. But once the music got closer thus louder, he agreed that somewhere there were indeed pipers. I gave him the well-deserved "I told you so" look. Down in the dark parking lot below huddled a group starting to warm up for a performance. I needed to find out where. I told my husband I'd see him later and off I ran down the hotel corridor to the lobby to inquire about my favorite Scottish musical sounds. At the same time, the band walked into the lobby and it turned out they were playing at a fundraising event in our hotel. I sat outside the dining room for some time listening to their distinctive and sometimes haunting melodies. What a perfect way to end a lovely day.

The next morning our destination was the famous and often frequented Blarney Castle. We'd been there twenty years before and were looking forward to revisiting this historical attraction with friends who were seeing it for the first time. I got great pleasure watching our friends' expressions seeing Ireland through their eyes, especially some having Irish roots like me. They were looking forward to kissing the stone, which we had agreed we would not repeat on the climb up especially since there were hundreds of people in the line. Before safeguards were installed, the kiss was performed with real risk to life and limb. Participants were grasped by the ankles and dangled from a great height.

We took pictures together and of other each with the castle in the background. My long-time "Sisterchick" Sue, and husband Dave, were having a marvelous adventure. Sue has Irish roots, too. What's a "Sisterchick," you ask? A Sisterchick is a friend who shares the deepest wonders of your heart, loves you like a sister, and loves you even when you're being a brat. Sue is my forever Sisterchick and even though we'd done a variety of vacations together, this one we'd been looking forward to for years and years. And here we finally were together. We shared laughter, tears and ah-ha moments on this adventure. Not only were these special friends along for this adventure but Sue's sister Jeanine and husband Chris were here also. All four were like children on Christmas morning. Sue gave me, Jeanine and Nancy a sweet sterling silver shamrock telling us anytime we wore it to remember our time together.

The stone castle reminded me of a soda cracker box standing on end with some cutouts on the top. Let's just say its curb appeal is less than spectacular. It's a five-story stone tower with windows all around it with a wedding cake like-topper that must have been erected to watch for marauding Vikings. Then there's an uneven yet walkable stone wall around the castle that's great for looking down on intruders or tourists, depending on your frame of mind or century you lived in. A crow or jackdaw was eyeing us from his perch above where we walked. I looked up and said, "Don't you dare," and hoped he wouldn't be depositing something white on my jacket.

Walking through a vine-covered wooden arbor and reaching the end, we stepped into magnificent gardens of flowers and humongous ancient trees. I noticed a crow hopping from one wooden arch to the next as we walked below. He looked like the same one from the castle wall.

We came to a ninety-foot long wooden pergola that spans the path through the area called the Herbaceous Border that runs along a south-facing stone wall in the upper arboretum. Extending more than one hundred yards it creates an impressive display of color using a wide range of perennials as well as unusual annuals. The pergola was bare of summertime flowers except for a late-blooming rose here and there. I stood imagining what all those vines would look like with thousands of colorful roses.

Hidden behind the castle battlements we discovered the Poison Garden which definitely wasn't here twenty years ago. Even the sign looked new and it read in bold font "DO NOT TOUCH, SMELL OR EAT ANY PLANT! CHILDREN MUST BE ACCOMPANIED AT ALL TIMES." We entered at our own risk made abundantly clear by the signage because these plants are so dangerous and toxic that some are kept in large cages. This garden contains a collection of poisonous plants from all over the world and are labelled with information about their toxicity and traditional and modern uses. What in the world? I highly recommend not going into this garden and we exited quickly.

The Jungle, complete with its own bamboo viewing platform, is the newest garden and trails along the back of the Tropical Border. It was designed to surprise visitors with exotic plants that can be grown in the Irish climate. There are banana plants, giant tree ferns and bamboo. I felt like I'd been transported to a completely different country somewhere in the Caribbean.

My favorite garden within the castle is The Seven Sisters that forms the central feature of a garden of grasses, and soft and colorful flowers which are a contrast to large, solid immobile gray rocks that dominate the space. Even the prickly purple thistle looked softer next to the hot pink Irish Heath. Rows and beds of different colors and types of dahlias and rows of a variety of colorful chrysanthemums, plus some surprising hibiscus, were all in full bloom creating a mixture of shapes and colors. Children were having a grand time climbing all over the boulders.

A plaque read that legend tells of a famous king who once ruled this area. He had seven daughters and two sons. His rival was also a powerful clan chief and the time came when the king had to defend his lands. One terrible day the army rode out to battle with the king, and his two sons led the way. Although victorious, it came at a great price as both sons were killed. The army marched back to the castle, passing the ancient druids' stone circle that had stood for millennia. The king dispatched a contingent of men to the sacred site and in his grief, instructed them to push over two of the nine standing stones commemorating his fallen sons. The Seven Sisters remains standing to this day. I made every effort to believe these stories of Irish history.

It seemed time for a break so we followed the signs through the stableyard a short walk from the castle, to the charming, appropriately named Stable Yard Café. Lined up in the display cases were beautiful cakes, fresh scones and other tasty treats.

They offered a large range of Bewley's coffees and varieties of teas. All cakes and scones are freshly made daily by a local baker and the selection of lemon drizzle, chocolate, carrot, coffee, apple tart, and Banoffi pie was overwhelming. We could have had Guinness stew, sausage rolls, pizza slices or snacks and crisps but we went with a little lighter fare. I had Banoffi pie in Scotland so knew it was a pastry base or crumbled biscuits, lots of butter and layered sliced bananas, topped with unsweetened whipped cream, toffee and a few thinly sliced bananas.

Instead, I enjoyed a cup of tea with cream and sugar along with a lemon scone with a drizzle of honey produced from a local beekeeper and a scoop of their loganberry ice cream. I mean, who doesn't have homemade ice cream at 10:30 in the morning? We were going to sit outside in the sunshine but I noticed a crow eyeing me that creeped me out so we sat inside and enjoyed the scenic Irish countryside posters scattered around the café walls. Garden flowers brightened each table from the mason jars that served as vases.

Then I noticed a crow standing in the doorway watching us intently. I surmised he was waiting for a speck of leftover scone. This one definitely followed us around and was getting on my nerves. Could a bird be spooky and disturbing? Yes. It was probably my imagination but I did take a few photos of him in these different locations and in each picture the crow looks identical. As we left the

Stable Yard Café, our crow stalker joined other inky black crows gathered on the rooftop. Or maybe they were jackdaws?

Slightly disturbed by the crow crowd, we headed directly to the Blarney Castle Shop for some browsing. Aimlessly wandering the aisles, I discovered a round rack with dozens of bookmarks with family crests and explanations of their origins:

CAMPBELL for my cousin Patti who is married to Donny whose family is mostly from northern Scotland. It means "crooked mouth." I laughed when I read this.

DALY for my friend Sally who volunteers at Meals on Wheels where I go each Thursday. Daly means "assembles frequently."

FINEGAN for my childhood friend Maleah and her parents who were some of my folks' best friends. Finegan means "little fair one."

MARTIN for my longtime friends Mike and Kathy. Mike's parents were best friends with my folks and like second parents to me. It means "devotee of St. Martin."

O'BRIEN for my great aunt Katie O'Brien with red hair and blue eyes who lived in Montana. I saw her several times in my youth. It means "exalted one."

WHITE for my friend Darrel who I worked with for years in nonprofit educational fundraising. He and his wife Charlene are originally from Canada but I was guessing he has roots in Ireland. White means "of fair complexion." I know Charlene has Irish roots.

However, I knew our next stop would be at the Blarney Woolen Mills, established in 1823, known as the home of Irish Knitwear and Belleek Irish China. Wanting a Christmas ornament in Belleek I saved my spending money for here. Inside are all types of clothing, blankets and anything else that you could ever imagine made of 95% merino and 5% cashmere woven in Ireland, discounted 10% just for us. Nancy smiled, as she was in her happy place—shopping. My husband purchased a traditional gray herringbone Irish flat cap; I bought a Christmas ornament for myself. At the end of our adventure, my traveling friends gave me a gorgeous 100% merino wool scarf of multiple pinks with light celery herringbone horizontal stripes and muted blue vertical stripes.

Driving through the countryside I noticed plenty of bunnies, frequently flattened as roadkill. Some locals purposely run them down as folklore reports that witches could disguise themselves as hares. Witch-hares were said to steal milk from cattle. I didn't need to see one of these.

Occasionally we'd see an Irish Wolfhound walking beside a human, or in an outside pen usually the size of a horse corral. These are big dogs with lots of hair. Folklore states a wolfhound named Adhnuall was the hound of Finn McCool, the giant who built the Causeway we'd visit the following week.

And as cats must have equal time, we learned that black cats were believed to be lucky and Irish black cats were said to understand human speech.

After lunch at the Woolen Mill Market we crossed into County Kerry for our final destination of the day—Killarney and views of the Gap of Dunloe. We stopped to stretch our legs looking down at the Gap of Dunloe. It is extremely rocky terrain with some trees and more Scotch Broom. I noticed something hanging from a solitary tree and went to explore. Someone had left a chain and lock hanging from a lower branch. I recognized it as a love lock that many couples leave on bridges in favorite cities they wish to return to. I could see why a couple left their lock here. I'd like to come back, too. As we crossed a stone bridge I looked down to see brown water flowing over the boulders; I knew that meant peat would be close by.

At the Killarney National Park, we boarded a boat and sailed through breathtaking lakes escorted by our expert boatman Captain Donal. A storm rolled in and sometimes the clouds touched the water and we couldn't even see the shoreline. The knowledgeable Captain Donal entertained us with witty one-liners and stories of the lakes and national park.

Late that afternoon we arrived at our next two nights' accommodations, Killarney Plaza Hotel. After dinner we were treated to some traditional Irish song, music and dance by the Gaelic Roots. We were exhausted by the end of the performance just watching them and concluded this was definitely for a younger generation of performers. The step dancing has always been my favorite type of dancing since I'd seen Michael Flatley in "Riverdance" twice after our first visit to Ireland. It was easy to recall the feeling of the beat of dozens of synchronized feet pounding and tapping the floor with a fast rhythm and catchy music. The twirling, leaping and jumping were truly amazing. My Irish roots were tingling then, too.

Our extraordinary guide April told us today's touring would be along the rugged coastline, looping around the picturesque Ring of Kerry, along pristine beaches, through quaint villages and over impressive landscapes.

Before leaving town and comfortably situated in my conveniently high vantage point looking out the bus window, I glanced over to my left where I sat eyeball-to-eyeball with a full-size bronze goat. Actually, it was a statue of a smiling goat with a crown on its head. April laughingly explained that he's really a quite popular goat called The King Puck and the statue represents a story of a goat which alerted the townspeople of impending disaster, or maybe something else, but he was widely popular. Someone had placed a necklace of white daisies around his neck.

Clouds covered the mountains lowering onto the hillsides but we could still see plenty of celadon pastures and farmland dotted with ponds and lakes and goldenrod broom. Unique and varied scenery would be the key words for the day.

Before the day ended we'd become familiar with names of places, villages and forts. Names like: Kilgarvan, the Battle of Callan in 1261, Cloonee Lakes, Uragh Stone Circle, Blackwater, Parknasilla, Sneem, Staigue Fort, Derrynane Abbey, Ballinskelligs Bay, Ballycarbery Castle, Leacanabuaile and Cahergal Forts, Coomasaharn Rock Art, Caragh Lake and McGillycuddy Reeks. Not likely to ever remember these names, I was glad to have maps I picked up along the way.

A stop at the Kerry Bog Village almost teleports one back to the 18th and 19th centuries. We were greeted by two friendly Irish Wolfhounds who obviously owned this place. One white house had a green front door and windows. I loved the front door because it is what we call a Dutch Door, where you can open the top and bottom separately. We had one in our last home and it reminded me of a favorite television series when I was young called "Petticoat Junction." Of course, I had to go in. Looking up on the inside, bog scraw (our straw but larger) was used to insulate the house during cold winters. Using flagstones made the floors uneven.

An iron bed and cot were in one bedroom. Coming out, I heard my name and stopped as Sisterchick Sue took my picture. Complete with a thatched river reed roof, this house belonged to the turf cutter. Large families were the norm despite the fact that they lived in small dwellings. Outside, above a pile of peat, hung a basket of red geraniums.

Off to the left is an old 19th century Romany caravan. These were used by those known as "traveling people" who navigated the roads of Ireland. A single black and white cob or a piebald horse pulled the caravan. Many families lived in these rolling homes.

The blacksmith, O'Sullivan's Old Forge, lived in the next building. The walls of the forge were thick with the center section made of loose stone. Several windows helped with good ventilation along with double doors and a large chimney. When a hot horseshoe plopped into cold water to cool, it created a lot of steam.

The stable dwelling had been the home of the McGillycuddy family. This was a typical home with a stable side for valuable animals like pigs, horses and cows in calf, and their body heat helped warm the house. The family lived on the other side of the residence. Families made their own cheese and butter.

The Laborer's Cottage is considerably smaller and showed a different class among village residents. A man worked in the boglands cutting and transporting turf. There is a neatly stacked mound of peat against the front of the house. The front door and window trim were painted bright yellow and inside is a mud floor. The few windows were small and the reason given, as in most cottages of this era, is for tax purposes. You had to pay higher taxes for having larger windows as light was considered a luxury. This tax started the famous phrase "daylight robbery."' Of course, cottages did not have toilets; instead they used a special pot placed under the bed.

The Thatcher's Dwelling with its thatched roof appeared amazingly perfect and thatchers of this time were in high demand because they were responsible for building and repairing the majority of cottages in their area. Displayed on the walls were teapots, pitchers, plates of several sizes and patterns, lanterns and other items used daily. This cottage even has an upstairs and a much airier and spacious interior.

I'd had enough of cottages, tools and machinery so I walked behind the complex to discover some beautiful horses munching in a field of dandelions. However, to my surprise, the informational sign told me that, in fact, these are Kerry Bog Ponies. They are a native breed to Ireland, recognized by the Irish Horse Board. The breed had been dangerously close to extinction in the late 1980s; however, with the perseverance of John Mulvihill and the Kerry Bog Pony Co-Op Society, the breed is back in healthy numbers. A dark brown pony with a black mane, really the size of many of our horses, ambled over as if to say hello. Another brown one with a matching brown mane had all white socks at the bottom on his sturdy legs. A lighter chestnut one also came over. Each had some white from the top of its head down to its black nose. Petting whichever one came closest, I knew they were friendly and had no doubt they could tell I had Irish blood coursing through my veins and that I have always loved horses. These ponies were used for farm work such as bringing home turf from the bog, seaweed from the beach and taking milk to the creamery. They are smaller, thus easier to keep, eat less and take up less space. They are also faster and more athletic than donkeys.

Milling through the farmyard and gardens, I happened across a pile of stones tucked away in a small arch. Little blue wildflowers poked through any open space they could find reaching toward the sunshine. Hearing a little rustling among the flowers, in my wildest dreams I hoped it might be a fairy but sadly it was just a light puff of wind that moved the flowers. But maybe?

The sign at The Red Fox Inn said OPEN and in we went to enjoy an Irish Coffee or Bailey's Coffee. None of us passed up this treat. Our souvenir was the recipe for making homemade Irish Coffee and a delightful memory ending this adventure.

Riding in our motorcoach provided us the gift of height, therefore sight, as we were able to see much more than those driving in their lower cars. We were above the hedgerows and stone walls so able to peek into people's second story windows if we could see through the lace curtains.

Streams wound like ribbon through farms and Scotch Broom. Occasionally we would see clumps of standing stones and ruins of castles, forts and stone homes.

We stopped for a hearty lunch and one of us had corned beef with a lemon sauce and three, yes, three mounds of mashed potatoes. I had the Shepherd's Pie that I swear had a four-inch layer of mashed potatoes on top. Dessert was warm bread pudding with deep rich cream poured over the top, settling in the bottom of the bowl with plenty of liquid to soak up the pudding. Not one drop of the delicious cream was left.

The Ring of Kerry has many small villages sprinkled along the coastline and countryside. We drove through one particular village where the businesses stretched out in a straight line all butting up against each other. They are all two stories high with the first one painted orange, then a blue store with wording on the front indicating its name, Green Chair, Haberdashery and Vintage Gifts, followed by an all-white building with green trim, another white one with red trim, then ending the row with a bright lime building. I just loved all these colors.

About ten miles from Killarney we pulled off at Ladies View, a scenic overlook and understandably one of the most photographed places in Ireland. Before me lay gently sloping emerald hills covered in grasses and low bushes. Beyond is a lake nestled at the base of mountains, and white cotton ball clouds against a blue sky; yes, indeed, it is a sight to behold.

Returning to Killarney by 6 p.m. was important because we had reservations for a Jaunting Car Ride through the national park. It's not really a car but a horse-drawn buggy ride. We wound through the lakes, saw small deer, a pheasant, squirrels and lots of bird life, and as we drove along our driver filled us in on what we were seeing, historical facts and always entertaining Irish folklore.

While walking to dinner, we saw a display in the window of Katie's Luxury Chocolates and Aunt Nellie's Sweet Shop which showed off various elegant trays lined with white lace doilies. On each doily was arranged a parade of chocolate delicacies, and each hand-dipped frippery was decorated with a different design on top. Almost drooling, that's all we needed and in we went.

Opening the door, I breathed in the fragrance of chocolate that smelled better than any perfume. I made a beeline for the dark chocolate exhibition while admiring the artwork depicting what type of soft center, delectable delight I would bite into. It felt like I was in a chocolate art gallery or museum. One dark chocolate with a right-hand swirl indicated a buttercream center. Another dark chocolate wore a white polka dot top indicating coconut inside. A dollop of red frosting revealed this filling was hot from chili pepper. A round dark chocolate patty with a gold embossed twist was filled with white cream mint. A deep pink twirl indicated berry cream inside. Next to it was a three-inch long stick filled with orange jelly. I bought three of these because it is a favorite candy that my husband enjoyed as a child. There were other displays of milk chocolate bars, toffees, caramels and marzipan but I wasn't interested. I selected one each of lavender buttercream, banoffee and a sea salt toffee. I chose some gifts for my special chocoholic friends and family, carefully hand-selecting sets of four chocolates that were cushioned in boxes, each sealed with gold stickers and each wrapped with a dainty ribbon tied in a perfect green bow.

We went to dinner at a well-known family restaurant called Treyvaud's and we also discovered why it received such a high recommendation. I had organic Irish salmon with sundried tomatoes and herb crust. Fresh green beans were included. My husband had prime Irish beef meatballs (two the size of baseballs) with a sweet and spicy red wine sauce and colcannon. Colcannon is cabbage and potatoes boiled and pounded together and much better than it might sound. The single bite of the mammoth meatball tasted scrumptious. For dessert we had our own Bailey's Irish Liqueur cheesecake with butterscotch sauce, a perfect way to end a delightful day.

We bid farewell to Killarney as we drove toward the Shannon River into County Clare. I like saying the word 'county' first then the name. I live in Marion County but prefer it as County Marion. The sun graced us with her presence and the scenery appeared different as we headed into dairy country. Hundreds of black and white cows munched lush grasses where some farmland was separated by streams, some fences and some hedgerows. We saw in the distance a group of standing stones, broken down stone buildings and little villages with stores and homes painted some delightful color. Some homes displayed flower baskets on their windowsills and pots at their front doors. Occasionally there would be a round satellite TV dish mounted on the side or top of the house.

A road sign showed Ballybunion R511 to the left and N67 Kilrush (to the ferry) straight ahead. We continued on the N67 and pulled in line behind seven touring motorcycles, some with sidecars. Clearly boomer-aged friends were on their holiday together. We got the all-clear to enter onto the three-story ferry and we were free to roam during the forty-five minute cruise, eliminating a two hundred mile road trip or at least three hours. We were on the Shannon Dolphin gliding through slightly choppy gray water passing two smokestacks that dwarfed a white three-story lighthouse. The

Shannon Breeze, a sleek single-story red and white ferry, passed us quickly going the opposite direction.

When we unloaded from the ferry we were greeted by those familiar blackface sheep feeding on the grass that gently dropped off onto sand and then ocean. We drove by Rinn Na Spainneach (Spanish Point) where summer homes dot the hillside overlooking this pretty area. The tide was way out so lots of creamy sand beaches were open for those playing on its shores. The two-lane road in some coastal areas is lined with summer homes with nicely groomed yards and gardens. In one area surfers were enjoying the waves, even though not big waves, and there were even a few wind surfers. Down the road, golf courses started coming into view, course after course. Then we popped out of civilization to countryside again sprinkled with relics of old buildings and crumbing stone walls.

A must-see in Ireland is the Cliffs of Moher. Our first visit twenty years earlier was in harrowing high winds and not enough guardrails as I recall. This tourist site has changed significantly making it easier for tourists to walk toward the cliffs or in the opposite direction to the O'Brien Tower. The sun shone so brightly the normally green grass turned a shimmery silver, moving ever so slightly in the breeze.

Using my binoculars, I scanned the rock cliffs for bird life, particularly puffins. I have a fondness for puffins looking like a colorful sea parrot dressed in a black and white tuxedo, with day-glow orange around their black round eyes and bright scarlet bills. I had been fortunate to see colonies a couple of times in Iceland and I knew it wasn't likely here because they are usually gone by mid-August, but I hoped a few might still be in the area. I spotted black and white birds on nests tucked into the rocks and thought I'd found them but nope, they were gulls, not my beloved puffins.

The café is now built into the berm of the hillside and we went in for a lunch of loaded baked potatoes and tomato soup. Perfect for this day. The visitor's center and gift store are much more accessible and with a greater variety of must-have souvenirs.

On our way to Ennis, a large blue and red road sign caught my attention: "Matchmaking Festival, Lisdoonvarna, Willie Daly is the matchmaker. All September. Europe's biggest singles event."

Before going to our hotel, we stopped at Bunratty Castle for a tour. The large 15th century medieval tower house was partially covered in scarlet vines with a little green ivy tossed in for accent color. Six-foot high fuchsia bushes with bright red blooms covered the front and around the corner of the castle. It is named after the Raite River which runs alongside this strategic battlement. The castle has occupied this spot for over one thousand years.

We were warmly greeted at the front door by a woman wearing a long velvet dress in multiple hues of dark green with a bright red short jacket. She wore a hat with a wide ribbon hanging down her back. Inside we saw furniture and furnishings belonging to both the McNamara and O'Brien Clans, and the secret stairways to the rooftop. We would return later this evening for a medieval banquet.

Later that afternoon we arrived at Old Ground Hotel in Country Clare. More scarlet vines accented the outer walls. Baskets of hot pink geraniums sprinkled with little blue flowers and ivy were overflowing from cement pots and the baskets under the windows. The entrance is especially lovely with a huge fireplace, and off the lobby is a large room with overstuffed chairs and sofas for lounging, reading or just looking outside.

Returning to Bunratty Castle for dinner, we were in for a treat especially for those who never experienced a medieval banquet before. Fortunately, they allowed us to use eating utensils because some medieval banquet venues do not. Heavy crockery cups were full of red wine. A waiter delivered a salad of cucumbers, greens and raw smoked salmon, or sushi or lox, as some would refer to it. A hearty lentil soup was served in a bowl with no spoon so we each picked up our bowl and drank, often dipping a dense, multigrain piece of bread in it. Plates of a half chicken, root vegetables and mashed potatoes were delivered by servers dressed in period costumes. They were also the musicians and actors performing numbers while we ate. A warm, layered apple dessert with a crumble topping appeared with the grand finale along with rousing singing, acting and dancing numbers.

Leaving the next morning we knew we would be entering a new country, Northern Ireland. We were heading farther north and as we negotiated a roundabout I noticed in the center of the circle a faded red boat filled with orange, white, yellow and red poppies. I thought I spied a couple of blue ones but I wasn't positive. I'd seen blue ones in Scotland and knew they were uncommon. I enjoyed checking out the decorations in roundabouts which varied from extremes of weeds and wildflowers to manicured grass and sculpture gardens.

We stopped for an experience of the daily life of a traditional Irish family at Rathbaun Farm, not too far from Galway. We watched the farmer Fintan skillfully shear a sheep in about three minutes flat. My guess is years of experience and hard work made this look easy. I asked if the local weavers used the wool for the sweaters, scarves and other woolen items. He replied that they were mostly woven here but then wool is sent to China where it's made into a variety of garments and sent back with labels that read "Woven in Ireland." Rarely did one find something woven and then made in Ireland.

Fintan shared the daily chores of a rural farmer. While showing us around, his sidekick Ted arrived to help with the next demonstration. Ted is a

Border Collie, a valuable member of the staff who displayed how he rounds up the sheep from various corners of the field. All the sheep did end up in the pen with Ted just gently corralling them in. One sheep, maybe a cousin of Shaun the Sheep from Scotland, wasn't exactly cooperating but Ted was patient just circling and moving it toward the gate of the pen. There were darling lambs, one white with a black face and another solid black that we got to hand-feed bottles of milk.

Feeling like we'd accomplished something outdoorsy and were now skilled farmhands, we were treated to homemade warm scones right out of the oven with homemade rhubarb preserves, clotted cream and bright yellow butter along with hot tea in English tea cups. Frances introduced herself and offered seconds if we wanted, which no one declined. I asked her about a recipe and if I could purchase the scone cutters and she said, "Of course." I did purchase a few sets for a special niece and friend at home who I knew would appreciate this souvenir. If one has enough time, Frances even gives step-by-step instructions and you, too, can learn how to make your own delicious treats. I felt especially drawn to Frances because that's my middle name and when I told her she said she thought we should have our picture together. And that we did.

Departing down a tree-canopied, one-way single lane road we stopped for a bit because the Northern Ireland Highway Department was doing some repair work. Bill cautiously drove around a man on a bicycle as I overheard our skilled driver mumble something like eejit (my guess is idiot) with no shoulder on the road for non-vehicles.

What a contrast this was to Galway, the sixth most populated city in Ireland, with around eighty thousand. It lies on the River Corrib between Lough Corrib and Galway Bay. Rain poured like a faucet turned on full blast. Our second visit to this city wasn't turning out great, just like the first visit twenty years ago. But all in all, I preferred the countryside and smaller villages than the larger cities.

Several of us decided to skip the tour and headed directly for a dry mall where we wandered looking in local shop windows. Displayed in one store were two-inch round fluffy sheep all in different colors. I bought a cute teal magnet. In the mall stood a three-story stone round column that housed the Tower Gallery where people could purchase their family crest or name with historical explanation. I did.

We found another Aunty Nellie's Sweet Shop, the same name of the heavenly chocolateria that we heavily invested in while visiting Killarney. This shop had a totally different vibe with colorful fun walls lined with a massive selection of packaged candies offering everything from Harry Potter frogs to toffee mice, candy canes, and chocolate bars made by local artisans. Some hand-made chocolates were available but sweets, biscuits and regional specialties like salted and flavored licorice were the highlights here. I'd never seen so many licorice products: rounds, triangles, coins, diamonds, torpedoes, wheels, balls, and buttons in the shape of herring. I felt like a kid where a little money could go a long way. My dad loved licorice so I bought a few buttons in his honor and gave one to each of my traveling chums. This made up for not finding Murphy's Ice Cream.

We were about one hundred miles from our evening accommodations and were eager to get there because it was a manor house and highly regarded plus full of history. The Manor House in Enniskillen is a 19th century estate located on a secluded lake in the westernmost part of Northern Ireland.

When I first saw The Manor House I laughed out loud. It is a WOW property. And it stopped raining. Matching granite lions on the right and left greeted us as we walked up the wide staircase to the entrance. The outside is stunningly gorgeous with its well-manicured lawn, almost like you'd see on some program on PBS, though not quite Downton Abbey. Our large suite faced a multi-tiered fountain. Lounging rooms are extravagantly decorated yet comfortable and welcoming.

The Watergate Bar was done in dark warm woods and soft lighting with wing-backed chairs and a sofa that, when I sat down, sank so low I feared I might need assistance getting up.

We had dinner in the Belleck Restaurant starting with vegetable soup, a melon plate, and I had Atlantic prawns while my husband had the stuffed loin of pork. A scoop of custard about the size of a tennis ball with a round flat piece of chocolate with a calligraphed white M on the top added a touch of class, along with berry compote and a spoonful of unsweetened whipped cream on the side which topped off a delicious dinner.

After dinner we wandered around the house seeing marble columns, a grand ballroom, drawing room chandeliers, bars, cellar bar and restaurant, floor-to-ceiling windows, alcoves with statues, and fresh floral arrangements in antique vases, all darn impressive and stately. Down one corridor are two extra-large chairs, like king and queen chairs that we took turns sitting in and taking photos of each other. A glass of wine might have had something to do with our silliness or just plain giddiness because of our opulent surroundings.

After a great night's sleep in this quiet location we had breakfast in a room surrounded on three sides by windows overlooking the pristine grounds. Breakfast consisted of a full Irish breakfast plus a variety of pastries to select from a buffet line. At each place setting sat three butter patties delicately made in a flower pattern.

We strolled to the lake looking at the expensive boats, walked to the end of the fishing dock, and saw sheep grazing on the hillside across the way. I could have stayed several days.

We departed riding under a canopy of cushy tree limbs that brushed the top of our motorcoach. Our final destination today would be Derry. Our knowledgeable tour guide April provided verbal enlightenment and musical entertainment on our bus rides. Several days earlier on one afternoon during a two-hour drive she played soulful Irish songs. I cried most of the time just thinking about my dad and looking at the countryside. When the famous traditional song "Danny Boy" by The Irish Tenors played, I went through five tissues.

Today she shared a book from 1942 entitled, *Instructions for American Servicemen in Britain*. One page reads "No Time to Fight Old Wars. If you come from an Irish-American family, you may think of the English as persecutors of the Irish, or you may think of them as enemy redcoats who fought against us in the American Revolution and War of 1812. But there is no time today to fight old wars over again or bring up old grievances. We don't worry about which side our grandfathers fought on in the Civil War, because it doesn't mean anything now. We can defeat Hitler's propaganda with a weapon of our own. Plain, common horse sense; understanding of evident truths. The most evident truth of all is that in their major ways of life the British and American people are much alike. They speak the same language. They both believe in representative government, in freedom of worship, in freedom of speech. But each country has minor national characteristics which differ. It is by easing misunderstanding over these minor differences that Hitler hopes to make his propaganda effective."

We drove through rolling green hills, little villages where a grandmother was pushing a tram down the sidewalk, passing one home displaying a Canadian maple leaf flag along with the Northern Ireland flag, spired-churches, cemeteries, magpies, wind turbines, and ponds and streams.

Our first stop was in Donegal Town strolling the square happy for a designated shopping time which meant mandatory shopping to me. It sits on a charming harbor with a serene beach, with lots of stone ruins from the past including its own castle, abbey, churches, railway, heritage center, and gift and specialty shops. Some of us were in heaven, others not so much.

Along our trip I had been watching for some type of artwork to take home as a memento that would always remind me of this special time in my father's family homeland with Dave and Sue, Chris and Jeanine, Greg and Linda and Bruce and Nancy. Something depicting my roots. I surmised my family had sheep and worked hard on a farm. So, it seemed meant to be when we discovered at Triona, the Donegal Tweed Visitor Center, two eight-foot long woolen runners about one foot wide that I could hang together on a decorative ladder propped against our bedroom wall. We observed how wool is woven on a large loom. Each square of material is a different color in a herringbone weave—teal, jade, olive, berry, pastel pink and finally purple. Each has flecks of cream and white in the yarn, softening the colors to a muted hue. And they offered to ship them along with three open-weave scarves I purchased for my mother, sister-in-law and myself, thus preventing additional bulk in my already stuffed suitcase. And getting heavier by the day.

When we arrived in Derry, well known for its turbulent political history, we were greeted by a large fuchsia-colored, free-standing wall that reads "You Are Now Entering FREE DERRY."

As we drove by the Craigavon Bridge, I saw the statue of two men. April said that the inscription reads "Hands Across the Divide," and told us that the bronze sculpture, one Protestant and the other Catholic, with arms outstretched to each other and their hands almost touching but not quite, symbolizes the spirit of reconciliation and hope for the future. It was unveiled in 1992, twenty years after Bloody Sunday. Basically, one side wishes to form a united Ireland and the other side wants Northern Ireland to remain in the United Kingdom.

Derry is the one remaining intact walled city in Northern Ireland and the last walled city to be built in all of Europe. It's about one mile around the entire city and you can easily walk along the vast walls for various vantage points.

We checked into the City Hotel Derry with a view right out our fifth story room of a well-manicured roundabout with four beds of red flowers creating an outer ring on the grass, and the inner circle of ivy columns surrounded by a ring of yellow flowers. Off to the right stands the impressive red sandstone, neogothic styled Guildhall with clock tower, and to the left, the pedestrian Peace Bridge stretching across the River Foyle. We would discover more about this relatively new bridge after our walking tour.

That afternoon our local guide, Mo, led us on a walk to see the courthouse constructed in the Greek Revival style. St. Columba's Cathedral occupies the highest point of land within the walled city and was consecrated in 1633. Mo laughingly told us he'd be the only Iranian Muslim Irishman we'd meet in Ireland. His Iranian father married his Irish mother and he grew up in Northern Ireland. He and his wife were raising three children, including a son with special health needs. Our talk did include the dilemma of Brexit and the concerns about what that could mean for healthcare for their son. Also, his wife's parents, who often provided child care and only lived fifteen miles away, were on the other side of the border. If the border crossing were to be reinstated, this would make travel and work much more difficult. He did not want to take a step back in time.

The 17th century Derry Wall is the largest ancient monument in state care in Northern Ireland

and has the longest, complete circuit of ramparts of the remaining thirty walled towns in all of Ireland. There are four original gates to the Walled City and they are: Bishop's Gate, Ferryquay Gate, Butcher Gate, which stretches across a street, and Shipquay Gate, entry point to the commercial part of the city. Three others were added later, Magazine Gate, Castle Gate and New Gate.

On the wall at Guildhall Square Mo pointed out historic buildings, churches, architecture including brick chimneys on rooftops, and the cannons at the Double Bastion by the Verbal Arts Center. The Londonderry Guildhall, previously mentioned, is a majestic red sandstone building and the meeting place of the members of council.

Depending on what Mo knew we should see, we went up and down walking from the dry moat around the exterior and back up around the top of the ramparts which provided an excellent elevated view to see the city. Scattered among the building are huge murals.

Two brothers and a friend illustrated events of the Troubles on walls lining Rossville Street. The political murals listed below were just a few drawn to commemorate the events and educate those who didn't live through the struggles.

THE PETROL BOMBER. This one is the oldest and most famous dating back to 1969, done in black and white of a boy wearing a gas mask to protect himself while he holds a gas bomb. The boy's eyes stare dazed from behind the obstructing visor through which the teenager is trying to see. In the background are uniformed riot police and smoke rising from crumbling buildings.

BERNADETTE features Bernadette McAliskey, a social Republican activist addressing a crowd with a megaphone in her right hand. A woman is squatting, holding a shield that looks somewhat like a garbage can lid and a boy behind her with a shield in one hand and a metal rod in the other. A bulldog stands alone, with burning rubble in the background and a male holding a handkerchief over his nose and mouth next to a young boy. She received a prison sentence for initiating and participating in a riot. She would later be elected to Parliament at the age of twenty-one.

Another mural along our walk is called DEATH OF INNOCENCE. This is a mural of Annette McGavigan, a fourteen-year old girl killed in 1971. The mural is near where she died. A British soldier killed her while she stood at the side of the road. She is dressed in a white blouse with a green tie that matches her skirt. In the left corner is a butterfly with the top half painted light blue and the bottom is orange.

THE PEACE MURAL, portrayed on a wall at the end of a building, is an outline of a white swirling dove painted over colored blocks. The dove is a symbol of peace and Derry's patron saint, Columba. The dove emerges from an oak leaf. The squares are equal on all sides representing the equality of citizens. This one promises hope and a bright future.

There are other murals such as BLOODY SUNDAY COMMEMORATION, THE SATURDAY MATINEE, THE RUNNER, and many more around Derry. Whether political, optimistic, celebrating the city or merely artistic, each holds special significance.

Mo shared truthfully about his country's struggles, prejudices and hopes for the future. When he asked if anyone had been to Derry before, I told him we had visited twenty years ago. I told him we'd come to Northern Ireland a few days after the Omagh bombing in August 1998. He took in a little gasp of air and instantly had tears in his eyes. He said his best friend's son had been in that market and died in the bombing at age eight. It was something he'd never forget. Me either, I told him. We bid Mo farewell and thanked him for his honesty and insight.

We visited the Craft Village after the tour and looked at many handmade items by local artists. Two shelves lined with three-tiered cakes, almost like wedding cakes, showcased a baker's handiwork. Something else that caught my attention while meandering through the Craft Village was a closed black door on a building. Of course, there is nothing unusual about a closed door, but hanging on a nail was a brass ring with four large brass keys. It certainly seemed like an open invitation to me and I was tempted to try each key in the door but better judgment prevailed.

There was a house with a perfectly crafted thatched roof with two swans made of straw or thatch, facing beak to beak, resting on the rooftop with their necks forming a heart. The sign on the door said we were welcome to take Irish dancing classes.

The Derry Peace Flame is one of fifteen peace flames around the world. It's Northern Ireland's only eternal peace flame in a city that strives for harmony. The flame is inside a small park beside the Guildhall in the middle of town.

That night I watched the sunset turn the river shades of orange as the white lights of the Peace Bridge, buildings and churches flickered on. Reflecting on the day, the Derry murals, along with our discerning guide Mo, helped me understand a piece of this history.

The next morning, I peeked out to see bright sunshine and the clock on the cathedral showing 7:06 a.m. After breakfast we set out to see more new countryside heading even farther north. We drove through little burghs of ten to twelve homes and saw craggy rocks touching tall thriving grasses, while driving along the Inishowen Peninsula and Malin Head. The scenery on the ocean drive is spectacular.

Cionn Mhálanna or Malin Head is a region, not one particular place on the peninsula, in County Donegal. It comprises an area north of the Black Mountain and there is no specific point which details the location of Malin Head.

We stopped for a walk, fortunately on a paved path, to Hell's Hole, a cavern with waves crashing against the steep rocks nineteen hundred feet below. Flourishing grass disappeared when reaching the jagged rocks that dissolved into a black sand beach. Splotches of Scotch Broom brightened the hillsides.

We passed a small home painted white with a thatched roof and a red door, red-trimmed windows with red geraniums overflowing from red wooden boxes, and a red wagon wheel by the front door.

Pulling up to another vantage point, Banba's Crown, before seeing the sights, I knew where my group of friends and husband would be heading before anything else—to the mobile espresso bar, really a tricked-out extended white van. The sign read "Coffee, Cappuccino, Latte, Mocha, Hot Chocolate, by Caffe Banba, Ireland's most Northern and Extraordinary Coffee Shop and Bakery, in Ballyhillin." Turns out this unique treat stop was one of two mobile coffee shops run by a husband and wife team who make all the homebaked goods, and a barista makes the specialty beverages surprisingly fast. Most businesses in this area pridefully have the words "Ireland's most northern" or "northerly" in their name.

I took a photo of Bruce and Nancy, Dave and Sue, Chris and Jeanine and husband Mark all smiling with their hot brews. Their backdrop was a rocky bluff overlooking the white-capped waves on the blue sea. Greg and Linda were already off seeing the sights.

Our next stop was at the well-known Farren's Bar, "Ireland's Most Northerly Bar since 1825." At the outside of one end of the building is a large, round jade Yoda, from Star Wars fame. On the other end of the building is a large green-painted golfer, Rory McIlroy, who grew up in this area and is a favorite of all locals.

We were welcomed by friendly staff and a young man named Hugh Farren, who took our orders and gave us a little history. The bar is done in warm dark wood with dozens of mugs hanging overhead on hooks. Racks held bread loaves, cans of peas, sacks of flour and boxes of sugar and other staples. At the back of one room a stove radiating warmth is positioned in the center of cushioned benches and chairs.

Star Wars memorabilia is proudly displayed since the final movie, "The Last Jedi," was filmed in the area. Star Wars ships, Jedi pictures, posters, Guinness wall murals, pictures of famous people and sports teams are prominent. Another popular artifact is a large white shoe autographed Forcefully

Yours, Mark Hamill, really Luke Skywalker, and I got to hold it.

A Storm Trooper's white helmet is available for anyone to put on. While Dave drank coffee, wife Sue tried on the helmet. She started the parade of all of us donning the well-recognized movie icon standing in funny poses. I had hoped for Yoda's green or Darth's red lightsaber but nope, not one.

At a cozy table underneath pictures of sports teams, Greg drank a Coke, his favorite, and Linda sipped a spiced hot beverage. I also had one—warm mulled cider with a quarter of a thinly sliced lemon floating on top garnished with four cloves and smelled yummy.

Milling around the outside of the bar and homes clustered together, in the distance we could see Ireland's most northerly lighthouse, Inishtrahull, just off the coast. It looked lonely by itself. Homes are well kept and the one with a marine yellow front door and window trim popped from the otherwise white house. A matching house looked almost the same but blue. An empty clothesline sat stationary except when the breeze moved the wooden clothespins.

On the return trip, again there were hundreds of sheep but one field in particular had sheep that had been shorn then sprayed with a strip of red and then another with blue.

Back in Derry, we stopped for lunch at a favorite restaurant that our guide April knew we would enjoy. Primrose on the Quay had a painted sign on a wall inside that read "Purveyors of Primrose Fine Irish Foods original recipes."

The eye-catching pastry display drew the attention of Sue, Linda and me. A "confetti cake" as they called it, had five layers with each layer a different color. A watermelon-colored layer started the masterpiece, then orange, lemon, and lime, ending with teal blue. It was frosted with yellow icing with elongated sprinkles scattered on the sides. The bottom and top were lined with teal flowers. The top had more sprinkles and was dotted with flowers. I took a few photos hoping one of my nieces would make it sometime for a family gathering.

The lunch lived up to its fine reputation but the most memorable was when the hamburgers were delivered to Dave and a second one to Chris. The astonishment on Dave's face had the look of "How in the world am I going to eat this?" Under the top bun sat a fried onion ring, a layer of lettuce, another fried onion ring, then a half-inch thick beef patty, so including the bottom bun totaled at least ten inches high. Both men persevered and devoured their burgers. I had a Fentimans botanically brewed ginger beer (like our ginger ale but theirs has much more ginger flavor) and a bowl of tomato basil soup because I knew what I wanted next—a Millionaire Shortbread bar for dessert. I had discovered these delectable delights in Oxford a few years earlier. It's a combination of decadent ingredients: shortbread on the bottom, then gooey salted caramel topped with a thin layer of dark unsweetened chocolate. The first luscious bite brought back wonderful memories of our adventures in England. See "The Walnut Door" in *Because of Colorful Doors,* if you want to experience that adventure with me.

Conversations at meals could be recapping our adventures, what was coming up or mundane issues like laundry. At this point in the trip, washing clothes, particularly underclothes, by hand in the hotel sink had become tiresome for most, and burdensome for one procrastinator in particular who hadn't kept up with his wash. He mentioned cotton items would take too long to dry. I reminded him he could use the hand-held hair dryer on the wall in any bathroom if the items hadn't completely dried overnight. He whined that he had several pairs to wash that night and I suggested that, for efficiency, when showering he wear all three pairs at one time. Wide-eyed nodding heads seemed to agree with my newly introduced travel philosophy but I never heard back if anyone actually tried it.

While others in our tour group were finishing their lunches, we were loitering outside when we came upon a Dulux Decorate Centre, a paint store. Dave worked his entire life in the paint industry. He is still a marvel at applying paint but mostly is phenomenal at combining colors. We simply had to go in and Dave quickly struck up a conversation with the store manager talking paint and the industry. I picked up some samples because I had convinced myself we needed to paint our new home's front door some bright gorgeous color the minute we got home. Dave narrowed it down to three choices for me, taking into account the weather, heat and angle of the sun.

Not far from our hotel, we walked along the riverfront toward the Peace Bridge. I love walking along water, just about any water. The River Foyle is clean blue saltwater not far from the sea. Central to the city, the river is a peaceful spot with wide walkways and fencing lined with dozens of large overflowing baskets of bright fuchsia, all with some extra tiny purple daisies and small white flowers. Fuchsia blossoms reminded me of two-tone layered swirling skirts. I couldn't resist the temptation to gently squeeze a red one to hear the pop. It was a childhood fixation that my mother didn't particularly appreciate but it sure was fun, similar to stepping on a puff ball from an oak tree. There were red with white, orange with yellow, pink with blue, red with purple, red with deep burgundy and many more varieties. I didn't realize there were so many types of fuchsias but I knew my dear friend Heather would know what kind they were and undoubtedly had some in her gorgeous garden. I had a few varieties in pots on our patio but just the usual pink with white or red with purple. I would now be on the lookout for more interesting fuchsias in the future.

People were on the water riding in paddleboats, canoes and kayaks. As we got closer to the Peace Bridge, the two structural white arms heading in opposite directions from each other got bigger. They symbolize the coming together of both communities from the opposite sides of the river, the Protestant Waterside and Nationalist Bogside. The bridge is over two football fields long and thirteen feet wide making plenty of room for its curved footpath, track and cycleway. It stretches from Guildhall in the city center to Ebrington Square on the other side. There are seats where people can watch the river go by. Some people stopped to chat and one man was playing a guitar.

Reaching Ebrington Square, we wandered around a former military square and barracks that transformed itself into a public space with sitting area, flowerbeds, coffee carts, ice cream stands, and a space for multipurpose events. There is a statue of a soldier with a rolled tent on his right shoulder balancing it with his right hand and a large duffle bag carried in his left hand. Looking across, I centered the red sandstone Derry Guildhall between the white arms on the Peace Bridge for a memorable photo and added another postcard in my mind.

Back across this gorgeous tribute bridge and walking around the neighborhood, we came upon an art gallery that was up a flight of stairs. Sue and I had to go mainly because the staircase is unusual and amusing. Each stair is a different color. Starting at the bottom, I stepped on stairs of teal, cream, melon, lime, navy, pink, light gray, yellow, charcoal, cantaloupe, red, light blue, aqua, and purple, reaching the top to the delightful gallery with handmade jewelry, enamel painted sheep, watercolor paintings, even fridge magnets. I supported the local economy as best I could.

Winding our way back to our hotel we simply had to enter the impressive Guildhall, originally named Victoria Hall. It's not only a church; there is an exhibition hall featuring informative history of Derry. Walking down the hall there are beautiful views of the majestic painted windows next to tall plaques retelling the history of this building and the region. There are exhibitions of old books, and one ancient map shows details of what the region looked like in the past. Not only are the stained glass windows remarkable but there is an impressively large statue of Queen Victoria.

It has the second largest clock face in the British Isles, second to Big Ben in London. The building is made of Dumfries sandstone, marble oak paneling, ornate ceilings and those incredible stained glass windows. I perked up recognizing Dumfries sandstone because it is from Scotland, a mere twenty miles from where these sandstone quarries lie close to my ancestors' home in Sanquhar, where I visited the previous year.

Looking out our hotel window on our final evening in Derry, the Peace Bridge shone brightly bathed in white lights. To the right was the darkened Guildhall, except for the clock and tower, both awash in white light.

We woke up to sun and clouds with the knowledge that this would be a delightful day, though repeating some of what we did twenty years ago. The drive alone is spectacular with old castle ruins sitting atop cliffs jutting down into the sea, white beaches that stretch far and wide and fertile mossy hills.

On the Antrim Coast Road is the medieval Dunluce Castle, now ruins. Perched on the cliff edge, it was the seat of Clan McDonnell. We explored a few rooms, little nooks and crannies and the free info guide explained where to find a drawing of a medieval ship scratched into the castle wall and how they used the steps to climb onto their horses. There are steep drop-offs on the backside down to the ocean below which provided stunning views up and down the coastline.

Giants Causeway is jam-packed full of folklore but it's an area of basalt columns, some red, some gray or black, resulting from volcanic eruption. Forming a hexagonal shape, most of these columns appear arranged into little stepping stones of hills while others jut out into the sea. We all spent time climbing around on the columns and I sat for a while just looking at this marvel which reminded me of the basalt columns we'd seen in Iceland along the southern coastline at Reynisfjara. Looking at an imaginary map in my mind, I could see how one day they might have all been connected to Scotland, too. Because it was cool and breezy, we retreated for a hot chocolate at the visitor's center and gift shop. I had to remind Dave that the Finn McCool round shield would not fit in his one piece of luggage, and no swords are allowed in his carry-on.

Departing the Causeway, I thought to myself, I may not return again since I've been here twice and there are so many other places in the world to experience and explore. Now I'm not so sure.

It took less than an hour to reach Belfast driving through the scenic back roads of the Glens of Antrim countryside and seeing O'Connor's Bar painted in bright green with yellow trim next door to Donnelly's Family Butchers, its building painted cherry red.

We arrived at the Europa Hotel in the center of Belfast. During the Troubles, journalists from all over the world stayed here. The hotel was given the name "Europe's most bombed hotel," and is one of the biggest and most important in Belfast's history. It was bombed thirty-three times by the IRA between 1970 and 1994.

April handed us our room keys and we took the elevator to the eleventh floor but became slightly confused because the doors indicated these were suites. First the Clinton Suite, with a plaque that reads "President William Jefferson Clinton stayed here 30th November 1995." Then came the Titanic Suite. There is a plaque displayed here that reads "The Titanic Suite Welcomes Hilary Clinton US Secretary of State Sunday 11th October 2007." No, we were not in one of the suites but in a lovely room at the end of the corridor with a view down to the street and the lively Crown Bar.

That night we ordered room service and stayed in enjoying our luxuriously spacious room. The bathroom had a bathtub so I slid in for some soaking time before a good night's sleep.

After breakfast we went for a guided tour of Belfast with a local guide who joined us on our bus. We saw the Stormont, also called the Parliament buildings, City Hall, one of the most iconic buildings, River Lagan, St. George's Market, Victoria Square with four levels of shops, Titanic Quarter, Cathedral Quarter, St. Anne's Cathedral and Clifton Street Poor House, in the heart of the city. It opened in 1774 and was used as a nursing home and hospital for older people. Its Georgian elegance is now perfect for events. We drove slowly down the most famous of the peace walls painted with hundreds of murals that divides the Falls and Shankill Roads in the western part of Belfast. It runs for several miles and is interrupted at several junctions by enormous metal gates across the roads. At the height of the Troubles, these were used as security checkpoints.

My favorite mural is called Solidarity P.O.W.'s, showing two hands grasping together out of jail cell windows. One shirtsleeve is green, white and orange, the Irish flag colors. The other has green underneath the white with a red rumpled cuff. On the Shankill Road side, navy, red and white Union Jack flags hang from houses and poles on the streets. Ropes tied across the main street proudly display flags with the British colors, and images of the queen are everywhere. At one point there is a slogan written across a wall that reads "Open your arms to change but don't let go of your values."

Attached to a telephone pole is a sign that reads "Alcohol Free Area. It is an offence to drink alcohol in public places in this area. Maximum penalty 500 Pounds."

We drove by McHughs, established in 1711. It boasts "Welcome to the oldest building in Belfast. Home of the 'Potato Boxty' & 'Steak on the Stone'."

A public art metal sculpture constructed in 2007 is called the Beacon of Hope or Thanksgiving Square Beacon overlooking the pretty River Lagan and is sixty-six feet tall. It is made of stainless steel and cast bronze and spirals upward, holding the Ring of Thanksgiving. The globe indicates peace and harmony. It's not a traditional solid sculpture but see-through and light and airy.

Something else that was added since we were last here is the Titanic Experience. Samson and Goliath are the gigantic cranes at the shipyard that built the Titanic. Titanic Belfast opened in 2012, marking the one hundredth anniversary of the launching of the legendary liner. The striking building looks like the front of a large ship.

We were not going to miss a thing in this exhibit and our strategy is usually to start at the top and work our way down. We went up the elevator to the sixth floor. The self-guided tour lets you go at your own pace exploring sights, sounds, even smells and stories of the Titanic.

Located where the ship was originally created in 1912, the exhibition follows the story of the ship from her conception in Belfast, through her construction and launch to the famous maiden voyage and subsequent place in history. Using state-of-the-art design, explanations and technology, each of the nine galleries focuses on a unique part of the story and the context of the period.

-Boomtown Belfast, showing the city at the start of the 20th century through stories and pictures of the works.

-The Shipyard, a cool mini-car ride, up and around the rudder. I felt like I was right there helping to build the ship.

-The Launch, showing that process.

-The Fit Out, the fitting out of the ship on the maiden voyage, the journey from Belfast to Southampton, and from there to Cherbourg and westwards. At this point I felt really sad since I knew what was coming. Passengers' backgrounds and stories were told in this area through recorded voices.

-The Sinking, the tragic disaster of April 1912.

-The Aftermath, the legacy of the disaster. This phase includes testimonials from survivors who arrived in New York.

This is a place not to miss and part of history. It is meaningful, somber and educational, all wrapped up in one well-done exhibit. Departing Belfast, we drove through countryside dotted with sheep, cows, homes, schools, shops and low-lying hills.

Driving on a very long driveway, past a golf course, and up a hill we arrived at Cabra Castle in Kingscourt, back in the Republic of Ireland, for our final night of our two-week adventure. We walked respectfully by a wedding party who were in the picture-taking phase. The wedding couple stood by their parents, mothers dressed in floral attire with a hat, and feathers in each hat.

April selected the room keys hanging on a railing in an arched driveway. The keys were large and substantial and attached to a silver oval fob that would never fit in a pocket. We were sent out much like on a scavenger hunt to find our rooms. The numbering system had nothing to do with the location of the room and after helping everyone else get to their rooms, we found ours at the back of the property in the Carpenter's Workshop. Up the narrow stairs to the second floor, we entered a spacious room with a king-size bed, large bathroom, snacks and water in Cabra Castle bottles similar to a wine bottle.

We only unpacked what we would wear the following morning for our flight home. Anything delicate had already been wrapped in the bubble wrap that I always take on any trip. I didn't have room for much more in my carry-on.

Several of us meandered around the inside and outside of this marvelous castle but since it was nippy and misty outside, Sue, Nancy and I retreated to a cozy alcove inside to order a warm drink and split an order of sticky toffee pudding which neither of them had tasted before. Each bite was like a party in my mouth.

Supposedly this is an extremely haunted castle, apparently by the ghost of a woman who was killed here. While we stood in the lobby underneath a large chandelier listening to the story about her, the chandelier swayed and the ceiling creaked. We scattered like songbirds with a hawk overhead. I have no explanation for this coincidental occurrence. I suspect someone walked down the second floor at the exact time were heard the ghost story. What a letdown. Not a leprechaun, fairy, spirit or ghost the entire trip.

Greg and Linda, Chris and Jeanine, Dave and Sue, Bruce and Nancy, and Mark and I had our final dinner together feasting on lamb shank, chicken or sea bass. For dessert they served an anniversary cake celebrating one hundred years. This dessert would be equivalent to strawberry pie with about five inches of whipped cream on the top.

Then there's the story of the Cabra Castle water bottles on the dining room tables. I had to have one or two, if possible. I mean really, who doesn't want a bottle from their family's castle? I knew to check first with April and our motorcoach driver, Bill, about purchasing a bottle. After rambling on and on telling them my family story, that this could be my family castle (and the gift store wasn't open), it was suggested I take one from the table. Bill said indignantly with a wink, "It's your family castle, just take it." April agreed.

I told my tablemates what had been suggested. After dinner I found several at my disposal from perpetrators who had hidden them in their jackets. We drank a lot of water during that meal.

Later I wrote an elaborate note to the cleaning staff explaining my situation and I left a donation with instructions for them to kindly pass it along to the proper authorities in the gift shop. I packed two for home in my carry-on, one for my youngest brother and one for myself. I am quite sure we are the only residents in the state of Oregon with a Cabra Castle glass water bottle.

That night, standing outside in one of the many gardens at Cabra Castle, in my imaginary world I pictured my great-great grandmother Maggie as a young girl running out of the house down the well-trodden path cutting through the wild grasses and purple heather to her secret place. The noise of the blowing wind caused her to pull her coat tightly around her as she shivered in the cold. She recognized Michael, shouted and waved but her voice got lost in the gale and squawking birds squabbling above her.

Michael descended the hillside and ran to join her. He knew right where she'd be. My fantasy had turned itself into a romantic novelette, but it's what I wanted and it's my dream anyway.

Fantasy—take two—Then I saw Maggie peering in through a window, one no longer belonging to her married family, the O'Reillys, but now the English Cooch family. Her chest knotted with emotion as she crept carefully over the cobblestones toward something in the wind summoning her. In her overanxious imaginings she heard laughter or maybe crying but which one? Turned out to be a common pesky black and white magpie. In my imagination.

Flying out of Dublin, from my window seat I watched the giant jigsaw puzzle of lush greens and browns in various shapes and sizes getting smaller and smaller until we flew through a cloud bank and only white remained.

I thought about what was ahead of me when we returned home, a memorial service for my darlin' dad. I heard a familiar voice whisper, "Darlin' daughter, you must return one day." I will, Dad.

Trip Tips:

Remember to study up on the country you are visiting. There are many inventors and artists who got their start in Ireland.

Mary Robinson (first female president of Ireland from 1990-1997)
Actors: Pierce Brosnan, Liam Neeson, Saoirse Ronan, Enya, Bono, Oscar Wilde
Inventions:
Color photography, in 1894 by John Joly
Guided torpedo, in 1877 by Louis Brennan
Hypodermic Syringe, in 1844 by Francis Rynd
Induction Coil, 1836 by Rev. Nicholas Callan
Ejector seat, 1949 by Sir James Martin.

The Irish have proof and take credit for inventing modern chemistry, chocolate milk, croquet, tattoo machines, portable defibrillators, design of modern submarines, boycotts, and seismology.

Some Pronunciation help...well maybe.

Letters have the same phonetic values as in English except for the following:

A is pronounced like o in hot or aw in thaw.
Bh is pronounced like v or w.
Ch is like k, never like s.
Dh is like y or is unpronounced.
Fh is unpronounced.
Gh is like y or is unpronounced.

Mh is pronounced like v or w.
S is pronounced like sh when it precedes I or e.
Sh is pronounced like h.
Th is pronounced like h.

Some words that might help:

Fáilte	Welcome
Cheers	Thanks
An Lár	City center
Bonnet	Car hood
Boot	Car trunk
Car Park	Parking lot
Deadly, Brilliant	Great, Excellent
Garda	Police
Jumper	Sweater
Lift	Elevator
Quay (Key)	Waterfront
Ring	To telephone
Slainte	Cheers
Bangers	Sausages
Boxty	Potato pancakes with meats & vegetables
Champ	Mashed potatoes with green onions
Chips	French fries
Fry or Fry Up	Traditional Irish fried breakfast
Dublin Coddle	Thick stew with sausage, bacon, potatoes

Lemonade	Sprite or 7-Up
Ploughman's Lunch	Cheese, bread and pickles
Salad	Salad and garnish on sandwich
Shandy	Sprite/Lemonade and Lager
Starter	Appetizer

Don't forget items in your carry-on for your long flight like earplugs or noise canceling headphones, inflatable pillow, a shawl or large scarf that works well as a blanket or to block out light, eye mask, sanitizing wipes, compression socks, sleep aids, food and water, pen, paper and notepad or journal, chewing gum, and one set of extra clothing. And don't forget your prescription medications.

Don't forget your passport and make a copy to put somewhere else in your luggage. Make a copy to leave at home with a trusted friend or relative.

Don't talk too much and keep it small talk unless you are friends. Let them do the talking.

Don't ask them to repeat themselves if you don't understand them. And don't speak slowly or loudly when talking with them; they are not deaf.

Don't talk about politics and religion unless you are asked, then state your opinions and don't get in a debate about Irish independence.

Don't get hit by a car or bus. Like the rest of the United Kingdom (U.K.), they drive on the opposite side of the street. Look right, left and right again before stepping out in the street.

Don't forget good walking shoes for meandering out to castle ruins, on the ocean shore or uneven cobblestone walkways.

Don't forget a rain poncho for any time of year; forget the umbrella and don't complain about the quick-changing weather.

Don't tell them how you've heard it always rains in Ireland. That's why it is so green.

Don't astound them with your lack of Irish geographical knowledge. Remember there is the Republic of Ireland and Northern Ireland.

Don't take a photo of someone unless you ask first.

Don't make remarks about Irish people as they are extremely proud of their country.

Don't skip the national foods.

Don't avoid people; be polite and greet everyone with a hello. Always say "please" and "thank you" as the Irish are polite and may become offended if you do not mind your manners. If you bump into someone, say "sorry."

Don't avoid trying to say some words in Irish. Even though they speak English, they have their own dialect with a thick accent and their own words. Get a list of commonly used words and practice before you go and don't say them wrong. Don't pronounce "Loch" like "lock." Review on YouTube.

Don't ever snap your fingers or wave your hand at a waiter in a restaurant.

Don't ask to take home food as leftovers. If you can afford to eat out at a restaurant, you can afford to buy other food to eat later.

Don't forget a hostess gift if you are invited to someone's home; a gift from home or a bottle of something always works.

Don't mention that you don't like the host's food; try to eat everything that is on your plate. Just don't take too much if you don't think you will like it.

Don't burp or wipe your nose at the dinner table; excuse yourself.

Don't worry about tipping at a restaurant because it is automatically added to your bill as a service charge. This is common practice in most countries around the world except the U.S. You can leave a bit more if the service is exceptional but it is not expected.

Don't forget to smile. The Irish are gracious and kind and as long as you smile and mean well, you will get along just fine.

Don't forget most British words are the same in England, Ireland, Northern Ireland and Scotland. And what Americans call the second floor of a building is the first floor in the U.K.

Don't forget the metric system is used almost everywhere in the world so weight and volume are calculated in metric. A kilogram is 2.2 pounds and one liter is about a quart. Temperatures are generally given in Celsius. Twenty-eight Celsius is a perfect eighty-two degrees to us. Twenty is sixty-eight and zero is our thirty-two degrees.

Don't forget clothing and shoe sizes are different.

Before visiting Ireland, you may wish to purchase a vocabulary guide; it's educational and humorous. And please buy a well-respected travel authority's book on Ireland like *Rick Steves' Ireland*, and read every word.

Traditional Gaelic Blessing

May the road rise to meet you.
May the wind be always at your back.
May the sun shine warm upon your face;
the rain fall soft upon your field
And until we meet again,
May God hold you in the palm of His hand.

"Travel opens your eyes and your heart."
Deleen Wills

"The Green Door" is dedicated to:

My dear friend, Pearl, who is like a sister to me. I cherish every memory of our times of exploration and visits together in our Oregon home, throughout the USA and gallivanting around the globe. She laughed at every word in "The Walnut Door," a story based at Mansfield College, Oxford University, in *Because of Colorful Doors* published two years before her diagnosis. I remember these precious times with Pearl but tragically she cannot. Inflicted with the hideousness of Alzheimer's disease, she resided for seventeen months in a memory care facility until her passing in September 2020.

Greg Jurgenson, a once active healthy man in his mid-sixties, recently passed after a two-year battle with the incurable, degenerative disease called Progressive Supranuclear Palsy that gradually deteriorated specific parts of his brain.

And the spouses of both these friends who I admire greatly: Howard married to Pearl, and Linda married to Greg, for their strength, perseverance and unconditional love of their spouses.

The Ivory Door
Ecuador & The Galápagos Islands

November 2011

In a chartreuse field of broad leaf grass, I sat on the ground cross-legged with my elbows on my knees, and my head resting on the top of my clasped hands, looking straight into the eyes of an old soul. And not human. Then he breathed on me—the noise of a loud puff. I hoped it wasn't from exasperation but from pleasure. It reminded me of the sound of a whale surfacing and exhaling. His breath felt slightly warm and smelled like grass in the fresh, earthy morning dew. Nose-to-nose, well almost, with me not moving, the one-hundred-year-old giant tortoise looked like he couldn't care less that I'd traveled over four thousand miles just to see him. He slowly walked around me and down the hill into a murky pond where he joined others, like children playing in the slimy green mud bowl.

Awaking from my dream, I acknowledged we had been watching way too many *National Geographic* programs and reading too many articles on The Galápagos Islands. I considered this official research because two months later we would be going with friends to this one-of-a-kind-place on planet Earth. By golly, I would be prepared to commune with wildlife in nature.

In autumn 2011 we were happy to escape the United States as a protest movement called Occupy had begun in September. It began in New York City's Wall Street financial district. The movement was against economic inequality. The Occupy movement will be remembered as a year of revolution, the beginning of the end of an unsustainable global system on poverty, oppression and violence. It spread around the globe. There were Occupy This and Occupy That signs and protests everywhere. I had the bright idea to make 8 x 11-inch printed signs that read "OCCUPY GALÁPAGOS" to use on our trip for a different purpose but only when appropriate.

Late November had been the time of the year when most research and advice from others who had gone before us had determined is the best time to explore this region. With friends Dave and Sharon, we flew from Portland, Oregon to Atlanta, Georgia, where we changed planes with the next stop Quito, Ecuador, elevation nine thousand three hundred fifty feet above sea level, nestled in the Andes Mountains. About one million people live in this capital city. We live in the hills of our capital city, Salem, Oregon, at about four hundred feet elevation. We were warned about possible altitude sickness. It is the second highest capital city in the world and the official capital city closest to the equator. High in the Andes, and built on the grounds of an ancient Inca city, Quito is known for Spanish-colonial designs and construction dating back more than five hundred years.

I read up on the Inca Empire on the flight. The region we would be in was mostly inhabited by the Tupac Incas, one of five sects. As with other ancient cultures indigenous to the Americas, the historical origins of the Incas are difficult to unscramble from the founding myths they themselves created. According to legend, in the beginning the creator god Viracocha came out of the Pacific Ocean and when he arrived at Lake Titicaca, he created the sun and all the ethnic groups. Lake Titicaca is on the border of Peru and Bolivia almost four hundred miles south and east from Machu Picchu. So, the Incas were brought into existence from the sun god Inti and they regarded themselves as the chosen few. There are a couple of versions of the creation myth.

There is a lot of archaeological evidence that has revealed that the first settlements in the Cusco Valley date to four thousand five hundred BCE (Before Christian Era) when hunter-gatherer communities occupied the area. Cusco is also in Peru but the Incas were all over Ecuador, Peru and farther south. The rise of the Inca Empire was incredibly quick. First, all speakers of the Inca language were given privileged status and this noble class then dominated all important roles within the empire. Cusco was considered the navel of the world, radiating out were highways and sacred sightings to each quarter. It spread across ancient Ecuador, Chile, Bolivia, Argentina and Columbia stretching thirty-four hundred miles with over ten million subjects speaking over thirty different languages. Now I really wanted to explore more of this region.

Sadly, the empire was founded on and maintained by force and the ruling Incas were very unpopular with their subjects. Rebellions were common and the Incas were engaged in a war in Ecuador where a second Inca capital had been established in Quito. Even more serious, the Incas were hit by an epidemic of European diseases such as smallpox, which had spread from Central America even faster than the European invaders themselves. A wave of illness killed a staggering sixty-five to ninety percent of the population. One of the diseases killed the king and two of his sons who battled in a civil war for control of the empire just when the European treasure hunters arrived. It was this perfect storm of rebellion, disease and invasion which brought the downfall of the mighty Inca Empire. This was an extremely sad demise of this civilization.

We landed right at midnight and all I could see from the airplane window were bazillions of city lights large and bright, to smaller and dim. This indicated to me that there were some hills close by. After waiting for a couple more passengers to arrive, we departed the airport on our charter bus taking us to the J.W. Marriott hotel in the heart of the city. It didn't take long to check in and find our spacious luxurious room on the eighth floor with curtains closed on the floor-to-ceiling windows. I just had to peek out. There were lots of lights but I couldn't really determine lights on what. The bathroom seemed large enough for a party. After a shower, we fell into bed and went fast to sleep.

Throwing open the curtains the next morning, I saw a square below of greenery, people, bikes and vehicles, the typical hustle and bustle of a work day. In the distance rose a mountain with just a touch of white on top. It was my first Andes mountain.

Before breakfast, I had a question and decided to visit the reception desk in person rather than trying to figure out the telephone system. With my question answered, back in the elevator I stood with a couple about our age and politely said hello. I've always thought it awkward being in an elevator and not speaking to whomever else shared that small space. This would be one of the most significant serendipitous hellos of my life.

After a delicious breakfast of fresh fruits, eggs and bacon, and some light fluffy pastry, I had seconds and thirds on the flavorful deep red watermelon. We were told to drink twice the amount of water we normally do at home. High elevations deplete your system fast and H_2O puts more oxygen into your body.

In the ninth grade at Calapooya Junior High, I had a teacher, Mr. Halstead, who instilled in me, and others who paid attention, a passion for exploring the world. He required us to memorize capitals of countries and his lectures somehow made these foreign places come alive. He talked about The

Galápagos Islands and Machu Picchu plus the interesting Inca Empire. He was my favorite teacher.

Several decades later my dad occasionally saw Mr. Halstead who mentioned he would like to see me. I met him and his wife in their home not far from my parents in a retirement village. When I told him of my many adventures and exploits his eyes and smile beamed with pride and said I'd given him the best gift a teacher could ever receive—the gift of knowing that one of his students had listened, learned and acted. It was a sad day when this exceptional teacher passed. He'd instilled wanderlust in me yet he himself had never travelled outside of the United States.

I had high hopes for a marvelous day touring this ancient city. While waiting in the reception area, I recognized the couple from yesterday's elevator encounter standing alone and pointed them out to my husband. He has never been as outgoing as I am but I waved and then motioned them over to join our foursome. Their names were Jon and Beth and they had come from Indiana for this adventure.

We knew that the Republic of Ecuador is located in the northwestern part of South America bordered by Colombia, Peru and the Pacific Ocean. The Galápagos Islands are part of Ecuador and located eight hundred miles from Quito and crisscross the Equator. And we were here in person.

Departing from the neighborhood of our hotel, I noticed a jet coming in for a landing. Criminy, it looked like it was landing right in the middle of the city. When we landed the night before at Mariscal Sucre International Airport, we basically dropped out of the sky into a bowl surrounded by ginormous mountains. The airport, named after a hero of Ecuadorian and Latin American independence, opened in 1960. It is one of the highest airports in the world at nine thousand two hundred feet.

I'd seen a lot of lights when landing and indeed there were thousands of dwellings inching their way up the hills, actually the Andes mountains. In broad daylight I could see at the end of the runway there were more homes, and to the other side, more and more. Millions of homes, businesses and restaurants crept upward. I was relieved that I hadn't been able to see all of this in darkness because landing in a basin with no wide-open spaces wasn't my idea of a comfortable touchdown. Obviously, these pilots knew what they were doing landing in high altitude density at nine thousand feet and probably, well hopefully, doing it daily was somewhat comforting.

The airport is located in the northern part of the city, five minutes from the financial center, and some terminals were located at major street intersections. This certainly turned out to be the most unusual airport I had been in.

Our Ecuadorian guide for the day said that due to its location in the middle of this huge city surrounded by mountains, the airport could no longer be expanded to accommodate any larger aircraft or an increase in traffic. Since its operation posed risks and several serious accidents and incidents had occurred in previous years, it would be closed with a new one opening in 2013. Great, just great, we were there in November 2011.

The Andes Mountains is the enormous spine which cuts South America in two from south to north, crossing seven countries: Argentina, Bolivia, Chile, Colombia, Ecuador, Peru and Venezuela and stretches about four thousand six hundred miles. On the other side of this mountain range is the Amazon River and basin. These magnificent mountains were created over fifty million years ago when the South American and Pacific tectonic plates collided. There are high-altitude plateaus that have allowed for human settlements and modern-day cities like Quito. One of the easiest peaks to reach is Cotopaxi, only forty-five miles south of Quito.

We had a full day of ahead of us visiting the city's historical landmarks. Our mode of transportation was a luxury bus with a friendly driver and our Ecuadorian guide.

I always take the window seat on any tour bus, airplane, boat, train or basically any mode of transportation, and my kind husband seemed fine with this over the years. He knew I'd be snapping lots of photos of things we were passing plus he could turn his long legs into the aisle.

As we approached our first stop, standing on the sidewalk was a darling little girl, probably six or seven years old, with long black hair showing underneath a black hat. She wore a colorful dress belted at her little waist with black boots to her knees. She held a stack of probably forty colorful scarves. Our eyes met as I heard my husband say, "Remember, NO eye contact," but it was too late, much too late. He knew I'd been had. We always laughed about the no eye contact principle. I stepped off the bus and went directly to her as she smiled wide, white teeth gleaming and a twinkle in her soft hazel eyes. Sharon came along and yes, even though this was just our first stop of our journey, I simply had to purchase something from her. And of course, buying three was cheaper than buying just two, so I got two and Sharon one. I selected one with blue colors of peacock, cobalt, teal, ocean, and lapis, and another with shades of purple with a ribbon of gold throughout. As she said thank you in broken English I waved farewell and wished I could take her home with us.

Looming directly behind my now favorite-little-girl-in-the-whole-wide-world stood one side of the humongous neo-gothic gray Basílica del Voto Nacional, the tallest church in Ecuador. This neo-gothic building's construction began in the 1800s and was finished late in the 20th century. On one end of the building are two five-hundred-foot twin clock towers with seven gates. This building is so massive I knew we'd be able to see it anywhere from the city.

Stats: It is almost five hundred feet long, one hundred fifteen feet wide, ninety feet high at the nave, fifty feet high in the twenty-four chapels— mammoth, colossal, in other words, gigantic.

Walking in, there is one long central nave with two smaller adjoining naves, an ornate colorful dome and stained glass windows. Around the central nave are twenty-four small chapels, each dedicated to a province of Ecuador. A crypt and a pantheon are also connected to the basilica. As a stained glass lover, I found this church's works amazing with real stained glass with lead and iron structural supports, not just painted glass. The famous Rose Window required binoculars to see the details.

The pink stone, from the Pichincha Mountains, gives the entire interior an inviting, cheery feeling. When the sun came through a window, the entire inside was aglow in a brighter pink. Columns and soaring arches all the way to the front altar crafted in neo-gothic architecture were amazing.

Gawking too long, I quickened my pace to cover the entire church and discovered a smaller side chapel and the stations of the cross, a series of painted images depicting Jesus Christ on the day of his crucifixion.

We walked up a flight of stairs to get a closer look at the Rose Window but one flight felt like five flights. This famous Rose Window was not all pink tones of stained glass but a series of separate partitions. The design reminded me of a spoke, like on a bicycle, that points to the outer rim. I think I counted sixteen three-petal flowers on the outer ring all in different colors. But the unique thing about these flowers is that they are actual native flowers of Ecuador. The next inner group is in a cross-shaped pattern. An odd puff of air reminded me of playing in a front yard as a child when the daphne bush was blooming in early spring.

We opted not to take the rickety catwalk to the high vaulted ceiling of the main chamber. Nor did we climb even higher to reach the rear towers on at least a twenty-step ladder that would not have been legal in the US. Instead, we took the elevator to the top for magnificent city views and a few close-ups with unique gargoyles.

Outside there is a series of gargoyles that looked more familiar than the fantastical beasts that normally adorn the facades of churches and cathedral. These all represent animals of Ecuador.

Searching carefully, I spotted rock-carved alligators, Blue-Footed Boobies, armadillos, monkeys, pumas, foxes, pelicans, falcons or maybe eagles (I couldn't really tell), parrots, winged albatross, sea turtles, iguanas, a ram, and a condor on the tower, which is the national symbol of Ecuador. Above the carved tortoise, a bird's nest was tucked safely into the stone curvatures protecting the two little heads anxiously looking for their next meal. I appreciated species native to the

Galápagos and the rest of the country rather than mythical creepy creatures on most cathedrals in Europe. Above the tallest spire hung a half-moon in the clear cobalt sky.

In the middle of the square were yellow lily flowers on tall stalks. Looking down a narrow street to the end, the green mountains rose sharply. Wrought iron was used liberally and molded into intricate patterns and designs on gates, fences and balconies. Small shops and stalls sold fresh fruit including the reddest watermelon I've ever seen, clothing, shoes, and vegetables, mostly for local residents. The national flag of horizontal bands of yellow at the top half, with blue then red occupying the other half, hung proudly from most buildings. The crest symbolizes the fertility of the land and mineral deposits, blue represents the sea and sky, and red represents the blood spilled during the nation's struggle for independence.

Looking down the street just on the outskirts of the main downtown area stood the Madonna watching over her city. This famous winged angel stands in Southern Old Town on El Panecillo, a six hundred fifty-foot-high hill. She overlooks Quito and was constructed in 1976 of seven thousand pieces of aluminum. Her official name is Virgen de Quito and she glowed in the sunshine.

Wandering around this historical Old Town, plazas break up the crisscross of the streets. There is an all-white square church, and buildings with many statues of important men. Stalls lined the avenues with artisanal handcrafts and foods. Doves searched for scraps fallen from careless or caring people and purple flowers lined a cement foundation.

We went to Central Grand Square where the central monument pays homage to people who fought in an important battle in history. Monumento a los Heroes Ignotos was erected in 1906 to commemorate independence against Spanish rule in 1809. A man points toward heaven with a lion at the base.

Through a stone archway several colorful buildings stood out like a bright rainbow. Along another narrow avenue there were houses in colors of soft green, peach, then a rosy pink, each with ornate ironwork on the windows and over the doorways. On another street the buildings were separately painted bright orange, periwinkle, pink, and lime, ending in pastel orange. The lime house had a sherbet orange front door that was slightly ajar. In my memories I was transported back to my childhood when we walked with our parents to the local ice cream parlor for a sweet treat. I always got one scoop each of lime and orange sherbet. The house had exactly the same colors.

Back in reality, I admit I am obsessed with colorful doors and discovering what might lie beyond. It started with our first trip to Scotland in 1997, searching for my roots. I call this regular travel occurrence my made-up word, "graviosity" (curiosity and gravity). My husband had seen me in action before on many adventures where I simply HAD to discover what was behind that colorful door. That's why I'd learned it was best that I discover these revelations on my own. But I couldn't wander away and peek behind the orange door on the lime house, darn it.

The central square is surrounded by old buildings except for one to the south, a city administrative building, and the president's residence on the north. There are small shops and vendor stalls with flowers, candies, fresh fruit, handmade wares and goods. At the end of each street there was a different and interesting view of stunningly high mountains.

We picked up some Ecuadorian dark chocolates made with seventy percent cocoa. It tasted too bitter for novices who ate milk chocolate M&Ms, but not me; I love the full-bodied, strong pure flavor. This country's Amazon region produces some of the most highly prized chocolate in the world. It is all because of the rare Arriba cocoa beans and these are used to make high-end chocolates for discerning chocolate lovers, or so the sign read.

Cocoa beans ripen inside football-shaped pods which start out green and gradually turn shades of yellow and orange. Inside the pods is a soft, white coating around each cluster of ruby beans. Chocolatiers ferment and then roast the beans to get the best flavor, a process that turns the beans to a warm shade of chestnut. This sounded similar to the process used for roasting beans for coffee, a beverage I have never acquired a taste for.

The National Cathedral borders the entire length of the south side Plaza de la República. The names of the original two hundred four Spanish conquerors are listed on its wall. Inside is the mausoleum of Antonio José de Sucre, founder of Ecuador; and some of the country's most important historical figures are buried here. Adjacent is the Sagrario Church built on top of a ravine that cuts the city in two. Across the plaza is the Conception Church and Convent, Quito's first female monastery and is one of the five cloistered convents in this historical center.

The Palacio de Carondelet or Presidential Palace forms one entire side of Plaza Grande Square, also called Independence Plaza. It is the seat of the government for Ecuador with a historic residence that's built around a central courtyard smack dab in the middle of the city. The building dates back to the mid-1500s, when the area consisted of several private homes. It is the seat of the president. Around the building were some nice little shops selling alpaca shawls and remarkable vivid, multicolored embroidered dresses with exquisite detailed work.

The long arched atrium to the northwest lines the front of the palace. The ironwork on the balconies overlooking the plaza, original from a palace in Paris, were purchased just after the French

Revolution. We strolled along the lengthy outside corridor lined with white stone columns. At the end of one section, antique farm equipment sat on display.

An unfamiliar tree caught my attention. The balls of foliage looked like cheerleaders' pompoms but these were bright green, and against the clear blue sky looked dramatic. Now, I know what a blue sky looks like. We have blue skies in Oregon; I've seen bluer skies in Alaska, and we've even seen supposedly the bluest in Siena, Italy, but this blue was exceptionally sapphire, true cobalt blue. My hunch was that altitude and no evidence of pollution had a lot to do with it. This blue reminded me of nature's blue like our Oregon blueberries, or the feathers on a Western Mountain Bluebird that migrated through our backyard visiting our feeders, or was it a blue morning glory flower or the blue poppies I had seen in Scotland? Yes, simply yes to all.

Pulling myself away from marveling at the blue sky, back at the palace, two soldiers guarded the entrance. They looked uncommonly tall until I noticed each standing on at least an eighteen-inch granite block. Their uniforms were colorful and impressive. The jacket reminded me of a formal tux with tails but in royal blue. Their white pants were tucked into knee-high black boots. Each held a long thin pole (really a not very strong-looking spear) made of a medium toned wood and, from the ground up, about ten feet tall. The jacket had red cuffs on the sleeves and red epaulets on the shoulders. Across the front of the jacket were six gold rods. The hat was held on by a black chinstrap, and had a white crest on the front with a top notch of one gold and one scarlet round bobble. And their bleached white gloves added an elegant touch to the entire uniform.

Iglesia de la Compañía de Jesús, often called La Compañía, is an ornately carved gray stone church with a massive cross on the corner and double wooden front doors. Tucked into four naves on the front of the building are impressively large, yet peaceful-looking angels. Above the arched entrance is an oval painting of Mary and baby Jesus and this is the only color besides the walnut door on the all-gray building. It has two ornate domes with plenty of gold trim, one sitting higher than the other and is located in the historical center of Quito, one block southwest of Plaza Grande.

Walking in through wooden double doors I stood surrounded by gray stone and was temporarily stunned into silence. I was silent because I almost couldn't breathe. I'd never seen anything like this. It was like being dropped into a vat of gold.

The interior is bathed in gold paint and twenty-three carat gold leaf including the main nave, altar, ceilings and side altars. There is gold leaf on the long ceiling in intricate patterns and gold leaf on the main altar with the lapis blue recessed top giving it the feeling of sky. The nave is capped by

189

two green and gold domes. At the front, they installed a magnification mirror to help you see the concave ceiling without straining your neck. I had to sit down on the pew for a while to take it all in.

The pillars and column are beautifully carved as well. Some religious artworks are displayed on the columns and, given the intricate carvings in the back, statues and architecture, "spectacular" would be an understatement. I've never seen so much golden decoration in any church and I'd been in dozens and dozens of cathedrals and churches around the world. It's so abundantly decorated I doubt there was an empty inch anywhere except pews. There is a reflection that the gold altar makes on the floor. The organ is circa 1889 and made in the USA.

Although baroque is most prominent, the Moorish influence is easily seen in the geometrical figures on the pillars. The floor plan makes a Latin cross with central, northern and southern arms. Gilded plaster and wood carving abound. I really like the Moorish touches that remind me of the Alhambra Palace in Granada, Spain.

On one wall hung a large canvas called "Hell and Final Judgement" from 1879 and it's still a mystery what happened to the original, painted in 1620.

The incredibly lavish, maybe even flamboyant, church with religious paintings by artists of the Quito School was constructed by the Church of the Society of Jesus Christ from 1605 to 1765. During this time the church's bell tower was the tallest in Quito but destroyed by an earthquake in 1859. Reconstructed in only six years, it again collapsed from another earthquake and never rebuilt.

Quito's School of Art was founded by Jesuit priests who arrived in Quito in 1586 with a mission to establish a church, school and monastery. They trained indigenous artists in European art forms, which led to the creation of the Quito School.

There are no photos allowed here so I bought some postcards to help me remember its remarkable qualities and uniqueness. The location of this church was chosen to experience the spring equinox so as the sun passes and hits each window, it goes dark inside and certain items are spotlighted.

Plaza de San Francisco is a major public plaza in the historic center. It is vast but quite plain with only a fountain on the right side but it's an old fountain built in the 16th century. Composed of cobblestones, water bubbled from its top down into the large bowl. Old pictures around the plaza displayed local indigenous people selling their produce in the exact same spot where we were standing with no shade trees or shelters. The photos showed how they coped with this situation, using awnings made of some sort of material stretched on a frame to provide protection from the sun or rain. Today, large umbrellas cover stalls and carts selling food and drinks, gelato, crafts, scarves, rosaries, produce and other foods.

Iglesia y Convento de San Francisco, church and monastery, which is the home of the Franciscan Order, fronts onto its namesake Plaza de San Francisco. The plaza is dominated by this largest colonial structure, spanning about four blocks, and the 16th century Roman Catholic complex which houses the city's beloved Virgin of Quito and the oldest church in the city. Twin towers sit above the rest of the baroque-style building.

It looked like it had been started in gray stone, then maybe somebody decided it was too dark and depressing so finished it in white stone with two matching square towers as its topper. The style changed over almost one hundred forty-three years of construction through earthquakes and variations in architectural style preferences.

Inside, the baroque main altar and side altars are beautifully gilded and carved. Its decorated ceilings reminded me again of the Moorish designs of the Alhambra in Spain. Every inch of the interior is covered with gold plating or art. Gold is prevalent causing the blue on the dome's interior to really pop.

San Francisco Square was a market in the 16th century when the Spaniards built the church and plaza. What really interested me was the history before the actual church was built on the ruins of Atahualpa's Palace.

Atahualpa, the last Inca ruler, refused to adopt the Roman Catholic faith and become a follower of the King of Spain. He was executed by strangulation. After killing the leaders, the big project of Christianization of the indigenous population started. The San Francisco order was instrumental in bringing this about. Knowing this history, I looked at this order in a different way as they tried to impress the locals and evangelize them on the very spot where their subordination began.

Lots of people sat on the steps eating fruit, sipping frosty drinks, many wearing authentic vibrant Ecuadorian clothing. The exterior gardens and courtyard were well maintained with a variety of brightly-colored flowers, green grass and artwork. From the bottom of the plaza is a beautiful view of the church complex, old elegant houses across the square and the mountains with the imposing statue of the Virgin.

This eclectic square felt alive with local vendors and I watched one elderly couple sitting on a bench sharing a sandwich while several pigeons waited for some crumbs to fall their way.

Driving along N2 Bolivar I looked down on carts full of watermelon and sat eye level with balconies crafted in delicate iron scrollwork overflowing with flowers.

We lunched at the newly opened Sucres Theatrum Restaurant, where the second floor had been known as the Plaza of the Butchers, in other words, the old slaughterhouse. Also, bullfights were held in this area.

They proudly boasted that they exclusively use Ecuadorian regional food from the coast, sierra and Amazon. The Amazon is on the other side of the Andes mountain range and about a thousand miles away. We were hearing news about this particular region because of a new virus that was causing harm to many, including pregnant women. A nasty daytime-active mosquito was causing infections known as Zika fever or virus that was often asymptomatic or caused only a mild form of dengue fever. With no specific treatment, the use of acetaminophen and lots of rest had been advised. However, they were finding it could spread from a pregnant woman to her baby which could result in severe brain malformations and other birth defects. More needed to be discovered about this bug but we were fine because it didn't fly over the Andes.

A lavish spread of local foods was set out in a buffet. I started with shrimp ceviche which the sign described as being "In Traditional Ecuadorian Style." One in our group had the Jipijapa ceviche, a sea bass ceviche variety invented in the town of Jipijapa pronounced Hippyhappa, which I enjoyed repeating several times. It is marinated in lime juice and seasoned with peanut sauce and avocado. None of us had the seafood ceviche which included octopus and other unfamiliar, questionable sea-things.

Signs explained what the dishes were. La fritada quiteña is slow-cooked pork, a traditional Quito-style frittata with cheese-filled potato patties. Another hearty choice was grilled beef tenderloin tournedos with corn cake and sautéed baby vegetables. Red snapper, pea purée, artichoke, zucchini and herbed Andean mushrooms looked good, so I took a scoop of this but scraped off the pea purée. Grilled red tuna pepper steak in a lemon butter and herb sauce smelled so good. We all took a small portion of each just to try them out.

A bowl of what we presumed to be corn nuts turned out to be our favorite go-to snack. The crunchy-toasted, lightly-salted large grain corn was addictive. Bags of this would need to go home with us.

There were several choices of reasonably small-size desserts to sample: fried baby Ecuadorian banana with a warm chocolate soup and homemade vanilla ice cream, creamy rice pudding with a caramelized crust, and lava cake made of seventy percent Ecuadorian chocolate with mint ice cream. Stop the madness. I would have the lava cake and passed on everything else including the Ecuadorian fruits of different textures and colors. Labels read: naranjilla, chirimoya, guayaba, babaco, guanabana. But wait, there's more. The mango tart with vanilla ice cream looked refreshing, and finally a chocolate soufflé with sautéed banana and honey crumble, in a mini dish. This was a fun way to try a sampler platter of many items; I love buffets for that very reason.

Back on our bus we drove by a square with statues, street art on the cement walls, and came to a sign that looked familiar—red with the word PARE, meaning STOP. I noticed a light blue Tucson like I drove at home. We would see many Hyundai dealerships all over the area as common as a mom and pop corner grocery store.

Out on the open road, we drove through lush greenery, homes, and nearby saw even more rugged Andes Mountains. The scenery alone was worth the short drive.

About thirty minutes from Quito we arrived at the Mitad del Mundo monument. This huge stone monument is a close calculation of the Equatorial Line which is painted in bright yellow. We all took turns hopping from the southern hemisphere to the northern and some of us straddled the line standing in both at the same time. The monument's yellow line read "Equator Latitude 0° 0′ 0″ with the dramatic snow-covered mountains in the distance.

Several shops surround the monument and include a museum. The downstairs pertains to Ecuador's people, food, climate and more. There is some history about the monument and its construction as well as interesting examples of physics. An elevator took us several stories to the top and then we walked down looking at the various exhibits about science and culture on the different levels.

The little shops making up a tiny city sell every imaginable trinket and I purchased postcards to send out the next day in hopes they would be received before we got home. I read a quote on a postcard that said "You know you've traveled when standing in both hemispheres at once."

I bought a hand-painted fridge magnet of the monument with S and N divided by the walkway with the Andes in the background, Mitad Del Mundo printed at the top, and Ecuador at the bottom—a perfect little souvenir.

Even though not mentioning it much, we could tell the elevation was a bit bothersome. We drank several bottles of water not only for hydration but water is H_2O, with O for oxygen that we needed in our systems. My doctor had given me some pills in case we developed headaches from the altitude but we didn't need them. My best recollection is a slight, dull headache. Instructions that had been given to us included "For your health we recommend the first day until you are acclimated to the altitude in Quito, do not drink any alcoholic beverage." We did not.

Returning to the hotel and after a shower and change of clothes, we were bussed to Carmine Ristorante, clearly Italian and one of our favorite types of foods. Chilean red wine bottles greeted us on each table set for four or six guests. We'd been in Quito almost twenty-four hours.

The restaurant is gorgeous on two floors and our group had a spacious section on the second floor. It was open to the cool night air and leafy bushes gently brushed my shoulder. It felt elegant yet not formal. The attentive staff hovered making sure we had enough water and wine. The owner came around to each table and greeted us, made sure all was well, and thanked us for coming.

The menu was extensive but I opted for one of my favorite salads, Insalata Caprese: mozzarella, tomato, a basil leaf or two and a drizzle of olive oil and a dot or two of balsamic vinaigrette. The tomatoes tasted like they had just been plucked from the vines. Oodles of pasta choices all looked delicious. A couple at our table had the penne Bolognese and I had pappardelle boscaiola, pasta in a creamy cognac sauce with prosciutto. It was scrumptious. And for dessert we all chose tiramisu or, as the menu showed, tiramisãs.

The next morning, I pushed open the curtains to let the bright sunshine in and looking out our eighth story window saw hundreds of people running a marathon. One man was bent over at his waist undoubtedly trying to breath. Really?! A marathon at nine thousand feet, seriously people?! I felt really rested after a great night's sleep but somehow felt exhausted watching those below. I had become winded the previous afternoon just going up one flight of stairs which felt like five.

After a buffet breakfast at Bistro Latino Restaurant we bid farewell to this lovely hotel at 8:15 a.m., got on our bus, picked up our boarding passes and returned to the airport for our two-hour flight to Baltra Island. I took a window seat on AeroGal.

I looked out the window as we took off, now seeing in broad daylight the aerial view of what I hadn't seen when we landed a few days earlier at midnight. Right beyond the airport property were streets lined with businesses and dwellings. Buildings inched upward as far as they could safely build next to the mountains. All around the airport were millions of buildings.

We circled, flying over several flat green plateaus where I spotted some dwellings. Some plots were the hues of mint, seafoam, emerald and then auburn, cinnamon and terracotta. And so many jagged mountains. The land disappeared as we banked over the azure ocean.

While I intently stared out the window my husband was having a conversation with a couple across from us. The English accent had caught his attention so he explained we had dear friends who lived in the Oxford area. This couple, Clive and Greta, lived in St. Ives on the south coast, promoted as the dazzling jewel in Cornwall's crown. Mark told them we'd been in the area thirteen years earlier staying at Marazion, Cornwall's oldest town. Turned out they lived in the next little town only six miles away.

They mentioned they were looking forward to their first visit to Alaska taking a cruise the next summer. My husband explained I organized group travel and told them we had a group of friends going also. That's where I got pulled into the conversation instead of sightseeing. Mark asked me when we were going and on what ship. Low and behold, the Brits were on the exact same cruise. We vowed to meet up in Alaska.

It didn't seem like two hours had passed before we landed on a parched austere island. The airport had two runways and another AeroGal was parked on the other one. My memory is of the overpowering scent of salty sea air during many family trips to the beach as a child. It's funny how some smells remind you of your childhood. This happens with my favorite songs too, a transference back to early days growing up.

One of the reasons we chose Celebrity Xpedition for this adventure was because I had done copious research and wanted a vessel and company with the same environmental policies we believed in. Celebrity goes above and beyond regular compliance. They do pollution prevention, reduce, reuse and recycle wastes, and use the most advanced system in the region to treat wastewater, a desalination system that provides most of the freshwater needs of the ships, and the hull is coated with slippery silicone to prevent biologic growth. They support the local community with fish ordered from local fishermen; local farmers provide the coffee and much of the fresh fruit and vegetables on board. They offered the opportunity for us to support the Galápagos Fund, where hundreds of thousands of dollars have supported local conservation projects, education, job training and habitat restoration. And they hired local people as guides. There was no casino, nor were there stage shows, staff pushing beverages or photographers with a camera in your face.

After going through proper channels and waiting for further instructions, looking across the runway and barrenness of the land, there in the bay floated our navy and white Xpedition just waiting for us. Pacing a bit and excitedly awaiting our departure, I wandered around the end of the open building and there he was, my first land iguana with mahogany leathery hide, long sharp dark spikes running down the entire length of his body, and flat feet with toes spread out, sunning himself.

I heard the announcement that we would soon be boarding our transportation, our first Zodiac ride, which would deliver us to Xpedition. Donning our orange life vests, awkwardly climbing in, holding on, a dozen of us in shorts, cotton shirts, most hatless wearing sunglasses, everyone was smiling as we got closer and closer to our home away from home for the next week. The Zodiac is an inflatable boat made of black rigid fabric that felt slippery like rubber. I could hardly contain my excitement and really didn't. If I could have jumped up and down in the Zodiac I would have.

Swaying streamers and flags with a variety of colors draped the top decks creating a party atmosphere. The Ecuadorian flag hung on the top deck at the front of the ship. Within hours of stepping off our plane we were on a rubberized boat that delivered us to the gleaming white ninety-eight-passenger boutique ship, really a super-yacht, Celebrity Xpedition, with her crew awaiting our arrival. She was built in 2001 in Germany by another company and named Sun Bay. She entered service for Celebrity in 2004 as a one-of-a-kind vessel for the company offering travelers a premium experience. Galápagos has eighteen major islands with twenty-one total. Xpedition has an easy on and off boarding platform built for those of us who are less-than-nimble. Our Zodiac was made to hold twelve people.

We were greeted with a glass of chilled champagne, some reading materials and our room keys, much like a credit card but this was unique because of the blue feet in the top right corner. There was my name, and stateroom 412 M/S Xpedition. Now it was official. I freely admit I am obsessed with colorful doors and discovering what might lay beyond. It started with our first trip to Scotland in 1997, searching for my roots.

As I pushed open the ivory painted stateroom door I just knew each time it opened we'd be in store for something incredible. We checked out our room and unpacked our luggage that had mysteriously arrived before us. Our stateroom was the smallest we'd ever sailed in although smartly designed and minimalist chic, and even though snug, it had a nice big picture window. Flopping on the king-size bed, it was deemed comfortable enough. A loveseat sat against the wall across from the desk and chair that would also serve as a grooming area. The window was slightly above water level and in the distance we saw parched, russet land and a faraway coned-shaped island.

Buffet lunch was served at Darwin's Restaurant, where we would have most of our meals over the next week. Salads, meats, pasta and much more would tide us over until dinner. The dessert selection was excellent with cups of pudding that surrounded a chocolate layer cake that read "Wellcome On Board." I figured the extra "l" in welcome was the Ecuadorian version. But what caught my eye was a key lime pie, one of my favorites. Turned out my new friend from the elevator, Beth, loved it, too. We were off to a great start. Staff greeted us warmly letting us know all we had to do was ask and they'd try to meet our requests. Darwin's, a stylishly modern restaurant, seated all of us at small tables or large banquettes.

At exactly 2 o'clock we sailed away toward North Seymour Island, not far from Baltra. During our sail-away, music was playing and we took ourselves on a self-guided tour of our new home. We started at the top deck, a spacious sunny area with lounge chairs and a large whirlpool tub. The gym, with a few pieces of equipment, served as the massage room, too. Down a deck was more café seating and one more down in the back would be where some buffets would be laid out.

Three small fishing boats zoomed by us and all occupants waved. They were between us and a large rock with a flat top, maybe a volcano that blew its lid. The Discovery Lounge is spacious enough to compare with smaller lounges found on big ocean cruise ships. This is where most events such as classes in Spanish cooking and how to mix a minty mojito would occur.

Our self-guided tour was interrupted at three o'clock for our first Xpedition briefing providing information about the upcoming itinerary and safety regulations followed by a mandatory boat drill.

You must be accompanied by a naturalist guide certified by the Galapagos National Park Department to enter any area designated as a national park. There are specific requirements to become an approved naturalist guide. They generally study under the auspices of the Darwin Foundation. Examinations are conducted by the Galapagos National Park Authority. Once qualified, they have to attend seminars and workshops in order to remain up to date with the latest information.

The Ecuadorian guides demonstrated how to correctly put on the bright orange life vest, then how to properly and safely get into a Zodiac without falling in or rolling off the side. It looked simple enough. And turned out it really was, well, for most. One sits down on the top of the side of Zodiac, turning or swinging your entire body including legs into the boat. There were rope loops to hang onto when skimming across the water. A rule: If we saw an animal or bird, we were to let the guide know by quietly sharing the exciting news so everyone could enjoy the encounter.

During the briefing, we got an idea of what animals and birds we could expect to see and why the environment would vary from flat beaches of white sand to black lava sand, to steep cliffs and rocky coastlines.

At four o'clock we were putting on the life jackets and climbing into our Zodiac with Garcia taking care of us for our first landing, called a dry landing, which meant we were not stepping out into the water.

This was one heck of a way to start as the land was all rocks, big rocks. Probably the most challenging landing of the week as we had to time our leap off the boat just as the surf receded. With the help of our experienced guides, we fortunately made our leaps at just the right time. A couple of folks wearing shorts had bloody scrapes to show how they missed the mark.

On shore, we were greeted by a young sea lion flipping its right paw which looked like it was welcoming us with a forward wave. Mom or dad was asleep on the warm rocks not caring at all.

We were told we'd hike about one mile and immediately I was very appreciative of our sturdy hiking shoes. On this rocky trail which fortunately was flat, we stepped from rock to the next uneven rock to the next rock. There was no rhyme or reason so you couldn't pick up a pace or get in a flow. It was the hardest flat one-mile walk I'd ever been on.

Paying attention to walking on the rocks prevented me from glancing around for birds and wildlife. When I finally did look down, I saw a pair of White-Cheeked Pintails side by side, like they were looking for something between rocks. I had a waterproof trifold *Galápagos Wildlife Guide* for reference and started a log of wildlife sightings so I wouldn't forget what I would see over the next week.

Overhead flew a large black bird with a long wingspan. Our guide said it was a Magnificent Frigatebird. "Magnificent" is actually part of its name, not just an adjective. It took one and a half hours to go one mile from rock to rock. These stones never were flat and smooth but more like uneven boulders. This walk would be totally worth it as we were very near to a Magnificent Frigatebird nesting area.

A familiar sight flying overhead were several noisy gulls but these were totally black whereas ours are normally white or gray. These are appropriately called Lava Gulls and we would often see them and their cousin, the Swallow-Tailed Gull.

I heard a sweet birdsong and looking in the direction of its melody, I spotted a smallish bright yellow bird in a leafless bush, almost as bright yellow as a canary. It had a scarlet crest on its head. How marvelous—our first Galápagos Yellow Warbler.

Several of us stepped off the path getting out of the way as a large land iguana grandly promenaded down its runway, not ours. It was different than the one at the airport in Baltra. This one had gold coloring under its chin and throat and not many spikes along its back.

Then we spotted a fluffy white and black bird with a long bill, our first baby Magnificent Frigatebird nesting in a sprawling thicket called saltbush, a perfect nesting site. The reason for the harrowing hike was to get to this out-of-the-way nesting area for these incredible birds. Adults when flying can have a wingspan of seven to eight feet. When flying overhead, their shadows on the ground are about the size of an airplane. They are the largest seabird of the frigate family. They look black but actually have brownish-black plumage with long narrow wings and a forked tail.

Three males took a position on the ground and inflated the ruby pouch on their breasts. It's supposed to impress a female flying overhead; sometimes it works and sometimes not. These sacks are called gular pouches. We were already learning new terminology from our guide.

An adult female was close to her chick. They feed on fish from the surface of the ocean. More gray and white puffballs, as I called them, came into view. They were in various stages of fuzz with their soft-looking fluff or plumage. These babies were mostly white with black wings. One was sound asleep on the ground next to an all-white rock, which turned out was covered in droppings. About twenty feet away was a male with his full red pouch trying to impress some of the females who were standing around like a bunch of hens in a chicken coop. But he wasn't getting the attention he probably had hoped for.

Another iguana that sauntered by was even more colorful than the last. Its legs and head were orangish yellow and only its torso was dark. The spikes on its back started yellow then blended into orange. It stopped and looked up at me as I squatted to take a close-up photo of its face. Its eyes were a goldish hazel; nose holes and the top and bottom of its mouth were aqua. If an iguana could be pretty, it was this one. We moved over to let it by because it was her right of way, not ours. From now on all pretty iguanas became a Her not an It.

As we walked back to the dock, there stood a Prickly Pear Cactus in the shape of Mickey Mouse ears. Disney would have loved this. This cactus is a favorite food of land iguanas and giant tortoises. The flat jointed stem is covered with small stiff hairs and spines. Our guide said that the yellow flowers along the bottom rim will turn crimson, then become fruit. They say the fruit has health benefits for diabetics, high cholesterol and hangovers. I wondered if the hangovers would be from too many prickly pear margaritas? It's supposedly also helpful as an antiviral and anti-inflammatory.

We stumbled, almost literally, upon dozing sea lions, motionless as shiny beach boulders. Only the adorable pups paid us any notice. Back at our dock, our guide helped us put the life vests back on and get into the Zodiac. We returned in time to get cleaned up for our first daily briefing before dinner. Captain Pacheco welcomed us and we all said "Cheers" as we toasted with champagne.

We could tell this was our kind of cruising with a relaxed dress code and open bridge policy which meant that after we made an appointment at guest relations we could learn about the navigation and communications systems on board. We booked ours for a few days out.

The setting sun turned the sky ginger, and as it eased downward the sky turned multiple shades of burgundy. A Magnificent Frigatebird with his deflated red pouch was the only thing between us and the perfectly round bright orange orb as it sank lower and lower until it was sliced in half at the edge of the horizon and then slid into the ocean.

Dinner menus were distributed and items selected. A marinated grated cabbage salad that somehow molded perfectly into a four-inch-tall cylindrical shape was still holding together. It was decorated with a swirl of red tomato sauce. I selected shrimp as my main course, always a favorite. Dessert was a no-brainer for me, my second favorite dessert—crème brûlée with mango sorbet in a cone, shaped as a cup. And as much Chilean wine as anyone wanted. Two of my favorite desserts on the first day of this journey.

Who would have guessed our first day would be so remarkable?

Slits of sunlight crept in through the curtains where I hadn't tightly secured them together the night before. I brought old-fashioned wooden clothespins for this exact situation. I just had to find them. Daylight meant I probably was missing something so I peeked out to a view overlooking Kicker Rock at San Cristóbal Island. I learned quickly this would be the rhythm of life on board Xpedition beginning with a morning wake-up call, buffet breakfast, then all aboard our Zodiac at the appointed time adorned with life jackets, dressed accordingly for dry or wet landings. And exploration with many firsts.

Kicker Rock, or Sleeping Lion, is an island of the remains of a satellite volcanic cone off the northwest shore of San Cristóbal Island. I couldn't see the Sleeping Lion at all. Two groups went on a seven o'clock Zodiac ride circumnavigating the rock. We had slept in so enjoyed the views from the top deck of two Zodiacs sailing around the flat rock barely sticking above water with four sea lions barking their greetings. This rock was an extension of the others to make the lion look like it was sleeping. I still didn't see it.

Among a bank of clouds, the sun popped through an opening with shafts of shimmering light radiating to the ocean. An azure sky won out as the clouds disappeared. Waving from a returning Zodiac were Dave and Sharon. As soon as passengers returned, a winch and line nabbed the rubberized boats and returned them to their resting place on board.

After breakfast we gathered below to board, starting our first full day in the Galápagos Islands. Littering the bay of Puerto Baquerizo Moreno on San Cristóbal Island were a variety of fishing boats and one larger all-gray Coast Guard ship. Tatiana II looked like it could house several people for overnight fishing trips or maybe even tours. Verito, Carla and other smaller boats seemed suitable for one or maybe two to go fishing.

Diego, our guide for the day, delivered us to this town of about seven thousand people. This island is the capital of the archipelago. First to greet us was an iguana whose camouflage skin blended with the rocks, barely noticeable. This was contrary to six bright orange-legged, funny-looking small Sally Lightfoot Crabs, also sunning themselves sharing one rock. A good-size sea lion stretched out on the warm cobblestones and couldn't have cared less that we had arrived. Diego mentioned this was just the beginning of seeing hundreds of these crabs, also called Red Rock Crabs, which are one of the most common crabs along the western coast of South America.

The bodies of these Sallys are auburn, then the colors change to orange and yellow legs. Sally is a typically shaped crab with five pairs of legs, the front two bearing small, black symmetrical pincers. The other legs are broad and flat. They are not huge crabs like we have in the Pacific Northwest but only three to five inches long. Flat and low to the ground, they sort of looked like spiders. They don't have the best reputation, being the ultimate coastal scavenger consuming nearly everything in its path. But they were a lot more pleasing and sort of fascinating to look at than Dungeness Crab at home or King Crab from Alaska. One Sally had bright blue coloring between its center auburn body and red-orange front legs. Rumor has it they got the name after a Caribbean dancer because of swiftness while jumping from rock to rock, their ability to run in four directions, and to climb up vertical slopes. This combination makes them difficult to catch and I thought, "Why go to all the trouble because their crab legs looked too small to bother with for eating?"

Several buildings lined the cobbled streets and we walked through a pleasant waterfront on Charles Darwin Avenue before boarding a small bus. There were nice paintings extending along the main street but this wasn't a shopping stop; we had scenery and wildlife to see.

As we took a short bus ride our guide explained that this island, the farthest east, is one of the oldest islands and the fifth largest. It is comprised of several volcanoes and is an area of two hundred fifteen square miles with an elevation of twenty-four hundred feet. The name "San Cristóbal" comes from the patron saint of seafarers, St. Christopher, and was the first island Darwin visited. He didn't find the lush tropical richness he expected. This is where he collected his first species.

For each of the morning and afternoon outings, we were offered two options: 1) usually a longer more active walk or 2) a short walk and less strenuous. We opted for the Las Tijeretas fitness walk of one and a half miles even though we were warned about boulders, hills and stairs. No problem. Option two was wandering around the little town and shopping. This was not on my agenda for this trip. It was all about wildlife.

Arriving at the trail head, it was even with gravel. Hallelujah. The only obstacles were branches of leafless trees hanging over the trail. Several times we bent down to avoid a possible prickly encounter. One bush held interesting flowers or maybe pods. The flower was crimpled light yellowish-green, about ten inches long with a pink middle and looked like soft crêpe material. But I didn't touch it to find out.

Then it happened, that nice flat gravel path turned into rocks and more rocks, rock after rock after rock. All uneven and possible ankle-twisters which I certainly didn't want to happen at the beginning of our exploration. It was slow going over this uneven terrain.

There were several different shapes and sizes of cacti, some bushes with soft to bright green just starting to show, and brown bushes with even browner branches. Then a lovely pastel yellow flower about the size of a fully-opened poppy stood out dramatically from all the brownness. It had six rounded petals with five round red clumps of fuzz tucked into its base with a yellow center. It is called a Cotton Flower.

During our walk, guide Diego heard a mockingbird and I realized then how impressive our guides were. He told us that the mockingbird is endemic to this island and how it evolved to survive according to plant and food availability. This island's mockingbird had mostly a white body with dark wings and tail. Still not seeing the bird itself, I asked if a mockingbird mocks; how did he know if it was actually a mockingbird and not the bird it was mocking?

He pointed out where the bird was sitting and said that birdsong is from a Galápagos Dove, making a coo, coo, coo, sound. This bird was not a dove but only mocking it. He mentioned that researchers had found there appears to be no limit to the number of songs and sounds mockingbirds can pick up. The male mockingbird does most of the singing, especially when trying to attract a girlfriend. He said he'd heard some of the island's mocking-birds mimic bugs, frogs and seals.

There are three other species of mocking-birds in the Galápagos, each different on the separate islands but all were from one original colony. I hoped to see each kind.

A short way up the rocky trail something scampered by me then stopped on a rock. It looked like a baby iguana but it moved too fast. Another first—a tawny and beige Lava Lizard with two white stripes down its sides. I determined quickly that most wildlife either started with Darwin, Galápagos or Lava, case in point.

In the distance was Shipwreck Bay and Kicker Rock. Below where we stood was a small bay of clear aqua water through which we could see to the bottom. Swimming there were two sea turtles. Another first—sea turtles. This is called Tijeretas Bay and not far from the town.

Kicker Rock or Leon Dormido in Spanish, Sleeping Lion to us, from this vantage point was now clear how it had gotten its name. One definitely needed to be some distance away to see the image.

Walking a short way, we climbed some steps up to a platform that overlooked the bay and as far as my eyes could see were water and islands. This very spot is where Darwin and his crew from the HMS Beagle came ashore.

An over-size Darwin statue is surrounded by a sea lion, giant tortoise and iguana at his feet. A picture of us taken by friends shows us barely reaching Darwin's waist. Several took turns straddling the tortoise about as wide as a horse.

Ending this morning's adventure at the Interpretation Center we learned about volcanic beginnings, seclusion from the continent, ocean currents, climate, and the arrival of different species and their establishment. Human history is also highlighted, chronologically described by the most important events related to discovery and colonization of the islands along with San Cristóbal history, too.

At the pier, a snoozing sea lion stretched out on the bench that would ordinarily be for people to sit on. We boarded a Zodiac back to our ship.

After lunch at the buffet, we had a snorkeling and water safety briefing. While we were eating, the captain cruised to our next stop for the afternoon, Española Island.

We opted for the long walk at Puerto Suarez, which would be a boulder-covered trail that required good balance and sturdy shoes, about two and a half hours of a really rocky hike and we were warned it was slow going and difficult. What the heck, we weren't missing out on anything.

Fortunately, we were in the arid season so it wasn't muggy yet. We selected this time of year because we could see animals clearly through the leafless brush; there were no bugs or humidity. Plus, certain animals and birds were doing things only once a year and this time of year was for some having babies or mating. We definitely weren't bug and humidity lovers which was just one result when coming in the rainy season. And walking on slick boulders and lava wearing plastic ponchos and rain gear sounded cumbersome and somewhat dangerous.

We hadn't walked far before coming upon a Brown Pelican with its head tucked under its wing napping and one rock away were two marine iguanas. One had a rosy body and halfway down its tail it turned ebony, with pine-colored front legs and matching spikes. The other had Christmassy-red on its left side and stomach, and coal black on the other side matching his head and legs.

A different one walked in front of Sharon, who stopped abruptly, giving it the right of way as it meandered slowly joining a squad of four others having about the same coloring and size, clearly its tribe.

A baby sea lion lying under a bush didn't even have its eyes open yet. Near the newborn were marine iguanas everywhere on every rock surface in varying colors. If I had been squeamish about these prehistoric-looking creatures it would have been here.

The Xpedition sat anchored just off shore from where we were, and while everyone gawked at the colorful iguanas some movement caught my eye. There it stood—my first Blue-Footed Booby using its grayish-blue beak to preen its chest. With the Xpedition in the background and booby front and center, it made for a most excellent picture. This one's blue feet weren't quite as blue as I'd seen on National Geographic but it was my first booby. I got a few photos before abiding by the rule letting our guide know of the sighting. Everyone went booby crazy. We learned they have nostrils on their bills that are permanently closed. Instead of breathing through nostrils they breathe through the corners of their mouths. This adaptation occurred because these seabirds dive after their food, and closed nostrils provide better protection from breathing saltwater.

Back on the trail, guide Lucia pointed out another mockingbird, then sea lions on the rocks and surf swirling around them as they barked at each other. Walking by iguanas, we saw a Galápagos Flycatcher (white underneath with gray head, back and tail) perched on a white post. Another first.

It took a while walking through and over the rocks when we came upon the cutest, fluffiest big baby bird I'd ever seen. There sat our first Galápagos Albatross or Waved Albatross, with its parents flying overhead. These birds have milk chocolate-colored bodies, bright yellow legs and feet with an equally bright yellow bill. There were dozens of adults soaring above us.

November brought some color to this island. Some low bushes had turned lime, brick, magenta and yellow, and as I took a photo of the flora I noticed a black and white bird on a rock. It was a Nazca Booby, all white except for black wings and cream bill. Another first but too far away.

Walking back, the colorful vegetation flattens out, and with the Xpedition off shore, another memorable photo. To my left I noticed a head tucked under its black wing; it was another Nazca Booby with a pal standing in brush close by. There was another one on the rocky shoreline not far below. The waves hit the rocks causing water to shoot through a hole, changing to a mist coming out the other side. Several more Nazca Boobies didn't mind me looking at them. Walking back, we were instructed to stay within pole markers as birds were nesting in the brush nearby. Another young albatross nestled among the low rocks with its head towering over them. Not far away sat a momma and her two little ones, almost as big as she was, just fluffier and beige and hazel.

About the cutest thing of the day was a baby Blue-Footed Booby, actually called a chick, covered in shades of brown including its feet. He turned toward me with head down, beak over his belly, wings at its side, and feet camouflaged in the soft dirt. He tipped his head up and his eyes were right on me. He made me laugh out loud.

A few steps away standing on a boulder was a Blue-Footed Booby, probably dad, with the right color blue feet, bright blue and the bluest ones I'd seen, along with duller blue beak. Dad with his mahogany head, wings and stark white body was preoccupied with his afternoon bathing practices. No one knows for sure why Blue-Footed Boobies have blue feet, or why Red-Footed Boobies have red feet, but the sight of these bright feet is startling. They sort of waddle back and forth like Charlie Chaplin in the old black and white movies. Their vacant wide-eyed expression made me chuckle. Some say their feet color is because of the food they eat which is mackerel, sardines, flying fish and anchovies. They fly above the water and dive into the ocean after their prey. Sort of like the idea that a flamingo is pink because it eats pink shrimp. But I doubt it because Red-Footed Bobbies eat the same menu items as their blue cousins. The name "booby" comes from the Spanish "bobo" meaning stupid. I disagree; they were smart enough to adapt to this barren environment.

A medium-size, walnut-colored Galápagos Dove, with red legs and feet and cobalt eyes, pecked around the brush for bugs. Probably two dozen red and black iguanas sunned themselves on white rocks sandwiched between green bushes. Below them were layers of white foam from the sapphire waves, and Xpedition dressed in navy and white. Large lizards, no matter how passive or gentle they might be, were a bit disconcerting at first, and being surrounded by hundreds had creeped me out but no more. Marine iguanas up to three feet long blanketed the rocky shores, almost motionless in the warmth. These are the only lizards in the world that have adapted to the sea. Mostly gray and spiky, they blend in perfectly with jagged lava. I had to step delicately from one sharp rock to the next to avoid falling onto dozens of sleeping spiky creatures.

Some yellow Lava Cactus added the only color with its microphone-shaped clumps. This plant has soft furry spines and grows in clusters to a height of about two feet. New growth coloring is yellow turning to gold to brown which darkens to gray with age.

The birds and sea lions were engaged in their activities, seemingly oblivious to our presence. We felt as if we were part of their world as opposed to being on the outside looking in, like at a zoo. A Galápagos Hawk, mostly black with yellow legs and feet, and white bill with black on the curved tip looked like a vicious raptor, but he didn't care that I took his photo as he posed on a rock for me. What a day. This was better than any television program I'd seen.

When we arrived back on board, we had a surprise in our room—a bottle of cabernet sauvignon along with six chocolate-dipped strawberries and six canapés. Wow. We quickly got cleaned up and changed, gobbled our unexpected treats and went to the top deck because I wasn't about to miss the Piña Colada cocktail party.

I could tell the sunset would be extraordinary because of a thin layer of clouds reaching from end-to-end in the sky already turning the sky apricot. As the orb dropped lower it was briefly completely hidden by the cloud bank. When it dropped slowly below the clouds the sky turned cantaloupe to mandarin then tangerine, bleeding to cherry and strawberry. The clouds were trimmed in silver along the bottom. The closer the red ball got to the navy water the brighter the reflection. As portions of the sun gently disappeared into the water the colors changed to cardinal. Just before it totally disappeared below the horizon, the flat horizon line turned fiery like hot magma flowing from a volcano and the ruby sky turned the deepest wine color I'd ever seen. It looked like a gigantic fruit salad of colors created just for me. I took a sequence of photos to remember this remarkable performance.

At 7:30 each night we would have our briefing in the Discovery Lounge about the next day's activities. Dinner was served at 7:45 and we ate every morsel. A pianist on board provided live music as after-dinner drinks were served.

I couldn't imagine each day continuing to amaze me more. But they did.

Tuesday morning we awoke to a different island, Floreana, once a penal colony for Ecuador and this is one of the four islands that Charles Darwin visited aboard the HMS Beagle. During the 19th century it was also the first capital of the archipelago. Very early, looking out our window at a cloudless sky I saw the silhouette of an island and I counted six cone-shaped volcanoes. Around 5:30 a.m. the sunrise made an appearance creating a wide swath of gleaming light on the indigo ocean. I went back to bed for another hour.

After breakfast, before boarding our Zodiacs, many picked up snorkel gear for later. We learned from Manuel, our guide for the day, that the HMS Beagle was a Cherokee class ten-gun brig of the Royal Navy, named after the beagle dog breed. The ship launched in May 1820 from England, took part in a fleet review celebrating the coronation of King George IV, and was the first ship to sail under the new London Bridge. But being in no immediate need, they put her in reserve for five years moored afloat without masts or rigging. Then she was adapted as a survey ship and took part in three expeditions. On the second survey voyage the young naturalist Charles Darwin was on board.

This would be our first wet landing so I wore my waterproof Keen sandals. Sliding off the side of the Zodiac into a foot of cool ocean water felt refreshing. People dropped their gear on the white-sand beach before we took an easy trail of sand and gravel looking at cone volcanoes, trees and bushes. A white daisy-like flower, with its double layer of white petals with a pink center, was the only flower on one bush.

We were on a Great Flamingo hunt. We were told they usually pack together and go from island to island as they please to find whatever menu item sounds good to them. We learned that a group of flamingos is called, not a flock, but a flamboyance. They are pink because they like pink shrimp. There it stood knee-deep in a shallow aqua lagoon—our first Great Flamingo. And the only one. Single, solitary, just one. It took a few steps then gracefully glided off to another location where, if we were lucky, we might see it again.

We heard a sweet bird song before spotting exactly what and where it was. This would be the case with most bird sightings. Manuel pointed out a small light brown Warbler Finch perched on a branch of a tree. He mentioned that its beak is not as thick as other types of finches we would see.

It was so quiet that hearing bird songs was easy and delightful. A few steps beyond sat an all-black Sharp-Beaked Ground Finch about the size of my hand with feathers fluffed. Maybe he'd taken a bath and was drying out. Its tweeting song plus the Warbler Finch together sounded like nature's radio station.

Around another hill in another lagoon was our solo Great Flamingo again. Just one but it was good enough. Looking down at a bush I noticed a pod that looked just like a white jelly bean but it was actually a pepper. The white bean would turn red when it was mature. A short distance away was a parched bush with a batch of bright yellow flowers called Yellow Cordia; they stood out from the stark brownness.

We turned toward the ocean and walked along a white sand beach watching sea turtles along the shoreline floating in the surf. An American Oystercatcher with its black and white body and bright tangerine legs and feet with matching eyes, and a Sanderling with a white and black body, and black legs, bill and eyes, shared the waterline searching for nibbles.

We came upon sea turtle craters about four to five feet in diameter where the turtles go to lay eggs and sleep. Their feet left a unique pattern in the sand leading to the water's edge.

We walked over a small hill back to the white sand beach and the bay where snorkelers and swimmers would frolic in the water. About half the group donned their black body, knee-high wetsuits, goggles, snorkel masks and tubes, and were ready to go. Mark, Dave and Sharon geared up. I saw Clive and Greta heading in with no protective gear and the water was chilly.

Not really an underwater person, while they snorkeled I combed the beach for pretty shells that I did not pick up to bring home, watched colorful Sally Lightfoot crabs scampering around the rocks, several Blue-Footed Boobies doing their morning grooming, and sea lions basking in the warmth of the sun on smooth flat rocks. A couple of these Sallys had stripes or spots and sported magenta claws and pink eyes. I sat on the warm, clean white sand and watched the thin line of lacy white foam trace the edge of the uncurling waves, each wave as flat as the next.

I could see Mark and kept an eye on him as he seemed to be getting farther and farther out. I hoped he was paying attention to his whereabouts. Fortunately, a line of Zodiacs made sure no one went past the imaginary boundary and hung around in case a ride back to shore would be required. Several birds plunged into the water around him like they were bombarding him; it was a flock of those silly Blue-Footed Boobies diving for their meal. Amazingly, they soar at heights up to three hundred thirty feet above the ocean and when they spot a group of fish they will dive below the surface, and during this dive they can swim up to eight-two feet deep chasing their lunch. They can plunge at speeds up to sixty miles per hour. To survive the impact of hitting the water and the pressure of diving below the surface, they have air sacs in their skulls to cushion and protect them. These are impressive birds indeed.

We were told that when a sea lion blows bubbles in your face, it means he wants to play. I guessed my husband was watching the underwater ballerinas zip around him wanting him to participate. In a black wetsuit he probably looked like a sea lion but his lack of marine experience and limitations were dead giveaways.

A Swallowtail Gull performed by diving then soaring upward. Along the rocks I spotted a Pencil-Spined Sea Urchin and a green Pyramid Sea Star with five bright green legs. I felt so relaxed in the sunshine slathered in sunscreen, toes in the water, listening to birdlife and waiting with anticipation of snorkel stories.

Seal lions snoozed on the rocks along the shoreline not caring one bit about these bigger wet-suited black bodies on their beach or in their water. I could see the top half of Dave, like a partially submerged submarine, and watched a large pelican plop down beside him about three feet away.

Our Zodiacs returned us to Xpedition for lunch and some down time. At lunch we heard about Mark's encounter with his new sea-pal. Gazing down at colorful marine life and taking pictures with the Kodak underwater disposable camera we brought with us, he looked up and was nose-to-nose with a playful juvenile sea lion. Both were apparently startled, Mark the most. This would be an experience he wouldn't forget. He got photos of a pufferfish, Golden Guineafowl, a blueberry-colored parrotfish, a colorful but ugly Mexican Hogfish, plus others that I couldn't locate on my Galápagos marine life guide.

For lunch the chef prepared an Italian buffet but we also had the daily choice of crêpes and hamburgers at the Beagle Grill. Our decision was the Italian buffet.

We enjoyed the BBC film, Galápagos, *Born of Fire*, before our afternoon Zodiac ride and another wet landing, which I really liked best. It usually meant sliding into less than a foot of water. Jon and Beth were in the same boat. We walked a shorter distance than we had been doing yet it was an incline, sandy with small rocks, and very brown and arid. It had its own beauty and a feeling of desolation.

We trekked up a short but steep hill and some steps to a wooden viewing platform overlooking this island and ocean. It is called Baroness Outlook. I had a brochure that I picked up at the cultural center on San Cristóbal that lends some intrigue to Floreana Island and at this very spot where we stood, a woman kept her watch for incoming ships. The self-proclaimed European Baroness bizarrely disappeared with her lovers in the 1930s.

Here are the sordid details condensed to my version: Back in the 1930s, these islands were largely uninhabited. For a doctor in Germany, Friedrich Ritter and his lover and former patient, Dore Strauch, the promise of seclusion was too much to resist. They embarked on a four-week journey from Berlin to South America where they waited a month in Guayaquil before sailing to the island of Floreana. When they landed, the volcanic island was harsh and subject to droughts and heat, yet the pair managed to carve a home for themselves among the elements. They were even called the Adam and Eve of the Galápagos. When they wrote home, friends and family sent letters to the press, so even searching for solitude they became somewhat famous.

With the press speculating, another German family, the Wittmers, found the couple's story inspiring and soon embarked for Floreana themselves. The Wittmers were a "salt of the earth" type whose down-home personalities clashed heavily with the free-thinking and intellectualism of Dr. Ritter and his lover, Miss Strauch.

At first the neighbors largely avoided each other, living about an hour's walk apart. Enter Eloise Wehrborn de Wanger-Bosquet, a self-proclaimed Baroness who had come to Floreana with two male companions, Robert Philippson and Rudolf Lorenz. The Baroness was a modern woman with self-absorbed tales of her life back in Europe. Regarded as stubborn, sexy and wild, she landed on Floreana and the island was instantly hers, or so she thought.

Parading around the island in skimpy outfits, the Baroness was not shy about her male lovers. It was said she'd greet passing ships in sheer outfits (standing at the lookout where we stood) with a pistol on her hip. According to the documentary, *A Galápagos Affair*, the Baroness was intent on building a hotel on the island, declaring herself Empress of Floreana. Her boastful attitude ruffled the feathers of her few neighbors and petty conflicts arose frequently. At the same time, the Baroness had begun to favor Philippson over Lorenz, who was supposedly mistreated by the preferred lover, seeking refuge with the sympathetic Wittmers.

On March 27, 1932, the island of Floreana was eerie and quiet, and a sense of foreboding, according to the writings of Strauch, had settled over paradise. A prolonged scream is said to have pierced the silence, then nothing. The Baroness and her lover, Philippson, disappeared.

So, this is where the murder and mystery of the Galápagos' earliest inhabitants get dramatic as written accounts by the salt-of-the-earth Wittmers and Dr. Ritter's lover, Miss Strauch, conflict. The Wittmers and ex-lover Lorenz claim the Baroness and Philippson had embarked on a boat to Tahiti, asking the family to watch their home and belongings until they returned. Miss Strauch, on the other hand, recalls in her writings that the Baroness' most prized possessions had tellingly been left at her house, while no sighting of an approaching ship had caught her or Dr. Ritter's attention.

The Baroness and Philippson were never heard from again; her eclectic personality and questionable presence forever lost to the island of Floreana. Suspiciously, Lorenz became eager to go back to Germany after the disappearance and soon made haste to the island of San Cristóbal, where his boat disappeared en route only to be discovered months later with his mummified remains on Marchena Island. It is one hundred eight miles between islands.

Then Mr. Ritter died months later from sour chicken that many suspect his lover, Miss Strauch, had poisoned. Claiming to have eaten as much of the rotten bird as her partner, the Wittmers remarked on the oddity of Miss Strauch waiting until Dr. Ritter was beyond saving before calling for help. While Dore Strauch retold the death of Dr. Ritter with loving sorrow and detail, the Wittmers claim his dying words were to curse Dore's very existence.

So, perhaps Lorenz and the Wittmers did murder the Baroness and Philippson. Maybe Ritter and Strauch were equally involved in the killings. It is possible Strauch had killed Ritter out of spite for his cold and unloving demeanor. But as with most great mysteries, the answers are forever lost to time. As for the Wittmer family, their stay on Floreana outlasted their unfortunate neighbors as they continued to live and die on the Galápagos, even opening a hotel on Floreana that remains open to this day.

Called the "*Galápagos Affair*," it's said the legend surrounds the famous tortoise, for which the archipelago is named. Supposedly these prehistoric creatures are able to see the intentions of those who visit the Galápagos and, if decidedly armed with bad intentions, can seal a person's fate with a curse. Whether the tragic fate of the Galápagos' earliest settlers was human nature or the mystical workings of the Galápagos tortoise, one will never know the fate of the Empress of Floreana, her lover or the ill-fated Dr. Ritter. Now that's a legend.

We walked through tall trees with a gray and white bark called Palo Santo trees that are endemic to the Islands and were scattered around this area. In a few months during the rainy season it displays bright green leaves. It's special because it is only found on three islands in the Galápagos. This tree is sometimes called the Holy Stick, not only because of its appearance, but also because of the incense-like scent that comes from the oil and resin in its branches. It is known as the frankincense-and-myrrh tree. Folk medicine says it helps cure stomach aches, and is a liniment for rheumatism. It is in critical danger and there is a ban on cutting live trees. The wood is commonly used for crafting objects and burning sticks for the pleasant smell of incense.

We returned to our rubber boat and cruised around the island. Manuel pointed out a flat Eagle Ray and a Marble Ray on the other side of our craft. He showed us mangroves, and in the crystal-clear water where nothing could hide from our gazes, a Pacific Green Sea Turtle swam by.

Winding around the island, a motion caught my eye as I quickly pointed out something black and white falling from a rocky outcropping. Turned out he wasn't falling but jumping into the water. Another first—a Galápagos Penguin. I was so excited I almost forgot the important Zodiac rule of "No Standing." Several little black and white bodies were frolicking about, darting around in the water. One squatted on a rock while another stood close by oblivious to all of us taking its picture. It looked about twenty inches tall. This was my first penguin sighting ever in the wild and it wasn't very big, actually the second smallest in the world, after the Tiny Penguins in Australia. The Galápagos Penguins are called Banded Penguins and are the most northerly penguins and the only ones living in the northern hemisphere because the Humboldt Current carries frigid water all the way from Antarctica. Clumsy on land, these four-to-five-pound penguins are masters at zipping and zooming, and twisting and twirling through the sea.

Back on board we enjoyed the cheese and wine tasting in the Blue Finch Bar on deck five and recapped our day. We were so relaxed looking at unique views of volcanic islands in azure waters. A frigatebird flew overhead and as we pulled away from the island, Xpedition created a wide contrail in foaming white water.

I held up my arm for shade from the lowering sun. Clouds crept in as it set which didn't stop a coppery sky creating flame patches dancing on the dark water. It dawned on me that sunrise around 5:30 a.m. and sunset around 5:30 p.m. would vary by only a few minutes each day and easy to remember about twelve hours apart.

After a tasty dinner there was an Ecuadorian Naturalist Party which didn't mean "au naturel," but meant the nature guides sharing Ecuador's facts and history.

Our travel package on board included all complimentary beverages. That evening we took a bottle of champagne to the top deck for star gazing under the southern skies. Our cruise director pointed out the Southern Cross, composed of five stars forming the shape of a cross. It is notable for containing two bright stars, Acrux and Gacrux, which point the way to the Southern Celestial Pole.

Orion's Belt, sometimes called Three Kings or Three Sisters, is easy to spot once pointed out by our expert director. Looking for Orion's Belt in the night sky is the easiest way to locate Orion. He pointed out that the stars are more or less in a straight line. As he suggested, I visualized a belt on the hunter's clothing. It starts in the east and marches westwards across the sky throughout the night. To the indigenous people in the Andes regions, Orion's Belt is seen as a Celestial Bridge between the sky's northern and southern hemispheres. I loved our nightly outings to the top deck viewing the constellations and we had undivided time getting to know Beth and Jon better.

Pulling open the curtain in the morning was now becoming a treat. What would we behold outside our window? Today it was flat water about the color of denim, a cloudless sky and islands in the distance. Another day in paradise. This quiet moment felt like a rare privilege, seeing what I was seeing.

After breakfast tanking up on fuel, we piled into our Zodiacs today with Alfredo, for another morning anticipating wildlife encounters of different kinds. The easy wet landing in about six inches of water deposited us at Bachas Beach, a beautiful white sand beach on the northern coast of Santa Cruz Island. Las Bachas comes from the mispronunciation of the word "barges" by the local population during the 1950s when World War II barges broke from their moorings and ran aground on the beach. We would be entering the largest nesting area of the Pacific Green Sea Turtles this morning.

We walked along the beach with dozens of empty turtle nests and tracks that led to the water. It looked like hundreds of imprints. Up and back, up and back each day, not easy in the sand. They much prefer to swim.

A five-foot-tall Prickly Pear Cactus had soft yellow flowers blooming at the bottom. It was sort of like being in a designer showroom of cactus art all different shapes, sizes and colors. Walking through cactus and scrubby brush wound us back to the white sandy beach and more turtle craters. In the rocks along the shoreline stood a Striated Heron, about a foot tall, with a medium gray and white body and a slate blue hat on its head. With more turtle tracks to the water, I felt like I was trespassing on hallowed ground. A pelican sat on the rocks that jutted into shallow water in shades of aqua, and turquoise to teal.

A Great Egret stood tall on a strip of water squeezed between two narrow bands of rocks. The white egret looked about three feet tall and we were quite a distance from it. When the tidewater flowed in, it easily plucked a little fish for lunch. There were two oystercatchers, one hunkered down and the second standing beside it balanced easily on one leg.

From the beach straight out on a rocky outcropping was a lone tree or maybe a big bush and was a cheerful, refreshing color of green against the color of the sky and water.

Walking through the turtle paths, again I felt like a trespasser. At a brackish pond (brackish being a word used frequently on this trip), could there possibly be flamingos? This was one of their hangouts. Not today, however. Instead, iguanas were sunning themselves and a few were swimming with their black heads above the water, sort of reminding me of an otter back home.

Back on board for an oriental buffet lunch and lecture by our cruise director about the geology of the Galápagos Islands, it helped to understand this area even better. During our bodies' refueling lunch the captain moved us across the Equator to Bartolomé Island, reported to be one of the most spectacular geologic settings in the Galápagos.

From our Zodiac I pointed out to my husband the barren, lava-covered island with winding wooden steps leading up and up and up. He just looked at me sort of with a booby stare. After a dry landing and way too short of a walk on flat ground, we started up three hundred eighty steps totaling about one mile long, all uphill. I thought it best not to look up. The surroundings reminded me of Craters of the Moon National Monument & Preserve in Idaho with its moon-like landscape and volcanic cones.

We marched onward—To The Top—as it's called. Looming to the left and right, it was the same—lava, lava and more lava sometimes in rivers or waterfall effects. We stopped along the way at several viewing platforms for spectacular vistas and to catch our breath. Xpedition got smaller and smaller. Lava trails, lava cactus, lava lizards, everything was the same color except the lava cactus where some cucumber-shaped arms were a goldish color. Too bad the nice boardwalk wasn't an escalator. S-curve after S-curve were the same colors. At one platform Alfredo picked up a basketball-size piece of lava, or pumice, with one hand and lifted it straight up. He was either very strong or it was pretty light, which turned out to be the case, as we all had a turn holding the airy rock.

Pinnacle Rock is a sharp rock spire that is a local landmark. This island is really one of the younger islands and its volcanic origins are easy to see with the flowing rivers of lava not blown away by erosion. Our reward for ascending to three hundred seventy-five feet was the remarkable view from the top of the island, perhaps the most famous in all of the Galápagos. Pinnacle Rock was worth the view for possibly seeing dozens of the islands, as well as having our photos taken at the two-story orange and white lighthouse at the tip top.

Walking down was a lot quicker, easier, and even prettier. Squeezed between Pinnacle Rock and another body of water was a field of emerald moss or grasses meeting the shoreline. It looked out of place. The brownish colors weren't so bad now because beyond it was sapphire water.

I wondered how so many species here are found only in the Galápagos or are endemic, a word we heard a lot. The answers came from one of our guides who explained that animals, after arriving by swimming, floating on debris, on the wind, or being carried here, adapted to the unique environment of the Islands, competed with other local species, and over time evolved to be unlike any others of their kind throughout the world.

After the hike and back on our Zodiac, Alfredo took us to the base of Pinnacle Rock. On some nearby rocks were two penguins and several bright Sally Lightfoot crabs. One crab had blue eyes (the others I'd seen had pink ones), and it was munching on something green. One penguin had its flipper to the side of its head maybe trying to get water out of its ear. Penguins make me laugh. I just loved this untamed nature, unafraid of us and allowing us to invade its turf.

We saw a small shark swimming around our boat, not really interested in us. On the bank a Snowy Egret about two feet tall stood up to its ankles in water. This was the first time we had reference to a snowy anything and I have no clue how a Snowy Egret got to the Galápagos.

The sun was setting behind an island when we returned to Xpedition so I didn't get the opportunity to watch it drop into the ocean like on other nights. As it disappeared it ricocheted gold hues through the sky. After dinner we had our nightly stroll on the top deck looking at the stars that seemed so close you could pluck any from the sky. That evening the lounge had been transformed with local decorations for a Crossing the Line celebration with a special guest appearance, of who else, but King Neptune himself. Leaving Bartolomé

Island heading south we would cross the equator on the way to our next stop sometime that evening. In the next few days we would zigzag across the equator several times.

The King surprised Dave who bumped a glass of red wine that, when hitting the edge of a chair, created a wave of red wine splashing on a "guest" sitting nearby. That red wine never came out of his beige pants but sure made for a funny story and a spotted souvenir until we returned home and tossed them.

We were making a big loop in the ocean and this morning we would be at Isabela Island, the largest island in the chain, comprising five volcanoes with the latest eruption having occurred in 2008.

By the time I looked out our window, the morning orb was up sparkling light on the smooth water and our island for the morning, Isabela. Volcán Wolf straddles the equator on the northern edge of this island. This volcano is the tallest in the entire archipelago, around fifty-five hundred feet high, and has steeper slopes than the other Isabela volcanoes, reaching angles up to thirty-five degrees.

Elana, our guide, helped us at a wet landing onto a steep gravel beach with only two casualties sporting cut-up knees and legs, fortunately not ours. Once over the lava rocks, the trail of compacted ash and gravel leveled out. A mostly black Galápagos Hawk landed on a large vertical chunk of lava. From the base, it looked like it had leaked lava eventually reaching the ocean. Five pretty Yellow Cordia flowers were bunched together in a fairly green bush. There were noticeably greener vegetation patches on this island than the others.

In the middle of our pathway lay one of the largest land iguanas I'd seen yet. Spread out were all four legs, and his five fingers looked like a golden scaly glove.

Dozens of puffy white cotton balls hung from nutbrown stems on a bush. Around a corner tucked into cool green bushes, almost like a fort, hid our first giant tortoise. Elana said that, because of its size, it could be a teenager. I could see its shell and it looked like an interesting engraved geometric pattern. Turtles and tortoises have the same kind of shell which really looks like a Viking shield of some sort. The shell is covered in scutes that are made of keratin, a bony external plate or scale. This is like a horn, beak or nail in other species.

The shells completely enclose all the vital organs and sometimes even the head. The shells are constructed of modified bony elements such as the ribs, parts of the pelvis and other bones found in most reptiles. I was more interested in the unique patterns on the back and learned the shell is important not just because of the obvious protection it provides but also as an identification tool, in particular with fossils as the shell is one of the likely parts of a turtle to survive fossilization.

Wow, their shells have comparable material to fossils.

Our guide told us that as the scales (officially called scutes) shed, a turtle may slowly develop a new pattern as the scales are the separate square regions on a turtle's shell. The pattern is quite often the veins running beneath the shell, while the color is dependent on the type of animal, sunlight exposure of which these would get a lot, and diet.

This was one of the five different species of giant tortoises on this island and I don't know what kind we saw and didn't care; it was another first.

Scientists believe the first tortoises arrived in the Islands two to three million years ago by drifting six hundred miles from the South American coast on vegetation rafts or on their own. They were already big animals before arriving in the Galápagos. Colonizing the easternmost islands of Española and San Cristóbal first, they then dispersed through the archipelago, eventually establishing about sixteen separate populations on ten of the largest islands.

During the 16th and 17th centuries the islands were frequented by buccaneers, a nicer word for a pirate, preying on Spanish treasure ships. Filling a ship's hold with tortoises was an easy way to stock up on food because of their incredible adaption that allows these animals to survive one year without food or water.

They mainly eat cactus plants, grasses and native fruit and drink large quantities of water when available that can be stored in their bladders for long periods of time. They have two main types of shells, the saddle-backed and the domed shell. The saddle-backed are the smallest but present a very long neck and pair of legs and feed on cactus. The domed are bigger with shorter necks and legs and feed on grass. They spend sixteen hours a day resting and can weigh up to nine hundred pounds.

A hawk landed on the branch of a tree with yellow pods not too far from a Galápagos Mockingbird. Looking toward the water I spotted another hawk walking down the beach with its feathers fluffed out. He looked miffed, like he'd just survived a brawl, but also comical as he pranced along the sand. A third hawk on a boulder caught my attention because Xpedition was in the background. There is only one type of hawk in these islands and even though mostly black, some are gray and white. A smaller hawk perched on top of a green T-shaped sign that read, STOP, because something was nesting on the other side. Before returning to Xpedition we enjoyed the scenic cruising along the coasts of Isabela searching for colorful fish but mostly saw iguana and sea lions swimming.

Back on board, dropping our things in our room we discovered two gold swans made of towels that graced our bed. They were placed beak-to-beak creating a heart. Our personal laundry was piling up so we sent it out for service. It was returned the following day with a bill totaling $5.50. This was the only extra cost except for some souvenirs from the gift shop costing $22 for the entire trip plus a donation we made to the Galápagos Conservation. This all-inclusive trip was quickly becoming a real bargain compared to paying everything separately on most cruises.

We had a delicious barbecue at the Beagle Grill complete with Caribbean tunes played on an electric keyboard by one of our guides. A frigatebird landed on the handrailing near us. He knew that Thursday meant seafood grill day and possible treats for him. The grillers cooked up juicy, sweet lobster tails, corn on the cob, and shrimp about the diameter of a donut. They were huge, moist and succulent. Salads, fruit, and desserts of chocolate cake and a variety of puddings were plentiful but I had the watermelon that had been so flavorful over the entire trip. We ate with Jon and Beth and Dave and Sharon while a healthy Lava Gull landed not far away, waiting his turn. I had no eye contact with him; I wasn't sharing even a morsel.

We enjoyed the lecture entitled "Charles Darwin Theory and Its Implications" before heading out on another expedition. We learned Darwin's *Origin of Species* brought a completely new view of life on Earth: Species are not permanent but are continuously changing from one into another; what we see today is simply a snapshot of the ones that have struggled and survived, chosen by the blind forces of nature. He was only twenty-six-years-old when he first saw the Galápagos on September 15, 1835. He found a place where creatures had changed to adapt to the harsh environment. A finch in his homeland of England looked much different than the finch here with a thickened beak to enable it to peck in rocks and lava to find a bug. When he returned home one year after leaving the Galápagos he showed his collection of the many species he found.

Even though we were a full week into our adventure, I still found myself having a hard time understanding our guides' accent even though speaking English. I probably grasped about three-quarters of what they told us. They spoke clearly; I just didn't always pick it up. Sometimes I'd ask for interpretation but my husband or friends often hadn't caught it either. Ecuadorian Spanish, as in the rest of the Spanish-speaking world, includes a wide spectrum of variations. While all Spanish speakers understand each other, each has its own uniqueness. I wished I'd paid more attention in high school Spanish classes.

Donning our twice daily tangerine attire, on Fernandina we had a dry landing with Eduardo, but on sharp lava rocks and the tide wasn't cooperating very well as it was pretty wavy and hard to predict when to jump out of the Zodiac onto the rocks. Fortunately, our capable crew was right there to help without any mishaps.

This island is the youngest and westernmost of all the islands. It is also one of the most volcanically active in the region, the latest eruption having occurred two years earlier. In 1968, the floor of the caldera sank nine hundred ninety feet within a two-week period, and in the early 1970s the coastline at Punta Espinoza was uplifted some nine feet during an earthquake. Yikes.

We walked a short distance on lava, ducking under and climbing through brown brush along a narrow sandy trail and to smooth hardened lava flows, with a curvy wave pattern embedded in the lava. The black lava touching the white sand added drama to the landscape. We came upon a white sun-bleached skeleton of a small whale or dolphin. The lava flows created unique patterns and designs. This area reminded me of the gentle waves of water flowing softly onto the beach or scalloped edging on draperies like my grandmother had in her living room. Sometimes the waves trapped water in little ponds causing greenery to sprout nearby.

We were in the lead group of the afternoon. It was quiet except for some birds chirping and tweeting. Ahead of us, in one glimpse I saw black lava, white sand, blue water, lava outcroppings, more water, then another lava bed, and in the distance was our ship with its bow pointed straight at us like it was peeking over the rocks watching out for its people, making sure we were safe. And no people anywhere to be seen. It was one of those peaceful, astounding moments and I felt immensely grateful to be in one of the most natural, unique places on the globe.

This area had hundreds, correction, thousands of marine iguanas not only on the rocks but swimming and lazing along the path where we were walking. Several lay body to body to body, all black and red like they were from the same clan. Walking by the pack, I felt a light warm spray around my ankle. Three steps more and it happened again. I looked down as an iguana shot saltwater from its nostrils, then again. I even got one on film. I took a picture of one that was looking up at me and his curved mouth looked like he was smiling. I laughed out loud as I had with other humorous encounters.

Marine iguanas can stay underwater for up to forty-five minutes while feeding on algae. The excess salt in their diet requires them to get rid of it by sneezing it out their noses. I now could attest with first-hand knowledge that the largest iguanas in the islands are found at Punta Espinoza and can reach up to four feet long.

A Spot-Winged dragonfly darted right in front of me and almost landed on my shoulder but instead flitted onto a twig. I could see through its translucent spotted wings, thus its name. It had hazel and white patches on its tiny body.

Clearly in the iguana capital of the world again, it felt like I was in some prehistoric era. In one alcove there were some very light-skinned ones, almost white. Most were stark black ones. I wondered if it was their version of albino. Across from the iguanas in the water were five Ruddy Turnstones with carroty legs and feet, white bellies and bronze heads, backs and tails, pecking for bugs.

This was surely an island of lava and lots of amber and gold lava cacti. All were similar with the shape of a long cucumber but the baby ones were usually brownish with a gold nubbin on top. One clump had dozens of legs. The lava fissures created deep crevasses where we walked very carefully and could see sapphire water below. Our guide pointed out a Galápagos Martin, a white medium-size brown bird.

On the ocean, iguanas were in various stages of jumping in, swimming, eating and getting back out which looked harrowing since there were rough waves hitting the rocks. They had to time it just right. I watched one in particular as he rode the wave to the rock and I lost him for a bit so thought he hadn't made it. But he slowly emerged climbing the rock to soak up the sun and warm up his body temperature after eating as much algae as he could.

Sea lions slept in the sunshine and one youngster was covered in blotches of sand with its whiskers twitching, probably because a fly was bothering it. We didn't see many bugs because it wasn't the season for humidity and bugs, which we avoided on purpose. This area must be heaven for iguanas. I stopped for one of dozens of photos of them and another one smiled at me.

We walked to an area where several Flightless Cormorants were drying off after a swim. It was a popular nesting area. Their stubby wings looked pretty funny compared to those at home that soar. A pelican about the size of a small airplane flew overhead and glided in. It reminded me we hadn't seen or heard an airplane in days. A third cormorant extended its wings to dry out; its eyes were a bright turquoise color. These now flightless birds have developed shriveled wings that prevent flying, with the payoff being faster diving. We have plenty of flying cormorants along the Oregon coast, so these certainly looked different with short wings. With no natural predators here, going after fish proved more valuable than taking to the air. We stood just a few feet from several sitting on the rocks in the sunshine contemplating their next underwater meal.

A frigatebird landed on the upper rocks with iguanas nearby. I looked down and there, staring right at me, was a penguin. An oystercatcher was positioned over her solitary speckled egg with probably dad standing a foot or so away. The oystercatcher tipped his head to the left looking at me with one orange eye, then tilted his head to the right, doing the same look with the other orange eye. I wondered what in the world this shore bird was thinking. I laughed at him, or her.

The back of a sea lion in the water looked like a miniature submarine and I thought of Dave snorkeling a few days earlier. I took a photo of the frigatebird and two penguins with waves swirling at their feet, and then another photo of a pelican with the surf crashing against the rocks behind it with Xpedition in the background. It was a day of memories and lots of photos.

One sea lion was pressed flush against a lava embankment with one flipper resting along the top as if airing his armpit. Picture after picture made me smile and feel so fortunate to be there in person experiencing this incredible nature.

Walking back, I noticed a newborn sea lion tucked under a bush with mom asleep but close. Dad was in a pool of water enjoying himself. He barked something to mom who got up and around and waddled to the baby and nuzzled it awake. She opened her mouth and picked up the pup by its neck and hauled it down toward the water. This baby didn't have its eyes open yet. Two other sea lions went nose-to-nose and looked like they were kissing. There was a group of four pups, one almost white and others already tan. One baby was rolled up tight causing ripples in its fur.

Back on board, we went to the bridge for a tour. This included: electronics, maps and graphs, an impressive radar screen, and rows of books such as *Metrology for Seafarers* and *Bridge Procedures Guide;* a book or anything needed for navigating and protocol was here.

The sun went down while we were standing on the bridge. Clouds rolled in but there was a gap where sun rays squeezed through creating amber light beams touching the water.

We were ready for the special beverage of the day, Pisco Sour, which I read was a beverage from this South American region but originated in Peru. After our daily briefing about tomorrow's adventures we sat down for dinner, noticing the white napkin that had been folded in the shape of a penguin standing upright, placed in front of the solid black leather menu. The chef had prepared a full Thanksgiving meal for the Americans on board. Graciously we ate it but I really wanted the shrimp.

After a full day of wildlife sightings, I wasn't in the mood for a talent show at the Discovery Lounge. I preferred the star show from the top deck with our friends.

Friday morning dawned with high clouds and after breakfast we headed to the departing area where we grabbed our life jackets and went down the steps to our boats. Breakfasts on board became something to look forward to with the large assortment of fresh fruit and pastries. Yes, there was plenty of protein and starch but I always ate the papaya and mangos, plus the luscious watermelon, with eggs and a pastry or three. While growing up, our family never had extra money for exotic fruit so now, when they are readily available, I enjoy every bite. It would be hard readjusting to life at home after this special treatment. I mean, who wants to cut up their own fresh fruit or peel oranges, or carve out grapefruit sections? How depressing, so I stopped thinking about it.

Pablo, our guide for this morning, helped with the wet landing that wasn't far from a long beach where we walked in the surf. Iguanas were swimming with sea lions. We were on Santiago Island, destination Puerto Egas.

In the distance was a large extension of white rock that had a jagged oval-shaped hole in the middle like it had been carved with a serrated knife. A Swallowtail Gull sat on the rocky edge. Noticeably different were mossy rocks and areas with iguanas happily munching. At the official National Park of the Galápagos Island sign sat a Brown Noddy Tern, all charcoal except for an interesting head. The top half of its head being white was divided almost perfectly in half with the bottom going back to the matching charcoal. It had gold eyes.

On a scarlet twig of a bush was our first Large Tree Finch, all ebony with a thick solid bill like an Evening Grosbeak at home. These had changed over decades, developing a thicker bill to be able to peck through rocks and lava for food. Our wimpy-beaked finches at home would not survive here. A sleeping Ruddy Turnstone with ginger legs tucked itself into a circle of feathers. A Galápagos Dove walked along the grasses and sand looking for a morsel. A two-foot-tall gray and white Yellow-Crowned Night Heron standing on one gray leg showed off his expert balancing act. The yellow patch on its head looked fluorescent with the sun shining on it.

Hiking for some time mostly on lava we reached an area at the end of the coastal walk where lava tunnels had collapsed to form beautiful blue pools in which Galápagos fur seals reside. Several were asleep nestled in the cool rocks. We stood on a lava bridge looking down at the turquoise water with a green sea turtle swimming in it. More fur seals were lounging about not caring one bit about us watching them. A soaking wet Brown Noddy Tern flew from the water to a nearby rock. Another Yellow-Crowned Night Heron seemed to have a tough time walking on the lava. It was a cycle of doves, iguanas, fur seals and birdlife everywhere. A pelican stood on a green mossy rock with Xpedition in the background.

Strolling back, the empty oval hole in rock we'd seen earlier now had two occupants; two sea lions nose-to-nose were silhouetted against the Aegean sky. We dropped some snorkelers off then headed back to Xpedition to the top deck for R&R and beverages. A frigatebird flew overhead checking out his prospects. While sharing the complimentary bottle of wine we'd been given earlier, Dave came out with a luscious frosty-looking ice cream drink from the bar. I asked what it was and he said the bar guy called it a Moo Slah. I said, "A what?" Dave repeated, "Moo Slah." I knew he was having the same issues understanding the accents like I was but whatever the name, it looked refreshing and cool. I headed in and ordered Moo Slahs and came out with two just like Dave's. Then Beth and Jon arrived and Beth asked the same question, "What's that?" I replied, "Moo Slah." Jon shook his head and said, "No, it's a Mud Slide." How in the world did he know? He'd walked by the bar and heard the bar guy making one for another cruiser. It was the drink of the day printed on the sign. More laughter commenced.

The concoction combined vodka, coffee liqueur, Irish cream and heavy cream dumped into a blender with ice, thus the ice cream appearance. Drizzled down the inside of a hurricane glass were ribbons of chocolate syrup with some chocolate shavings on top. Some at our table had more than one Moo Slah, and we laughed all the way to lunch. Just another misinterpretation of the native tongue. Moo Slah, Mud Slide, whatever, it was delicious.

Our chef prepared an incredible Mexican buffet, then our naturalists shared stories and information about their homes and Life in the Galápagos. And the captain once again moved the Xpedition to another location.

With Roberto our guide, we donned our life jackets, got in our usual mode of transportation and had a dry landing on Santa Cruz Island heading to Cerro Dragon or Dragon Hill. Wonder why it's called Dragon Hill? Because of the zillions of iguanas.

After a short distance we came upon a small grove of tree-size cacti. I really enjoyed the forest of cacti and Palo Santo trees with curvy trunks and crooked limbs. They were turning from gray to showing green in some of the bark. We walked parallel to the beach where another new bird, a brown and white long-legged Whimbrel stood knee-high in water. His bill was slightly arched and there was an inky tip on its tail.

This portion of the island had completely different vegetation than we had seen elsewhere. Green and red ground cover, or maybe succulents, covered a large area of ground to the white sand. The wispy bushes had yellowish-green limbs. Another Whimbrel waded ankle-deep in the water around lava rocks.

I was quite intrigued with the lime-colored succulents or ground cactus. Our path became dusty and rocky and around a bend floated two White-Cheeked Pintails with red on the top of their bills. A Darwin's Finch as well as Yellow Warblers were frequent visitors along this trail. Roberto pointed out the Small Tree Finch and Medium Tree Finch but honestly, I couldn't tell the difference in size and hardly differentiated body color.

Reaching a rocky, low-lying hill on the northwest side of this island is Dragon Hill with its millions of land iguanas. These miniature dragons roam around nipping away at the fruits and flowers of their favorite food, the Opuntia Cactus or prickly pear to us. That's where we get the pink liquid that is used in beverages, candy, and other things.

Roberto mentioned that the iguanas are fortunate to still be on the island because it is the most populated human island, and domestic animals gone feral have plagued the countryside for decades. Wild goats, cats, and dogs were especially hard on the iguana population. But the Darwin Foundation and Galápagos Park Service have been very successful in their joint efforts to protect the iguanas, increasing their numbers and removing the offending animals. Not only did we see iguanas but we saw a light grayish-brown Galápagos Flycatcher. I'd hoped to see the Vermilion Flycatcher with crimson body and head, and its tar-colored back down to its tail but darn it, we didn't.

There are a couple of small brackish lagoons where flamingos like to hang around. Nope, we didn't see a one. By now, each time we were in a location where the flamingos are known to occupy, we knew they wouldn't be there. It was like they had a sixth sense that the Oregonians were coming so vacated to another favorite pond at another island.

The flora of Cerro Dragon is impressive as it passes through different vegetation zones. The transition between these zones was sometimes very sharp, as if someone had deliberately planted the trees and plants in their own personal garden. As we boarded our Zodiac and returned to Xpedition, I appreciated this afternoon of different colors and sights. Each day was its own unique adventure.

Back on board I didn't miss the Margarita Party but excused myself to see wispy layers of amber and coral clouds trailing across the sky as the sunset created basketball orange splotches dotting the water. More clouds meandered in from the left cutting the sun in half until it dropped behind a distant coffee-colored island turning the sky a now familiar crimson.

We went back and forth over the Equator several times. When we returned to our cabin, there was an official certificate on the bed and mine read (grammar errors included), "By order of the Ocean's Majestic King Neptune, we certify that Deleen Wills Has crossed the Equatorial Line on board M/S Xpedition during the voyage through the Galápagos Islands. Therefore, this carrier of this certificate is and should be known as: "Neptune's Kingdom Subservient". Signed on the High seas Fausto Pacheo, Master M/V Xpedition November 20-27, 2011. Latitude 0° 0′ 0″

Dinner was delicious with a salad of asparagus, grilled plantain, and half an avocado. The dessert of cream puffs that looked like open clam shells sitting in a pool of chocolate was spoon-licking good. We shared a bottle of Doña Dominga 2010 Shiraz from Chile.

But we passed on karaoke that night, instead going to our favorite nighttime hangout—the top deck watching for shooting stairs and hoping for a UFO or two. The evening was clear and the stars brightly twinkled in the night sky. I could almost touch them or so it seemed. This evening ritual became a favorite of mine. I suggested we should have a telescope at home.

We were nearing the end of our week of exploration and I was not at all happy about it. After breakfast we boarded our Zodiac for a dry landing as we disembarked at the Municipal Pier at Puerto Ayora (the largest town in the islands) on Santa Cruz Island, the second-largest island. In 1959, the Ecuadorian government declared all the islands, except areas already colonized, as a national park. In the same year, the Darwin Foundation was founded to promote scientific research and ensure the conservation of the Galápagos. In 1992, the waters surrounding the Galápagos were declared a marine reserve.

Taking a five-minute bus ride on the main street and a short walk down Charles Darwin Avenue past the General Cemetery, there was an abundance of owls painted on headstones, walls, crosses and almost anything else. It is widely believed that owls take our souls to heaven. Everything in the cemetery was painted stark, clean white, and above-ground tombs were prevalent.

A little farther along we reached the Charles Darwin Research Station and Giant Tortoise breeding center. The vegetation was greener and lush with bushes of Yellow Cordia, ferns and succulents.

At our first stop on a lower area, three giant tortoises huddled together. A Galápagos Mockingbird stood on the back of one. One tortoise stretched out its long neck and was gold underneath its chin and neck. Their front legs were splayed out and they looked like contortionists turning their legs both in and out. Close up I could see the bones of its neck and droopy thin skin draping down, like the skin of a really old person. A healthy large land iguana in multiple shades of gold stood in the path and was shedding its scaly layer showing smooth gray skin underneath.

The trio turtle pack looked like dinosaurs. I read a wooden sign "Back from the Brink." In the 1960s, the tortoise population of Española Island came so close to extinction that all the remaining tortoises, twelve females and two males, were brought here to the park and station headquarters for protection and breeding. The first successful hatchings occurred in 1970 and 1971. As with the other races, the young are reared to three to five years of age and then returned to their island. In 1977, another adult male was returned to the islands from the San Diego Zoo and joined the breeding population. The population of tortoises on Española, reduced to fifteen individuals, now numbers over one thousand and their offspring are reproducing in the wild. Tortoise #1000 returned to Española in 2001.

There were many types of cacti and someone pointed out a Candelabra Cactus, with tube-shaped pads. They can grow twenty-three feet tall. In addition, there were all those magnificent tortoises of different sizes, under trees, bushes and rock ledges.

We learned about the Española tortoise's nesting season. The research center had one male with five females and two males with seven females, permanently housed in two corrals, each with several nesting areas. The tortoises breed before and during the nesting season, from June to December. During that season, the corrals are checked daily for nesting activity. When choosing a site for building a nest and depositing eggs, a female looks for the right combination of soil, temperature and moisture conditions. A female tortoise builds her nest with her hind legs, forming a hole about fourteen to twenty inches deep and four to ten inches wide, slightly wider at the bottom. The mother buries the eggs and delicately pats down the soil with the underside of her shell and her feet.

Eggs are collected from nests in the field and brought to the Breeding Center where they are kept in incubators for one hundred twenty to one hundred fifty days. The tortoise's sex is determined by the temperature during incubation. Eggs incubated at 85.5 degrees Fahrenheit become females and those incubated at 82.4 degrees become males.

Tall barrel cacti with pokey spikes looked like the head of a woodpecker. There were so many cacti

I was beginning to see faces and shapes, as I often see in clouds. Walking on a wooden platform we spotted the cutest little baby tortoises about the size of a dollar pancake then medium ones in another area, really not a lot bigger than the previous pen of babies.

Reading the informational signs, we learned more about tortoise preservation. In these different ponds the babies to toddlers to teenagers were flourishing. Color-coded numbers on their backs indicate from which island the eggs were harvested so one day they could be returned to their rightful island home.

I then read a sign that famous Lonesome George, the last member of the Pinta Island species, was somewhere in the area. Sure enough, there he was. He was found in December 1971 and taken to the station in March 1972. An effort to find another specimen from that island had not been successful. He was sharing his pen with two female tortoises of the population from Wolf Volcano and reportedly didn't seem too keen on his female companions.

As we walked down a narrow dirt road, there sat a person at a small table carving into dark brown wood. When he finished the five-inch-high tortoise, he smiled and offered it to hold. I asked the price which seemed way too reasonable so paid him more and the carving is one of several remembrances of this extraordinary adventure.

Crafters in stalls sold items for a very affordable price. I stepped in looking for a Blue-Footed Booby fridge magnet and wasn't disappointed. I appreciated that everything was hand-painted and locally made. A folding table was set up by the waterfront where a fisherman was cutting up his catch or leaving it whole. Several large grouper were laid under the table where pelicans like bookends watched for anything to drop.

I always like to take a picture of the country's flag and a car license plate. Ecuador's license plate is solid orange with three black letters and three black numbers. A white police truck with royal blue striping and a rack of lights on the top was parked on the street. Printed on the side was "Policia" and "Servir y Proteger."

We stood in front of the Fuerza Naval base with the four of us holding my homemade OCCUPY GALÁPAGOS signs.

Zodiacs returned us to our ship where an art exhibit had been set up for us featuring Galápagos jewelry and local painter Edgar Jacome with his lovely artwork. My souvenir from any trip includes earrings so I purchased a pair of sterling silver starfish-shaped ones. A second pair, also silver, were about the size of a nickel and reminded me of the shape of an imperfect sand dollar. Etched in the silver was a design of a starfish with tiny turquoise stones on the tip of each one of its five arms. Most Ecuadorian art and jewelry depict nature using the sun, water, animals and water life. An Ecuadorian buffet lunch followed.

That afternoon we had a dry landing at the Municipal Pier and took a forty-five-minute bus ride through flourishing grassy and flower-packed scenery heading to a private farm in the highlands. Several farms on the boundary of Galápagos National Park are home to the free-ranging giant creatures. Looking out the window I spotted a big coal blob in the thick grass. It was a giant tortoise in the wild!

Before even getting to the farm, I noticed more massive tortoises munching on grass, some as large as pigs, if not cows, moving gently yet deliberately. These tortoises are monitored but are free to go anywhere they want. The farms provide the ideal conditions where food is plentiful and finding a mate, when it is time, is easy. Even though they could move around the island, they have little reason to do so; really why, life is good where they are.

At the farm that serves as a thoroughfare for these gentle giants, we were able to commune with them. The shell on one was ringed in green then gold, my guess from murky pond scum. A prehistoric-looking creature tolerated my close inspection of its leathery skin and tank-like armor. Behind one mammoth tortoise four of us stood holding our silly OCCUPY GALÁPAGOS signs. I wanted to Occupy the Galápagos permanently.

Sitting in the grass, one wandered by keeping his head straight ahead yet rolled his eyes toward me, reminding me of an evil eye; I chuckled. Its lips were tightly sealed in a straight line. This doesn't compare to the smile of an iguana. A pretty little gray bird with a lacy fluffy back and cherry beak, maybe a young one losing its plumage, became a willing passenger on the back of its tortoise. I couldn't find it in my bird guide. A black Sharp-Beaked Ground Finch hopped on the ground looking for food.

Large globs of coffee-colored tortoise poop, bigger than horse poop, were easily avoidable. Two creatures were on the move surprisingly fast down a slight embankment. They moved nose-to-nose then both backed away from each other. I assumed they were males. Tortoises were under brush, in the brush, and on top of brush. I watched one saunter to a mud pond where six others already were in their space. (I thought these might be females rejuvenating at their spa.) She went to the edge, stuck out her long neck, then stretched it out even longer and drank some gunky water with a loud lapping sound. Slowly, like the slowest motion ever, she eased herself into the water submerged about halfway. Her neck was partially immersed and she put her mouth even with the surface of the water and blew bubbles. What the heck?! I even got pictures to prove it. I have no clue what type of communication that meant but decided she was glad I was there.

After plenty of time communing with one-hundred-year-old creatures, we boarded the bus for a ride through pretty countryside to a lava tunnel and walked down extremely steep steps etched in the lava so that we were able to explore this long underground channel.

Not having much time left in the Galápagos, we strolled down one street lined with stalls and small shops but I found exactly what I was looking for: A hand-carved painted Blue-Footed Booby. And the feet were as bright blue as the live ones. The eyes, yellow with black centers, wings marvelously detailed in the carving and black and white paint on its head and back were all done exceedingly well for this piece of art. I found everything reasonably priced in this country and as is my practice in most places, I rounded up and always left a bit extra not only because I truly appreciated the workmanship but I never wanted to be referred to as an ugly American which is a common reputation around the world.

That night our sunset was just as colorful and impressive as all the other nights. Our farewell dinner was complete with entertainment by our local guides who we'd come to truly admire. We walked up a few decks to our usual evening hangout for a final moment admiring the southern sky.

I didn't dare open the curtains the next morning. I didn't want to have to admit we had returned to where we departed one week earlier—the dock at

Baltra. As we were standing on the deck looking in the water and waiting our turn to get in the Zodiac, Jon pointed out two White-Tipped Reef Sharks, one really big. Two Blue-Footed Boobies swam by the boat with their blue feet showing up nicely. The boats were tied together in a line for us to depart. Three Brown Pelicans stood on one boat and none on the others. Sitting in our Zodiac for our final ride, I watched Xpedition get smaller and smaller as we got closer to land. Our roundtrip cruise returned us to Baltra, home of the Galápagos airport. We walked onto AeroGal for our return flight to Quito.

As we flew away, from my window I recognized many of the places where we'd just had an adventure of a lifetime. The return flight treated us to plenty of blue water below as we quickly gained altitude and landed right in the middle of Quito with buildings surrounding the entire airport. Back to civilization, unfortunately.

After checking into our hotel, I left my napping husband and spent the afternoon shopping in an open market, slowly meandering as we'd gone from sea level back to nine thousand two hundred feet and the altitude difference was very noticeable. We had started high for a couple of days, then sea level for a week and now back to mountain level for less than twenty-four hours and my system felt a little off-kilter. I wondered if it would be easier to start at sea level then go higher for a week, then return to sea level, as would be the case should we ever get to experience Machu Picchu.

I stopped at a jewelry store looking for my typical memento. Everything made was tied to nature, which Ecuadorians cherish. A pair of round earrings with thin ribbons of colors in a spiral pattern caught my eye, the exact colors of our hot air balloon named Valley Sunrise: white, yellow, orange, red, light blue and dark blue. Chunks of the colors were placed randomly and in different proportions. A white dot in the middle started the silver thread that spiraled to the outer rim. Even though the colors were exactly the same as our balloon, it reminded me of different seasons of the earth, or simply a spiral rainbow. A second pair was sterling silver in a flower pattern with eight petals of different colored stones: dark orange, light orange, white, turquoise, teal, blue, purple with an orange center. And I bought more handmade colorful scarves, two dozen actually, for family and friends for Christmas presents.

Our final dinner as a group was at our hotel and we selected the traditional Ecuadorian meal of seafood with rice, beans and vegetables, and crème brûlée for dessert. After a fine meal, we regretfully said farewell to Jon and Beth who had different flights thus leaving at a different time in the morning. We vowed to stay in contact. I loved her smile, stories of their shelties at home and sparkling hazel eyes. Jon's British accent seemed to attract attention, mostly from the ladies. We had met some people on trips over the decades that became friends but none as dear and special as these two.

After breakfast we were escorted to the airport for our flights home from Quito to Miami, then Dallas Fort Worth onto Portland arriving home around 9 p.m. after an hour's drive. That morning we had been in Quito and it was hard to fathom what we'd just experienced.

Previously I referred to our trips as vacations; now they are all adventures. They are defined by a variety of moments that linger in my memory years after the trip has ended, maybe having been a first-time-ever happening—something thrilling, funny, inspirational, blissful or stirring. Some happenings create a postcard in my mind, like my Blue-Footed Booby encounter. This is why a visit to the Galápagos Islands is such an educational and inspirational experience. In just a week or so, you are served up with a lifetime's worth of extraordinary moments and forever memories.

I have three snapshots etched into my brain's photo album: The first Blue-Footed Booby, the Galápagos Penguin falling off the rock, and sitting on the grass communing with my own one-hundred-year-old giant tortoise.

This trip of exploration and enlightenment heartened and fortified my wanderlust—*a strong desire for or impulse to wander or travel and explore the world.* It had been instilled in me at an early age by my parents as our family of five traipsed around the Pacific Northwest camping in our fifteen-foot travel trailer.

Where would our next adventure be? After hearing many remarks about Machu Picchu and Peru, it moved further up our must-experience list.

Trip Tips:

Remember to study up on the country you are visiting. There are many inventors and artists who had their start in Ecuador. You may wish to use this information when striking up a conversation with a local.

-Rosalía Arteaga, first woman president 1997.

-Singer Christina Aguilera (half Ecuadorian, half German-Irish-Welsh-Dutch ancestry).

-Octavio Palacios in 1902 created a mechanical computer named Clave Poligráfica. The device translated words from one language to another.

-Panama Hats did not come from Panama but Ecuador by hatmaker Manuel Alfaro before moving to Panama where he made a fortune off the design.

-Ecuavoley, similar to volleyball, was invented in neighborhoods in the early 20th century and boomed in popularity in the 1950s.

-Graciela V.O. de Cuadros was granted US patents in 1980 and 1991 for her collapsible hammock support, a design that has spread all over the world to make relaxing anywhere that much easier.

-"Umbrella Newspaper" started printing issues with a plastic, waterproof front page which could also be used as a shield against the rain.

-HandEyes invented by four Ecuadorians is an electronic aid for blind people that prevents accidents and stumbles. Using a sensor to determine the distance of nearby objects, the device vibrates or sounds to warn the users of their surroundings.

-Ecuadorians have proof and take credit for inventing dark chocolate.

Some words that might help:

Adios	Good-bye
Amiguero	Extra friendly and amiable
Autobús	Bus
Banco	Bank
Bienvenida	Welcome
Bróder	Pal
Buen día	Have a nice day
Buenos días	Good Morning
Buenos tardes	Good Evening
Café	Coffee
Caramba	Exclamation to express surprise, anger or excitement
Cerveza	Beer
Cómo está?	How are you?
Dónde está?	Where is?
Dinero	Money
Es demasiado caro	It is too expensive
Estaba delicioso	It was delicious

Gracias	Thank you
La cuenta por favor	The bill, please
Loquillo	Crazy person
Me llamo	My name is
Mañana	Tomorrow
Marisco	Seafood
Me he perdido	I'm lost
No me jodas!	Don't mess with me
Ojo!	Watch out!
Pardón	Sorry
Por favor	Please
Qué cosa?	What was that? (when you didn't understand something)
Salud	Cheers
Si	Yes
Sorroche	Altitude sickness
Té	Tea
Vino	Wine

Easy for us, same as English:

Cool	Hospital
Hotel	No
Taxi	

Don't be disrespectful. Address locals as Señora (Mrs.) or Señorita (Miss) or Señor (Mr.).

Don't stand too close, about one to two feet or sometimes farther back is pretty common for an average friendly chat. Sustained eye contact is normal, even expected. It is customary to shake hands when you greet someone.

Don't use the wrong hand gestures. Beckoning someone using the index finger (like when we are trying to say "come here") is seen as provocative. Doing this same motion with your palm facing sideways or down is derogatory. The way locals signal someone without these connotations is to use all four fingers instead of the index finger. Pointing is generally rude. Instead, many pucker their lips or point their chin with a little upward nod to indicate direction.

Don't be paranoid, just be friendly. Occasionally visitors that refuse to make friendly eye contact and say a greeting can be perceived as scared. This highlights the fact that they are not from here and are out of their element. This can potentially put a target on them for theft.

Don't forget to smile. Ecuadorians are gracious and kind and as long as you smile and mean well, you will get along just fine.

Don't forget a rain poncho for the rainy season.

Don't avoid people; be polite and greet everyone with a hello. Always say "please" and "thank you" as the Ecuadorians are polite and may become offended if you don't mind your manners. If you bump into someone, say "sorry."

Don't avoid trying to say some words. Even though they speak English, get a list of commonly used words and practice them before you go so you don't say them wrong. Review on YouTube.

Don't or do, there is no cut-and-dried guide for tipping. The fixed menu lunch is popular throughout the country. You will rarely see an Ecuadorian tip a lunch server. You may see $2.75 rounded up to $3 to avoid the wait for change. In fancier restaurants you will often notice that, in addition, a service charge is tacked on to the bill. No more is needed. If there is no service charge added, standard is 10 percent though Ecuadorians usually tip far less, more like five percent. Taxi drivers are rarely tipped but you can round up by ten to twenty-five cents.

Baggage handlers are happy with $1 per bag. Give the hotel doorman a fifty-cent tip if he provides extra service such as hailing a cab for you; a tip of a dollar per day or $1.50 for exemplary service to the hotel housekeeper who cleans your room is recommended.

Don't forget to take some postcards from home to write thank you notes for staff, tour guides or bus drivers, anyone you'd like to show your appreciation.

Before visiting you may wish to purchase a vocabulary guide; it's educational and humorous. And please, please, please buy a well-respected travel authority's book or two and read every word.

"Travel opens your eyes and your heart."
Deleen Wills

The Stone Door

Planes, trains, buses and a wheelchair in Peru

April 2016

Having lunch at one of our favorite Chinese food restaurants, my husband and I talked about our greatly anticipated imminent departure the following day for Peru. Pulling the fortune from one cookie I found two stuck together. Jackpot! The first revealed, "Travelling to the south will bring you unexpected happiness." Peru, here we come. The second one read, "Your hidden creative talents will soon be revealed." Interesting, since my first book, *Behind Colorful Doors*, had just been published.

We'd watched many television programs over the years on Discovery and National Geographic and read copious articles from magazines and newspapers on Machu Picchu, Peru, the Lost City of the Incas in the Andes. A 1954 adventure film, "Secrets of the Incas," helped boost tourism and supposedly was the inspiration for the all-time great movie, "Raiders of the Lost Ark," that we'd watched several times and is still one of my favorite action flicks. I secretly had a small crush on Indiana Jones when it was released in the early 1980s. Then there was the animated movie by Disney, "The Emperor's New Groove." Other films had also been filmed in this region: "The Dancer Upstairs," a crime-thriller set in Lima; "Aguirre, the Wrath of God," a Werner Herzog film in the Amazon,

Peruvian rainforest and Machu Picchu; and the creepy slithering "Anaconda," about a crew searching for a tribe deep in the Amazon jungle and taken hostage by a snake hunter who is in search of a giant anaconda. I didn't make it through this movie.

I pretended that we were explorers, not greedy treasure hunters, and were about to embark on an adventure of a lifetime to a 15th century Inca citadel located in the eastern Cordillera of southern Peru on an eight-thousand-foot mountain ridge. Machu Picchu hides above the Sacred Valley northwest of Cusco.

From travel experience, we knew a land tour meant moving every night or two staying in a different location. We each packed light, learning this protocol decades earlier from our travel guru, Rick Steves, founder of his company, Europe Through the Backdoor. We each packed: Three pairs of pants, five shirts, one jacket with a hood, one pair of hiking shoes, one pair of lighter-weight shoes and other necessities. We'd do this trip with one carry-on bag each.

Passports - √
Currency Peruvian Nuevo sol, called Soles - √
Altitude and prescription medications - √
Adaptors and converters for 220 V - √
Open mind for an emerging country - √

I had my cheat-sheet printed with the conversion rates: 1 Sol = 31 cents; 5 Soles = $1.55; 25 Soles = $7.77; 100 Soles = $31.09; 500 Soles = $155.46. The paper Soles were in pristine condition because Soles could not have even the tiniest tear but I never learned why.

Our destination was Lima, Peru, Land of Ancient Mysteries, elevation about five hundred feet above sea level. One neighboring country is Ecuador where we had been five years earlier exploring Quito but mostly The Galápagos Islands. Since that experience in South America, I had been researching another new country in this region for us to explore. We were ready for this unique place.

But first we needed to get to Miami to meet up with other travelers on a Collette guided tour. We had traveled with Collette touring all around the globe and I trusted the company and considered their tour guides top-notch. I knew I didn't have to worry about a thing when traveling with them. And they carried our luggage; I love that.

Our policy is to never depart the same day as a tour or cruise begins. I am not willing to take the chance of late flights and missed connections, and in over thirty years I am relieved to say we've not missed an adventure because of self-induced mishaps causing unnecessary stress.

We departed a day early and stayed not far from the Miami airport knowing we'd be returning the next afternoon for our flight to Peru. We checked into the

Best Western around 6:30 p.m., walked down the road for a tasty, flavorful Mexican food dinner then tried to go to sleep. Even though it was nine o'clock on our body clocks, the digital clock on the nightstand read 12:00, Florida time. We had brunch scheduled the next day with longtime friend Mary Ann, who I worked with for years at a private university in Oregon. I always attempted to see her anytime we were going through Miami which wasn't often.

Mary Ann and partner Michele picked us up and we went to brunch at one of their favorite cool places called Morgan's Restaurant. We sat outdoors under patio umbrellas as the sun beat its toasty rays on our west coast winter-white skin. Starting with freshly-squeezed orange juice mimosas, I knew we were now officially on vacation. Eating tropical fruits and frittata along with lots of catching up was a marvelous way to start a trip, complete with parting hugs from dear friends.

At the airport at 3:15 p.m., we rendezvoused with other travelers from around the country to make the five and a half-hour flight to Lima, the capital of Peru, located on the Pacific Ocean. Promptly at six o'clock, April 23, LAN flight 2515 departed on time. I had my usual window seat.

All sorts of pre-trip thoughts were swimming around in my head. Is tap water safe to drink? A big NO on this. But bottled water is cheap and sold nearly everywhere. The advice was to drink as much water as you can; it'll help with preventing altitude sickness.

Will I get sick? I re-read my info that stomach bugs are a frequent problem for visitors, but if we could avoid fresh vegetable salads and only eat fruits that we peel, we'd reduce the likelihood of suffering from intestinal discomfort. Ceviche and other raw seafood dishes are popular in Lima, just make sure they are cooked ten minutes before eating anything and that should kill any bacteria. Finally, the information said to bring antidiarrheal medicines and play it by ear. Darn, I forgot the Imodium. Oh well, the pharmacies would have it. No worries on raw fish, no way.

I had read and heard from other travelers that altitude sickness could cause a headache for twenty hours but others might endure several days of fatigue and nausea, too. When we were in Quito, Ecuador, we did have altitude issues at nine thousand feet with a headache but we weren't there long. More tips for coping at high elevations were: Don't consume liquor for the first twenty-four hours, limit physical activity, hydrate twice as much as normal and drink lots of coca tea, suck coca hard candy or chew coca leaves. If the headache persists, take ibuprofen. I had that. Plus, I had meds from my doctor for possible elevation issues. Finally, if necessary, hydrate even more and sleep it off. Most hotels have oxygen, so don't hesitate to ask for it. OK, got it.

I reread my *Lonely Planet* Peru book just to refresh my memory as we chased the sun arriving in Lima at 10:30 p.m., in the same time zone as Dallas, Texas.

We knew no one on this trip except our guide Beth and that was from email only and this was unusual for us. I organize travel for groups, friends and family, and we normally went with someone. Neither of us being shy, we knew we'd meet somebody to pal around with as had been the case on other travels, some becoming lifelong friends like faux Scottish aunties Margaret and Wilma who we serendipitously met on a Caribbean cruise; Beth and Jon from Indiana who we met in Quito before the Galápagos Islands; Clive and Greta living in England who we also met in the Galápagos; this list can go on forever. One of my favorite things is meeting new friends from around the world. "Travel opens your eyes and your heart." That's my very own quote.

WELCOME TO LIMA flashed on the reader board and we followed the signs for "Visitors With Passports," and queued up to get a new country stamp in our passports. Others picked up their luggage and we passed it off to our Collette bus driver, about the only time we would need to haul our luggage on this trip.

We transited via motorcoach to our hotel, our first stop for a few days. The normal one-hour-ride would become two because it was some holiday plus being a Saturday night in a city of ten million people and country of about thirty-one million. I knew from reading that the three named languages spoken are Spanish, Quechua and Aymara, and religions are eighty percent Roman Catholic and twelve percent evangelical.

Along the shoreline there were fireworks or so we were told. We could hear deep bangs like cannons but only saw random bursts of light shrouded in coastal fog if we happened to be looking in the right spot.

Our cushy accommodations at the Hilton Lima in Miraflores, one neighborhood among dozens, weren't too far from the city center and the ocean. The snazzy bathroom had granite countertops and two sinks, complete with locally made toiletries and four bottles of water. Even though early in our trip, these exceptionally high-quality toiletries, minus the shampoo and bar soap, disappeared into a gallon Ziplock bag and were tucked away in my luggage, yes, to be carried for the rest of the vacation. The shower and large tub were big enough for a party which I greatly appreciated. Around one o'clock in the morning I sank into the deep tub for a bubble soak before a good night's sleep. My husband fell asleep in two seconds flat, which was normal.

Looking out our hotel window, we seemed about even with eight-to-ten-story buildings and I couldn't see any higher as a layer of fog blanketed our coastal neighborhood. A bright orange four-story building on the left stood circled by colorful one- , two- , and three-level homes with patios and balconies containing vibrant multicolored bushes and flowers, and palm trees, lots of them. To the right was a street lined with homes, sidewalks and front yards but with unconventional house colors. The first home was painted golden, then a lilac one, followed by slate, cinnamon, pumpkin, ivory, crimson, soft gray, and ending with a sunshine-yellow home, all with imperfect-size palm trees and fence-high, wall-climbing red and purple bougainvillea separating the properties. We needed to explore this street after breakfast.

At breakfast plenty of fresh fruits, cereals, pastries, eggs, meats and potatoes almost overwhelmed the buffet table. What a joy to rediscover the reddest, most flavorful watermelon that I'd ever tasted from five years earlier in Ecuador and on the Xpedition ship while cruising the Galápagos Islands. The server asked about beverages and my coffee-drinking husband had a cup topped with a heart designed in foam. It was the first time I'd seen a shape floating on coffee.

After breakfast, needing to stretch our legs, we changed into our walking shoes and stayed around the hotel having no desire to get lost the first day. We walked by a periwinkle painted colonial-style home, and next to it stood a purple grape-colored house with about six inches between each house, just wide enough for a dog or cat to slip through. A pastel pink home was next with a Toyota SUV parked in front of the house, fenced in by a black wrought iron decorative gate. They had transformed the typical front yard of grass and flowers into a convenient stone-lined driveway for their vehicle. The all-white license plate with Peru written in black at the top had three black letters and a blank space followed by three black numbers.

Cars were parked in front of nice homes because there wasn't room for garages. Some parking pads were made of decorative slate, stone or gravel. A Peruvian flag swayed in the light breeze at one home. In three equal portions the flag is red then white and red again. The middle section features a shield-shaped coat of arms with a llama against a blue background, and a green tree and a gold cornucopia below them. Green palm and laurel branches at the bottom are tied together with a ribbon and branch off to the right and left encasing the crest. At the top is a wreath. I informed my husband that actually what looked like a llama to us is really a vicuña, a free-roaming camelid brought in thousands of years ago and closely related to the llama and alpaca. The tree is a cinchona tree and the bark is used to make quinine. The cornucopia, which spills gold and silver coins, is symbolic of the nation's mineral wealth. If I am questioned about my story or accuracy, I had my guidebook to prove I wasn't making up facts. Exaggeration or spur-of-the-moment fabricated data had apparently happened in the past, not that I could ever remember when or where.

Along the edge of a sidewalk was a drive-in gasoline pump, only one. We watched as a man pulled in, inserted a credit card in the slot, pumped his gas then quickly got on his way. The area looked nicely kept up with orange and white geraniums that butted up next to a family home. I did wonder about safety from explosions or fire but didn't say anything. Colorful bushes of fuchsias and a cute black and white bird with a bright orange bill, appropriately called an Orange-billed Sparrow, lollygagged in the grass looking for grub.

Something we learned is that Peruvians also use natural gas to fuel their vehicles, with pumping stations situated around neighborhoods for convenience and efficiency. Using natural gas instead of gasoline had become cheaper and more fuel efficient. Taxi drivers really like it.

I brought a *Birds of Peru* laminated trifold by Rainforest Publications that my husband had purchased. We enjoy viewing birds and butterflies and instead of trying to remember what I'd seen, I started a log of birds. I really, really, really, wanted to see an Andean Condor which would be more likely seen the higher up we travel. Storks, herons, egrets, hawks, and a variety of vultures were expected sights. Then a bonus would be spotting a unique-looking bird called the Andean Cock-of-the-Rock, the national bird. It is famous because of its stunning headdress of red-orange feathers that remind some of the red-orange fringe that Incas used to wear as a badge of rank. The male bird has black wings and the bottom half of its body is black.

The Condor is a sacred bird of the Incas, part of the vulture family and can live fifty years and stands about four feet tall with a wingspan of about ten feet. Able to soar almost without moving its wings, the bird flies from its nest in the heights of the Andes down to the beaches where it feeds on dead sea lions. It has no song and the male makes a squawk with its tongue when courting. Monogamous, they have black plumage with white splashes at the ends of their extremities and a white collar; the head and neck have no feathers. They didn't sound all that attractive or majestic like our Bald Eagle but their commonality is that they are both opportunists and scavengers.

As we rounded the block back to the entrance of our hotel, another couple we'd greeted earlier, Mark and Nancy, were embarking on a walk and we joined them for another loop. Varying from our previous circle we discovered Miss Cupcakes, est. 2009, with a bright blue front door propped open, beckoning us. We faced a three-tier cupcake display with delicacies decorated with bright blue frosting on white with colorful sprinkles and a blue jigsaw puzzle piece decoration on the top. A neighborhood sports team had won some championship and blue and white were the team colors. I didn't understand the puzzle piece though.

There were at least a dozen others to try but I went for the dark chocolate with darker chocolate frosting. I would have had two different kinds if the shop had minis available.

Returning to the hotel we boarded our motorcoach in the sunshine but the closer we got to the ocean, just a mile or so away, the foggier it got. A local guide named Fidel joined us for the Lima portion of our trip. It would have been an easy walk but this was just the first stop on a day of exploring. Esplanade of Miraflores is a vista point on a hilltop overlooking the Pacific hundreds of feet below with stunning panoramas of Lima, Fidel assured us, but we could barely see through the dense fog. It reminded me of our Oregon coast in the summer. When temperatures in the Willamette (will-am-ette) Valley, some fifty miles away, reach ninety degrees then the coast can get fogged in.

The entire sprawling park is designed as an amphitheater from which you can enjoy specular views. Walking with Fidel, he told me his mother is Spanish and father Peruvian. He studied at the university and loves his job as a guide educating new friends about his culture and country.

Pretty purple flowers were in full bloom at Parque del Amor or Park of Love. Really, that's what it's called because of a daring, provocative, ten-times-larger-than-life, central sculpture created by a Peruvian artist and inaugurated appropriately on February 14, Valentine's Day, 1993. El Beso (The

Kiss) shows a reclining man and a woman wrapped in each other's arms locked in a passionate kiss.

The locked lovers aren't the only impressive thing about the park—there are mosaics adorning benches and walls plus a lot of green space on the bluffs overlooking the Pacific. There is a path through the brush on the hillside that winds down to the beach hundreds of feet below where surfers enjoyed the waves. I appreciated the tile work since I'd taken two classes some years ago and had a few unremarkable pieces to prove it.

Cement benches, walls, chairs and tables were covered in all different patterns and designs in about every color imaginable. Palms and other trees added a green splash of nature around the park built on rock cliffs. The incredible tile work reminded me of Barcelona, Spain. People were reading, talking on cell phones, strolling, watching hang gliders disappearing into the fog, and surfers in the gray water.

On the short bus ride our Collette guide, Beth, told us most speakers of English or Spanish know the first "c" is silent like in Picchu. The life expectancy is sixty-nine-years old, GDP per capita is $5,000 US and the literacy rate is ninety-one percent. Peru lies on the Pacific Ocean of South America just south of the Equator. Peru ranks among the world's top producers of silver, copper, lead and zinc. Its petroleum industry is one of the world's oldest and its fisheries are among the world's richest. It is about five hundred thousand square miles, a little less than the size of Alaska and about half the size of Texas. Lima is laid out like a checkerboard and has two large square plazas. Whew, this was lots of information to retain.

I could tell that Beth would be excellent as our guide. She would care for us on this trip and reminded us, even though Collette had sent repeated information on this topic, that everyone must only drink bottled water because the rivers and streams are now polluted due to animals depositing waste in the water supply. Plastic is considered trash but they didn't have a litter law or recycle program which quickly became evident.

We knew we might get some rain in April but this time of year the highland landscapes were supposed to be lush shades of green with fewer tourists. We were there in the autumn; it was springtime at home. We always preferred cooler temperatures to warmer on vacations. My philosophy is that it's much easier to add a layer or two of clothing when in cooler temperatures as one can only remove so much clothing when it's too hot.

We drove by Huaca Pucllana, an important archeological site located in the northern part of our neighborhood called Miraflores, Fidel said it was built with thousands of handmade bricks and is split into two main areas which were used for administrative and ceremonial purposes. Some might think it's just a pile of bricks but the story is that this pre-Inca temple is the most popular of Lima's archeological sites. It is an adobe-and-clay pyramid built by the people of Lima in 400 AD. These people built canals redirecting water from the three main rivers to irrigate the entire valley in order to raise crops. This innovation was monumental in Lima's development, without which it is doubtful the capital of Peru would have been founded on this site. While Lima's coastline is rich in fish, crops would support thriving civilizations for two thousand years. He explained this culture died out around 700 AD, after which the site was later converted into a tomb for the elites of the Wari Culture. Several mummies, including a child, have been unearthed. The tombs at the top of the pyramid were reserved for nobles who were buried with small animals and Lima-style pottery, done in a wave pattern. After the Wari Empire disintegrated, the Ichma Culture came to rule the region from around 11 AD until they were conquered by the Incas in 1470.

At the window, I sat even with the structure and fortunately a red stoplight gave me extra time to check this out. Looking across an adobe brick wall I could see the roofline of a tent decorated in the Lima style, with the curvy lines representing waves of the ocean. Crops of beans, quinoa, some goldish berries, cotton and other unrecognizable produce grew in a small garden fifty yards from the pyramid. Alongside the garden, a small farm displayed a sign showing pictures of llamas, alpacas and guinea pigs. We had been warned from a very experienced traveler friend, Russ, about the guinea pigs being a delicacy but I would not be sampling this meat even though it is a popular Sunday meal for families. And I certainly wouldn't be eating alpaca either. I'd stick with fish, pork, chicken and other non-cute products.

Looking back across the brick expanse it was certainly a contrast to the skyline of modern shiny buildings. Tree limbs drooped loaded with deep pink-colored, star-shaped blossoms that reminded me of an orchid. I wanted to get up close and smell them but wouldn't be able to jump off and get back on the bus fast enough.

We arrived at one of two of Lima's plazas with trees and well-manicured areas and a large old fountain in the center. The Plaza Mayor or Plaza de Armas of Lima is the birthplace of the city of Lima, as well as the core of the city. This square is located in the historic center and turning a complete three hundred sixty-degree circle, I saw the Government Palace, Cathedral of Lima, Archbishop's Palace, the Municipal Palace and Palace of the Union, and a few horse-pulled buggies available for rides.

The Archbishop's Palace had an extraordinary door with sixty-four round brass knobs about the size of a softball, and the biggest door knocker I'd ever seen. I doubt that anyone could actually pull it to knock.

Fidel shared fascinating history during a walking tour of the historic center, strolling through yellow five-story buildings trimmed with white windows, arches and doors.

A silver Hyundai Santé Fe with a yellow stripe along both sides had Policia displayed easily. I always take a photo of a police vehicle because my youngest brother worked in law enforcement. I appreciated knowing if I ever got in serious trouble and locked up, he'd come for me. Or so I hoped.

We entered the famous Cathedral of Lima through a smaller door to the side and friendly staff greeted us. Being in a sacred place, we spoke in whispers. A black and white checkerboard tile pattern is on the floor. Arched beams in the ceiling are all painted gold. There is a ten-foot-tall gold ornate candle holder. The main altar is totally made of wood and there was only one chair by one table. A larger-than-life wooden carved man holding two large keys in one hand and a book in the other stands by the table.

Several smaller chapels with displays and statues are open for people to pray and worship. Starting on the right and going around in a U-shape are fifteen chapels. I really liked the Chapel of Saint Joseph (as in the Holy Family, that Joseph), patron saint of carpenters. It's the only plain chapel with natural bare wood, very little adornment using hardly any gold, but left simple and elegant.

I spent some time in the Francisco Pizarro Burial Chapel which contains the mausoleum in which lie the authentic remains of the conquistador of the empire of the Incas and the founder of Lima. His remains were discovered by chance in 1977 in a small lead box and on the top this inscription is engraved: "Here lies the head of the Lord and Marquis Don Francisco Pizarro, who discovered and won for the Royal Crown of Castile the Kingdoms of Peru." I saw a photo of his living descendant, Hernando Pizarro, with a complete skeleton spread out on a table. After a lot of research based on biological anthropology carried out over several years, the positive identification of the remains put an end to a debate that had raged for more than three decades.

The crypt of Our Lady of Candelaria, a subterranean vaulted burial chamber was discovered by chance in 201, during work to restore the chapel's threshold. Seventy bodies were found including men, women and children, twenty-seven children to be exact. They were all arranged in five communal tombs in which the individuals were interred on top of one another and covered with lime and earth.

Then there is the Archbishop's Crypt or the Main Crypt that is as old as the actual cathedral, probably commissioned around 1566. This burial place was used to inter the mortal remains of archbishops, viceroys, canons and other illustrious types. Even though it was closed in 1808 when Lima's General Cemetery opened, burials within the crypt continued, probably clandestinely. Today, only archbishops have the right to be buried in the still-used crypt.

We walked by the celery green Casa de la Literatura Peruana, the home of Peruvian Literature housed in a renovated railway station located in the historic center. The clock on the tower read 4:10.

I spotted a myriad of delightfully bright buildings, the first being a burnt orange two-story building with three balconies painted lighter shades of orange. Next was a pea green building with white colonial balconies, then a tan building with dark wooden doors, and a building with a bell tower at the end.

Looking up I saw, perched on the top of one building's peak, a giant black bird. I was sure it would be my first condor. However, when excitedly pointing it out to my spouse, the skeptical birder burst my bird-spotting bubble when it turned out to be one extremely large black vulture. I pulled out my *Birds of Peru* guide to try to prove him wrong and shut it quickly.

Walking down the street, little shops were tucked into single car-size stalls where convenience items such as sodas, packaged chips and candies were being sold to locals. Another one sold fresh fruits.

A monumental façade looked like it had been slathered with deep rich butter. It contained a dramatic entrance and dark double doors about six stories tall. Above that there is an ornate balcony or porch that reminded me of the one where the pope stands at the Vatican. The façade shows statues of cherubs instead of typical gargoyles. It is flanked by two identical twin bell towers.

This impressive building complex is the Basílica y Convento de San Francisco. The church and convent are part of the historical center of Lima. It also contains a library and catacombs—terrific, more bones. Paintings, like frescos, show religious items and various maritime articles. There is an impressively large mosaic-tiled gold flag with a bird or maybe a dragon on each side and a colorful crest in the middle.

The church and monastery were blessed in 1673 and completed the next year. It survived several earthquakes and suffered extensive damage in 1970. The inside is a fine example of Spanish Baroque. The dome, vaults and two side naves are painted in a mix of Moorish and Spanish designs. It is normally referred to as the Monastery of San Francisco but it is actually two parts. The first is the Iglesia or Church of San Francisco and the second is the Convento de San Francisco, where the Franciscan monks lived, ate and studied.

I know that religion is seen in different ways by different people and the presentation of the Divinity differs depending on the country but it's really evident here. In the refectory of the monastery there is a fresco of the Last Supper, and looking closely, I noticed something peculiar—guinea pigs, one of the food specialties, is served instead of the usual sacrificial lamb that we typically see. I quietly chuckled but didn't point it out; pointing is rude. Sometimes viewing cathedral after cathedral in Europe one can get a bit burned out but the artwork at San Francisco Monastery wasn't overly stated or gaudy like many Catholic churches can be.

I got a warm fuzzy feeling seeing youth and older people together. A man maybe in his late twenties, dressed in medium gray cotton pants, and a pullover soccer-style shirt, chatted with an older woman. I only assumed her age because of her all-gray braided pony tail down her back. Her black and white heavy socks showing above her walking shoes were unique. The bottom third had a black and white geometric sun separated with zigzag lines or maybe a mountain ridgeline. The middle third had Inca-looking people and the top third were alpacas or llamas. She wore a bright purple-and-slate-colored skirt covered with a teal floral pattern, and a matching teal sweater. A red ribbon surrounded her straw hat with the fabric sown into a bow at the back.

Back at the hotel, we had learned over many trips how to become quick-change artists. Ninety minutes later we were at Café Café for dinner with its very welcoming owner, happy to have us. He proudly informed us that according to World Travel Awards, Peru had been voted the World's Leading

Culinary Destination for 2016 and had won the award every year since 2012. He acknowledged it was partially due to the large waves of immigrants from Africa, Japan, China and Europe who brought with them many new cuisines blended with Andean to produce some of the best foods in the world. He added that we would also be eating well when we reached the Sacred Valley.

Several different groups sang, danced and performed traditional numbers. Their musical instruments were as vibrant as their clothing.

We all tried a Maracupa, a Passion Fruit Sour, which is a traditional tasty beverage. For the first course I had Taquenos, mozzarella in fried bread dough with a passion fruit sauce followed by a main course of pumpkin and blue cheese ravioli, ending with flan for dessert. My husband had the Causa Limena, smashed (yes, smashed) potatoes, avocado and tomatoes, Chorrillana Fish (bass) served with Tacu Tacu, a mix of rice and beans, and finally Alfajores which are shortbread cookies filled with dulce de leche, a milk caramel. We always tried to order different meals and desserts to share at least a bite, usually only a tiny bite if sharing dessert.

We'd heard that Peru also offers some delicious specialties we simply had to try including ceviche (raw fish marinated in lime juice), papas a la huancaina or potatoes in cheese sauce, sort of potato dumplings, and pollo a la brasa, a grilled chicken. I'm not a persnickety person but I was not eating raw meat or fish.

I had to try the national drink created in Peru called a pisco sour. Pisco is sort of a miracle of the Peruvian desert and a concoction of both Indian and Spanish society. It is a grape alcohol in which the culture of the vine, the quality of the land, the climate and the casks in which it is stored, all play a part. It is stored in half-buried, large yet narrow clay vessels. A pisco sour is made with egg whites, sugar, pisco, lemon juice syrup, angostura bitters, crushed ice and ground cinnamon. Not only did it sound refreshing and light, I can attest that it is.

Also, lager beers, chichi (a fermented corn beer), and local wines are vastly popular. Coca tea is widely available and is also considered a remedy for effects from high altitude. Fresh juices of papaya, passion fruit, guanabanas (baby bananas), cherimoya and other exotic choices are easily available. There's also a popular beverage called chicha morada, a non-fermented spiced and fruity purple corn drink as well as Peruvian soda called Inka Kola. I mistakenly thought it might be a coke, but it tasted like carbonated Nyquil to me.

The seasons are flipped in the southern hemisphere and because northern Peru is on the equator, summer and winter change less in the northern half of the country than in its southern half. Lima is about in the middle. The dry season is from April until November in the southern Andes. It was a lovely, balmy night in Lima.

It had been an educational and entertaining day but I wanted out of the hubbub of the big city and was ecstatic soon to be getting a glimpse of the persevering cultures and breathtaking beauty of the Andes.

Each morning I thought it prudent to begin my day downing a bottle of water. We are not accustomed to this at home as we have some of the finest water on the west coast. The smell of the plastic bottle reminded me of summer afternoons spent in the kiddie pool at the neighbor's. Since tap water isn't safe to drink, brushing our teeth took on a new meaning when dipping a toothbrush into a glass of bottled water or remembering to pour bottled water onto the brush. And when taking a shower and washing one's hair, don't let any sneak in between your lips. We didn't want to take any chances getting the dreaded stomach issues we'd heard about. We were a bit proud of ourselves sharing our tips of success with each other. Plus, I had forgotten Imodium.

After a luscious breakfast we got on our bus for the one-hour ride returning to the airport and Fidel told us that about fifteen thousand years ago the first people filtered down from north and central America and were faced with diverse and extreme environments at varying altitudes. An ocean abundant in fish contrasts with bare coastal valleys that are only inhabitable where rivers wind through the desert. To the east, the valleys and high plateaus of the Andes mountains slope down to the Amazon rainforest, home to exotic foods, animals and medicinal plants.

In the 15th century the Incas achieved unprecedented control over people, food crops, plants and domesticated animals that incorporated coast, highlands and the semitropical valleys. When the Spaniards arrived in the 16th century, the search for El Dorado, the fabled City of Gold, extended into the Amazon lowlands. Since independence in 1821, disputes, wars and treaties over Amazon territory have been fueled increasingly by the knowledge of mineral oil and natural gas under the forest floor.

Peru means "land of abundance" to the Quechua Indians and the sites of Machu Picchu and Cusco recall the wealth of the Inca civilization that was destroyed in the early 16th century by Spaniards who built an empire on Peru's gold and silver.

The Inca capital was Cusco but the Spanish founded Lima in 1535 along the coast and made it their capital. The Spanish preferred the lowland coast because of the climate and for easier trade with Spain. The western seaboard is desert, where rain seldom falls. Lima is an oasis containing more than a quarter of Peru's population, most of European descent.

The Andean highlands occupy about a third of the country and contain mostly Quechua-speaking Indians. Quechua is the language of the Inca Empire.

Fidel said that Peru's recent history has seen it switch between periods of democracy and dictatorship. The desperate poverty of the Indian population gave rise to the ruthless Maoist guerrilla organization Sendero Luminoso. The guerrillas were largely defeated but problems with poverty and illegal coca production persist. He added that crops of coffee, cotton, sugarcane and rice, plus poultry and fish are exported. There is an abundance of gold, copper and zinc.

The Inca Empire dates between 1430-1532 AD but before that was the Chimu, Chincha, Chanka Confederation from 1200 to 1470 AD. Before this, between 800 and 1200 AD, were the Wari and Tiwanaku tribes.

Most archaeologists believe that Machu Picchu had been constructed as an estate for the Inca Emperor Pachacuti. Often mistakenly referred to as the Lost City of the Incas, it is the most familiar icon of Inca civilization. The Incas built the classical-style estate with polished dry-stone walls around 1450 but abandoned it a century later at the time of the Spanish conquest.

An hour later with all this wealth of information we reentered the airport property and noticed a gigantic six-pack of Coca Cola almost like a 3D billboard that maybe a giant would have enjoyed.

I did notice it when we arrived a few days earlier but in my weary state, wasn't sure what I was seeing.

When spelling Cuzco some use a "z" but we thought we should follow what the locals do, using an "s." We were off to Cusco on the 9:05 a.m. flight on LAN. I nabbed my usual window seat on Flight 2123 as we circled over the blue Pacific Ocean on this fogless morning. We climbed higher and higher from sea level over brown dry mountains. This was unusual for us because Oregon has mountains over ten thousand feet too, but ours are covered in some amount of snow year round. Two summits were haloed in light clouds. I thought about all those forest paths to explore and what the Incas must have felt.

Below I could see brown roads crisscrossing and large blue mirror-like lakes, flat plateaus, splotches of green patches around towns with one mountain and nestled in at its top sat a patch of snow, probably a long-lived glacier. As we banked right along a ridge of the Andes, I saw the slope of emerald grassy mountains and one narrow tan road slaloming for miles. Way in the distance were more mountains clustered together covered in snow.

While we flew one and a half hours from coastal Lima to mountainous Andes to Cusco, I divided my time between looking at the scenery and reading the airline magazine. There was an article about the Peruvian Andes saying, "These mountains occupy the central part of the Andean region of

South America. Divided into the northern Andes and southern Andes they are geographically indicated by the highlands or sierra, inhabited by man in the high valleys from 8,200 to 10,000 feet above sea level. With more than one thousand mountains at sixteen thousand feet high and dozens more than twenty thousand feet high, this colossal geographical formation is the most important articulate hub of Peruvian culture. The multiple weather varieties range from freezing at the summits to suffocating hot in the valleys."

Looking at the majestic mountains I was reminded of a favorite quote, "The World is a book and those who do not travel read only one page." This quote was written by St. Augustine born November 13, 354. He lived until he was seventy-five years old dying on August 28, 430. Now, that's a long time ago and his words are still true today.

Soon we'd be landing at eleven thousand five hundred feet. Off and on during the week we'd be spending time at even higher elevations in some areas. We were almost in the heart of the Inca civilization called the Sacred Valley, which is the agricultural center of the empire.

Coming in on approach to Cusco, I saw one-to-six-story buildings, trees, grasses, mostly red terracotta tiled roofs, and a school with a soccer field. The airport had nothing close around it but brown land unlike Quito, Ecuador, where buildings surround the airport. Just off the airport property were dwellings that crept to the edge of steep hills, actually the Andes mountains. I temporarily forgot we were already at eleven thousand feet, so these were definitely mountains not hills.

Beth had told us earlier that the best souvenir we could buy would be available when getting off the airplane. It would not only be ornamental but useful—a brightly-colored, hand-woven water bottle holder. Coming to a stop, I looked out the airplane window and there she stood, just as Beth said. A woman was laden with colorful woven items. Seven stacked hats, the top one crocheted with alpaca animals into the hat, sat on her head. Striped bags hung around her neck down one side. In her right hand were packages of coca leaves; the other hand held a doll and several more were tucked under her arm, all decked out in traditional colorful costumes.

I made the first purchase of woven art—two water bottle holders that we could drape across us and leave our hands free. Each had Machu Picchu embroidered on them and my teal one had ribbons of other colors. My husband's was green with colorful additions. And we bought a bag of coca leaves because I could already feel the elevation. And who doesn't try coca leaves at some point? What a great place on the runway at the Cusco airport parking lot to get a hat or water bottle holder and only 10 Soles! Beth had also mentioned that a man would take our pictures then he would appear the final morning at our Cusco hotel with prints. She didn't know how he did it but he did this with each tour group.

In the airport terminal while waiting for our bus to arrive, we were already sucking on the leaves, which basically were flavorless and at first crunchy. Then the next question was what to do with it—swallow or spit out? I forgot to ask. I spit the unsoftened leaves into a tissue but someone chewed his enough to pulverized mush and swallowed.

One of the airport workers helping with our luggage had a cool tattoo on his left arm. It reminded me of a Celtic cross but then again maybe a geometric sun. I'd have to find out. Already feeling a little lightheaded, I could tell I probably wouldn't be my normal effervescent self on this part of the trip.

A local guide, Holber, from Fiesta Tours Peru, would serve as guide extraordinaire and interpreter for our time in the Sacred Valley. Driving on streets that our Oregon Department of Transportation would classify as unimproved roads, we drove through Cusco. A garage repair shop with a lot full of cars only had two stalls for work. The names Frenso y Lubricentro, Ramos, Mobil 1, Mobil Supra, Mobil Delraz, made perfect sense and easy to understand. Another similar station showed Servicio Eléctrico; four were lined up for service or an electricity fill-up.

A familiar red road sign read PARE. We knew that meant STOP from our trip to Ecuador. Driving past a grove of thin trunked trees with wispy branches and leaves, I figured altitude had something to do with the sparse look.

Along the roadside it wasn't uncommon to spot one- or two-story crumbling ancient rock dwellings. The color of the clear blue sky reminded me of Quito. Also commonplace were discarded plastic bottles, way too many of them. On curvy roads, already slow going for our bus, became even slower when a truck loaded with cargo and people pulled in front of us, but it allowed me to get some photos of a crafter's set-up on the roadside selling all sorts of colorful items. This was obviously an ancient village that now had tourists milling around, stepping through doors of collapsing rock-walled homes and grass-covered floors where Incas probably lived hundreds of years ago.

Holber talked during the drive giving us helpful history and useful information. He said cotton had been an important product of Peruvians for centuries and from its fibers the first dresses were made and he proudly noted that they continue to astonish the world with quality. Cotton grows in colors. A rust-colored plant produces long and elastic fiber in brown, reddish, lilac and yellow tones. I thought that maybe I'd actually seen cotton in the fields below when flying into Cusco. Cotton also has medicinal purposes attributed to it and there are one hundred seventy-seven genetic derivations still not commercially developed. He stated that the most popular varieties are Tangüis and Impa, a Peruvian contribution that the international textile industry incessantly demands.

Switching topics, he said that over four hundred twenty species of birds have been identified and he'd point some out when he spotted them for us. There is an endemic Inca wren we might see in Machu Picchu. Speaking of Machu Picchu, he said it is home to three hundred seventy-seven types of butterflies, fifteen types of amphibians and twenty-five types of reptiles. I was surprised to learn so much could survive at that altitude.

Beth told us we would learn the old methods of spinning, dyeing and weaving textiles during our first stop at a living museum of the Peruvian Andes. The sign read "Welcome to Awana Kancha, Social Project" and explained all about the evolution of ancient camels, dromedaries, alpacas, and llamas.

Etched on a large board: "Over 3 million years ago, toward the end of the Pleistocene, Camelids which originated in North America migrated to South America where they settled in non-Andean areas. The first steps in domestication occurred around 4000 BC. For over 6000 years the domestication and semi-domestication of the Camelids have been controlled at altitudes of over thirteen thousand feet above sea level.

The domestication of the Camelids cumulated in the shepherding and appearance of a variety of Camelids that were clearly domesticated approximately 5500 years ago. There are two varieties of wild camelids, vicuña and guanaco, and two types of domestic camelids, llamas and alpacas.

The variability of forms and types originate from the process of domestication. These forms manifest themselves through the rich colors of fibers and the productive specialization of the animals (fibers, meat, skin, manure, transportation, fuel, religious rituals, tools, etc.)" Underneath the writing, eight different animals were pictured.

Just as we read on the board, each alpaca and llama is very different from the other. Tan, gray, black, or chestnut, some had smooth flat fur and others had dreadlocks hanging to the ground. We handed them grasses to eat, and a tan one with short hair on its body and a mop of curly hair on its head approached me. Some had long bangs that covered their large brown eyes and six-inch-long eyelashes. A baby with dark brown fur and a black face snuggled close to its mom.

I named one Cruella de Vil, with its all-black body and head except for her flashy bleached-white bangs along with gorgeous thick eyelashes and chin hairs. I laughed out aloud because she reminded me of my dear friend Carol, who has her own dramatic swish of white against her dark hair. I chuckled as one with brown stringy dreadlocks brushed the dusty ground. I couldn't see its eyes through all its hair but its mouth gaped open talking to somebody about something. Its ears stood straight up, and knowing that if dogs do this—one should move away. I did. A white one looked like it had just come out of a dryer with its hair poufed. One looked like a spotted appaloosa horse. Another lay all stretched out in the grass with brown and black spots on its legs, neck and head and a totally beige body. They were as different as people, each individual. And it's true they do spit as my husband can testify.

I wandered into the small store with racks of packaged snacks and caramelos, woven dolls, and Andean hard candies in various flavors. There were stacks of bars of green (their version of organic) chocolates and dark chocolates using seventy percent cocoa. Rows of local beers sat on the shelf; the sign listed Candelaria, Pale Ale, Golden Ale and Witbier. Lined up next to the beers stood metal bottles of manadarina, limón and lima Wasska Chilcanos, which I surmised was soda.

Then there were the coca products. The sacred plant of the Incas, this leaf has an important place in Andean culture, in which the essence is believed to evoke wisdom and knowledge. It is used in multiple ways medicinally, and as a palliative for fatigue and hunger. Nowadays the use of it in the illicit narcotic trade has had an extremely negative influence on the image of the plant which has significant symbolic and cultural worth.

Back outside, a woman demonstrated how they dye yarn. Ninety-eight clumps of yarn in different hues were spread between twenty-four long posts. Another lady sat on a rug on the ground with a loom in her lap, weaving. She had covered her head with what looked to me like a yellow cloth placemat and was dressed in authentic clothing. I assumed the headdress was specific to her region. Another woman sitting on the ground worked on a loom that had two posts stuck in the ground and the yarn sat on her lap. Her fingers moved quickly as she created patterns from straight rows of yarn. She wore a jacket the color of a deep purple cherry. Lovely finished pieces were for sale but it was too early in the trip for bulky purchases for me.

I appreciated the colorful textiles they were crafting and sharing information about the quality we should look for. Baby Alpaca is highly regarded and means the first sheering, the first one ever from this animal, therefore costing more than just plain old alpaca. After the demonstration we actually could tell the difference by the touch. We were pros now and knew what to watch for.

Back on the road passing by recognizable alder and cedar trees, Holber pointed out the random red cinchona, Brazilian coral trees and laurels. A bit farther along, we pulled over for a view back down from where we'd just come. It wasn't a wide valley and the road snaked parallel to the river through emerald and tawny patches of crops with mountains looming all around us. I took a good deep breath of the thin clean air having it fill my lungs with pure Andean sky.

We commonly saw numerous terraces built into the mountainside. These are one of the great accomplishments of Inca engineering. Holber pointed out that the Incas divided the slopes of the hills they were climbing into enormous steps, a perfect size for the giant in *Jack and the Beanstalk*. These terraces, separated by stone walls, were filled with fertile soil for planting crops, and rainwater irrigated them. The gigantic steps that combine function with beauty also prevented landslides due to rain.

It became clear that this area was an orchid paradise along the roadside, paths and popping from rock walls. On the side of the road a large statue of a rotund man pointed toward the next town called PISAC, spelled out in white rocks at his feet. Pisac is situated on the Vilcanota River. We were at eleven thousand two hundred feet, already one thousand seven hundred feet above the Sacred Valley floor, now twenty miles from Cusco. We drove down a road barely two lanes wide with us taking way more space than our share; glad I wasn't driving. Basic two-story buildings lined the roadway and were all painted shades of brown except one pink and the other one yellow, side-by-side. Sadly, in this land of natural wonder, there were a lot of plastic bottles scattered on the ground.

We parked and were forced to march through, not slowing down or stopping at all at the handcraft market, before reaching a sign that read "Restaurant, Café, Bar, Pizzeria, Inti Killa." Brickishbrown doves with gray heads pecked the ground at the entrance. My Peru bird guide showed a picture and they were Ruddy Ground Doves.

The restaurant sits above a beckoning gift shop called Joyeria Arte Mercedes. With invisible blinders on and perseverance high, I resisted temptation, instead walking up the one flight of steps as a sweet aroma wafted our way. One woman formed two round dough balls then flattened them into patties before she added sliced bananas to one, and cubed pineapple to the other. After a short time she gently picked up a side of the cooked dough and pulled it up over the other half and crimped it together; our version of a fruit turnover.

Another woman molded a similar dough but put savory meats and vegetables in it. We had one steaming hot pork and the other chicken; both were flavorful and delicious. The owners were gracious, coming around to make sure we had enough to eat. We selected the banana desserts.

From our table on the balcony decorated with hanging flower baskets, a couple of hummingbirds flitted around and chased each other off. I couldn't identify one due to their quickness but this country has several types and some birds that looked like hummers really weren't. One was mostly black with a tint of iridescent green with an orange band around its neck. My guidebook showed an identical photo of a Gould's Inca.

Below the restaurant stood two women and two little girls each dressed in Peruvian attire. I assumed they were mothers and daughters. They were at the market we'd just hurried through. After we'd finished our banana turnovers, I went downstairs to the market where one woman held a white and tan baby goat in her over-the-shoulder cloth bag. The other lady held black and white twin goats in her bag. I took a photo and got to donate one Sole for the remembrance photos. These were the cutest goats I'd ever seen. Then I wondered why I was so infatuated with these baby goats. I mean, we have goats, too. Why are animals so much cuter in a foreign country? I have dozens and dozens of sheep pictures from Scotland and Ireland, yet we have thousands of live ones in our valley at home.

The pathway through the market was made with uneven rocks about the same size but not placed evenly for walking. Again, for me it was too early for purchases but some in our group were already supporting the local economy. My time would come.

One fabric wall hanging depicted the entire market entitled "Mercado," with each embroidered stall intricately displaying the vendor's wares of fruits, vegetables, fish, poultry, plants, alpacas, flowers, yarn, clothing, and much more. Even though impressive, I resisted temptation. In two booths were trivets, hot pads, mitts, Christmas socks, towels, towels with holders for hanging, tablecloths, napkins, table runners, scarves, shawls, coats, baby clothing and darling hats, all showing off something special about Peru. Another stall had lovely hand-painted clay nativity scenes of people and animals. I had a feeling I'd see much of this again.

I remembered that in my carry-on I had stashed a foldable tote that I could fill with treasures then use as my one carry-on, and my original carry-on could become checked luggage of basically dirty clothes by the end of the trip.

Driving out through the center of town, we saw a white two-story building with a royal blue door and seven matching windows. School was over for the day as students dressed in uniforms poured out the doors. Girls wore plaid skirts in shades of blue, with a red vest and crisp white blouse. Boys wore red pants with a white stripe on the outside with a matching shirt or jacket. They walked or rode bikes. There was no bus or parent picking them up in a vehicle.

We drove by terraced grasses, maybe another ancient Inca village. Several men hand-worked an area surrounded by a decaying stone fence that most llamas, horses or cows could step over. One section was a lime green crop, one crop had a rusty-colored flower or grain, and other crop was a mossy color. The plot touched the lower side of a mountain that shot straight up as sharp as a fjord in Alaska, just one of many skinny valleys nestled in the steep Andes range.

We stopped next at the Pablo Seminario Ceramic Studio. The flyer read that Pablo Seminario is an oasis for tranquility named after the man of the same name, a soft spoken, gray-haired ceramicist who set up a small workshop with his wife Marilu over thirty years ago in Urubamba. There is a photo of him on the brochure and he looked like a throwback to the sixties in America.

An architect by trade, Pablo had always been interested in different Peruvian cultures so he started learning about their different pottery techniques, focusing particularly on the pre-Columbian style in an attempt to preserve the ancient art and give it life in today's modern world. He focuses on creating unique pieces of art and sculpture which, in the past, had been displayed at the Smithsonian and UN headquarters in New York as part of a Peruvian Art exhibition. What an extraordinary man.

We walked under a tree of gorgeous clusters of red trumpets with a white rounded tip like a Q-tip dangling out the end. I discovered later this is the Cantua, the national flower of Peru that can also be white, yellow, pink or red. It's also known as the Sacred Flower of the Incas. Then a pink hibiscus tree or bush was loaded with blossoms. I had a premonition I would be purchasing something remarkable here.

We started our unique education with a mini-seminar about the internationally known artist's techniques and designs, inspired by ancient Peruvian cultures. We then watched one artist form clay and water, crafting a pitcher by hand. Another woman formed a flower vase. A man covered bricks of damp clay, etched with famous Peruvian patterns, with a cloth. Then he etched an elongated angel into the clay. Drying in the sun were dozens of bowls and vases. Five-by-five-foot flat slabs of clay baked in the sun. A ten-foot-high prickly purple bougainvillea enveloped the area and I knew not to touch or get too close to them. Not only were we in an artist's studio but a lovely vibrant garden, too. On a telephone wire close by, three tan-bodied, black-and white-winged doves sat together watching us. Back inside, women were carving intricate designs into the red clay. Another lady expertly and unhurriedly painted designs on a medium-size vase dipping her brush quickly between clean water and at least two dozen paints in separate small clay bowls.

A terracotta bowl had an etched alpaca in the bottom painted with aurora borealis blues. One woman worked on a three-foot-tall floor vase, with one section of curled waves, the middle section of alpacas with mountains in the background, and the final portion of common Peruvian designs. Most items were in different phases of painting.

Clay miniature homes and buildings using no paint looked natural. In another room an older man intently worked on a five-foot-high Peruvian-style fish. There sat Pablo, the very owner and founder!

He had longer white hair than in the brochure photo, with bushy eyebrows and a mustache, and he wore a navy vest over a navy polo and jeans. He looked like an artist from the sixties in America. He was soft-spoken, almost shy, but he answered any questions we had and showed us the fish he was designing in the clay.

We had time to shop and I went to a room with shelves of multi-toned clay angels. Since this would be hand-carried, I searched for just the right size, about eight inches long. I looked and looked and found her. These do not stand upright but almost look like they are flying on their sides looking at you. In her dark brown hair is a silver sun right above her face and her brown eyes are sculpted out from her flatter face. Her hair flows onto her back between two outstretched arms, not wings, and down her terracotta body is a silver leaf, an upside-down girl, an alpaca with an Inca designer head, a fish, another leaf and a larger girl then a smaller one. Two clay feet in boots finish her off with a signature of the artist. On the back is a carved, half-inch thick piece of wood also in the same shape glued onto the clay piece with a sun stamped on it, and website writing with the studio name. Inserted is a little metal rod allowing her to be propped up for a nice display.

I selected one more memory—a five-inch long, hand-carved, dark brown, almost black wood alpaca lying down with a colorful blanket with Inca designs draped over its back. Pointy ears are painted

316

white outlined by a thin red line and instead of hair over its eyes, a tiny painted blanket of red, white and blue to add some artistic flair.

Back on the bus driving through the mountains, I saw a patch of snow glued into a deep ravine. My husband pointed out a hawk and I found that it's called a Roadside Hawk in my guide. A few miles later driving through a tiny settlement, a little girl wearing a red sweater and burgundy skirt sat on a cement block wall guarding her one free-roaming sheep below.

Sunset would be at 5:06 and my watch showed 4:30. As the sun dropped behind the mountains, the twilight seeped in around trees and buildings. We drove slowly down a bumpy, dusty road and I seriously questioned where in the world we would be sleeping for the next two nights.

When we then turned onto a one-lane dirt road, two men carelessly sped by on a motorbike. They stopped abruptly by two cows (with big horns) who'd clearly tried unsuccessfully to make a break for it. Flailing their arms and speaking rapidly, the two-legged duo tried coaxing the two four-legged perpetrators back from where they'd escaped. It reminded me of a humorous slow-motion cartoon.

Our talented driver tried to avoid potholes that could swallow a European SmartCar. Ahead I could see lights on sprawling hilly land. Our eight hours of daylight quickly disappeared. Now the only lights in the black night sky were from the hotel.

With no major towns around us, light pollution would not be an issue.

We arrived at our impressive 4-Star, off-the-beaten-track-hotel, the Casa Andina Premium Valle Sagrado or Private Collection Sacred Valley. It felt like we were at a ski resort totally surrounded by mountains. The airy lobby had rattan furniture and an open area with an unlit fireplace, frilly purple orchids floating in tall clear cylinder vases and somebody sitting on a sofa puffing oxygen. In another round flat bowl floated several green orchids. One was remarkable because of its shape. It looked like a caricature of a person with thick long squatty legs, a torso with no arms, and a head in which I could easily see eyes, nose and mouth, then two larger green petals forming an umbrella over its head. It looked bizarre.

When we picked up the keys to our room the host mentioned there was an observatory on the property should we wish to star gaze. We signed up immediately for the next evening when hearing there would be a full moon. I mean, who gets a planetarium at their hotel?!

It took a while with a bit of a climb to reach our rooms separated into complexes. The curtains gently moved from the breeze of the open doors to our private patio. Our spacious room had a king bed with lots of bedding and pillows, a large bathroom with a soaking bathtub, and a shower. There were no perimeter lights so I couldn't see anything but darkness and stars.

In the opulent bathroom on the counter were two-quart bottles of water, a package of Kleenex, and when lifting the red lid of a wicker basket I discovered local natural-made treats of soaps, shampoo, conditioner, hand lotion and a separate body lotion and sunscreen, most including the ingredient quinoa. I reminded myself and spouse we needed to be drinking all the water provided. A couple of the mini-products were removed and tucked into my Ziplock baggy to be taken home as mementos.

We hung up a few clothing items as we'd be here for two nights, then met with Mark and Nancy rooming next door and walked about seven minutes winding through the trees and flowers on the stone path following the Lobby sign. I already felt turned around. In the lobby, one in our group sat cross-legged on a chair puffing on oxygen. It wasn't in canisters but a box machine with a cord and headset with a white plastic piece that went under the left ear and then in one's nostrils. I picked up a headset at the reception desk and decided anytime oxygen would be offered I'd inhale five-minutes' worth.

Outside, part of our group stood around in the dark watching our dinner being prepared by the restaurant staff fixing us an authentic Pachamanca dinner, a unique process whereby food is placed on hot stones and buried in the ground to cook. Yes, much like a luau in Hawaii, except we were at eleven thousand feet and the stars seemed like we could pluck them out of the sky. This being our first real opportunity to easily gaze at the galaxy from a southern hemisphere perspective at The Southern Cross and Orion's Belt, I recognized these star patterns from five years earlier on our adventures in the Galápagos Islands.

A pit of red coals held layers of beef, pork, chicken and alpaca (absolutely not having this), then root vegetables and potatoes. They covered the top with wood and a covering of some sort. The woody aroma of the burning logs reminded me of our family campouts roasting s'mores around the fire. It would be served in forty-five minutes giving us plenty of time to star gaze. The moon shone full and brilliant in the night sky, illuminating our path back to the side door of the restaurant.

Inside a man was setting up an orange wooden full-size harp. It matched his several shades of orange-to-red coat and hat. His pants were a neutral gray. He'd be our evening's local entertainment. The harp is one of my favorite musical instruments and whenever I got to hear one in person, I felt enthralled or captivated and transported to heaven. I made another purchase that day—a CD of his music. Not only did he play marvelously and with such depth and feeling, he had been totally blind from childhood.

The hearty dinner had been dug up from the pit and presented buffet-style, tables overflowing with steamy food and tempting aromas. I vowed to try most anything local but I would certainly not be eating alpaca, instead selecting the other flavorful meats plus some long type of green bean, multiple varieties of potatoes, then some cubed fruit salad and a meringue cookie with sliced strawberries on top.

After a nice long soak in the tub and falling asleep in a comfy bed, sometime during the night I heard wild dogs barking but they didn't keep me awake long. Others heard the dogs also and we found out the next morning that there are no leash laws in Peru and they weren't wild.

We retraced our steps from the previous night winding through gardens in dusky morning light on our way to breakfast; sunrise wasn't until 8:33. As our days at home were gaining minutes of sunlight each day, here the days were shrinking. Breakfast at the Alma Restaurant blended a choice of protein, juicy flavorful fruits and round donut hole pastries. A sign read "Variedad de Panes, Variety of Breads." There were several types of doughy holes: deep fried, dipped in sugar, one sprinkled with seeds on top, another white-ish in color as if it hadn't been cooked at all. You can eat them as is or pull them apart and slather them with honey or jam. Honey dripped from a nearby honeycomb. Water carafes held milk products plus a pink runny yogurt that can be poured over cereal.

We boarded a smaller sixteen-person van because today we were going to experience the lifestyles of some local people and delve into their culture. A large motorcoach wouldn't get down these roads. We drove through small villages, more like a collection of hamlets, and didn't see any traffic except for a boy on a bike pulling a cart. In the terraced fields entering town, men were using foot plows to till the fields and plant potatoes. The town is framed by snowcapped mountains and surrounded on all sides by Inca ruins and terraces.

Holber pointed out a flock of six Speckle-faced Parrots but they were too far away and moving too fast for a photo. I could see that they were bright green.

We dropped in elevation into Ollantaytambo, a town that is an Inca archaeological site at over nine thousand feet on the Patakancha River and close to the point where it joins the Willkanuta River. During the empire, this had been the royal estate of Emperor Pachacuti who conquered the region and built the town and ceremonial center. The walls on the outside of homes and buildings were covered in bougainvillea that looked like lengthy strands of colorful plush garland.

An extraordinary local guide at the spectacular Ollantaytambo ruins took us around explaining what we were seeing—the only Inca settlement that has been continually inhabited since its inception. The extensive Inca fortress of

Ollantaytambo is one of the few locations where the Incas managed to defeat Spanish conquistadors.

A terraced complex topped with carved stone panels, narrow alleys, streets of water canals and trapezoidal doorways with an occasional alpaca wandering through, reflect ancient Inca architecture and heritage. Trapezoidal isn't a magical act trapdoor to escape below but a door of cut stone where the top is smaller than the bottom. Random White Amaryllis sprouting from the cliffsides created the illusion of snowballs in seventy degree weather.

The Inca temple and fortress above the town is second in beauty only to Machu Picchu, according to our guide. Since we hadn't seen Machu Picchu yet, we couldn't voice an opinion but I didn't doubt him one bit. He mentioned that this little town is also in the midst of a tremendous struggle to save its way of life against the mass forces of tourism and development.

This is the starting point for the four-day, three-night hike known as the Inca Trail. Verandas were sandwiched between rocks and grasses dotted with palms. Plastered on the side of the mountain hung a gigantic carved design. How did they do that? We walked through Templo Del Agua, a crumbled yet still waist-high stone village, with glassless uneven windows, revealing trees and mountains beyond.

The Inca Trail is one way of reaching the fortress at Machu Picchu, just as the ancient people of the Empire arrived on foot—by stone paths, steps and tunnels that cross the Urubamba River, extending for twenty-six miles. I didn't want to know how many people and animals perished on this trail.

Some in our group decided to hike several hundred feet to the top of the terrace made with the blocks of stone that were uneven and at least one foot high per step. We decided to save our energy for the next day at Machu Picchu.

A chestnut alpaca peeked around the corner of stone ruins and startled me. A creamy alpaca wandered through one stone home easily stepping over fallen, crumbling walls.

A plot of tall green bushy stalks with rusty tops displayed a sign that read "Quinoa, Chenopodium Quinoa." Our guide shared his book of ancient drawings. We walked along a creek that meanders through the property and across a small stone bridge that we probably could have jumped from one side to the other side. Clear water looked good enough to drink but we knew we would not. The tinkle of the water was the only sound; it was all ours.

It rained the afternoon before our arrival. I took a long deep breath—I love the smell of the earth after rain, the freshness in the cleansed air. I wished I had Incan ancestry but knew that was not the case.

Standing at the foot of the terraced ceremonial center looking up, we could see that it is sandwiched in the middle of the mountains, like an Oreo cookie. Rusty-top quinoa grows on the other side of a stone wall. Our guide said that crops of ten cereals are found around the world and four are native to Peru. And here was one growing many feet tall. He said that this is the last town in the Sacred Valley before the Urubamba river plunges through steep gorges toward Machu Picchu, tomorrow's destination. Having remained hidden from the world for more than four centuries, the architectural complex of Machu Picchu or "Old Mountain" in Quechua, was discovered in 1911 by Hiram Bingham III. It is seventy-five miles from Cusco on the edge of the Urubamba canyon, seven thousand seven hundred feet above sea level. It is said that the Incas built it as a religious sanctuary made up of houses, places of worship, hydraulic systems and terraces. But this would be tomorrow. I reminded myself to stay in the moment.

About fifteen minutes on the road that would take us to Machu Picchu, Beth explained we were stopping at a brewery, yes, a beer brewery and the first one in the Sacred Valley. We were the first Collette group to stop, guinea pigs, so to speak. We arrived a little early so we walked up one flight of stairs to the rooftop which offered views of majestic mountains and the river. I looked across the road and up to the vertical cliff and saw three white capsules affixed to the side of the mountain. Rock climbers could stay overnight if one summoned enough nerve. I couldn't figure out how they would even get there, then into the white oversize oblong shell.

We were familiar with the fast-growing brewing industry because Oregon had been a leader in this self-brew business and I have a nephew who was having fun creating his own concoctions. Brewery of the Sacred Valley sits above a rushing river with the establishment surrounded by bushes of fragrant flowers, flitting birds and peacefulness. Going downstairs I stayed on the walkway taking my time to view vibrant orange trumpet flowers, another tree with stark-white trumpets, passion flower vines with exotic white petals, and a soft purple orchid with a green sprout with three purple legs that looked like a miniature alien. There were tall leafy bushes with clusters of lilies: a yellow one shaped like a long tube, a pink lily that looked like a turban, and another type that was red in the form of an open cup or bowl. All were fragrant and I could understand why many shimmering green hummingbirds, their bodies gleaming in the sunshine, whizzed by on their private freeway between flowers. The entire garden seemed alive with movement and color and the photo ops were endless.

Inside the brewery hanging on the wall were the brewmaster's framed certifications. Alongside was a chalkboard with a list of Today's Drinks: Diña

Elsa Wheat, Lion's Tears, Inti Punka IPA, plus about eight more.

The owners, brown-bearded Joe Giammaetteo and shoulder length, brown-haired pregnant wife Louisa, were an energetic millennial couple—Joe originally from Washington, DC and Louisa from LA. She attended the University of Oregon where she obtained a degree in recycling management and a wealth of information on the lack of recycling in this incredible natural country. She committed herself to educating women on how to reduce plastics in the environment. She believed education starts with the mothers who could train their children. The brewery was established partially as a way to support a local nonprofit that supports education for young girls in nearby villages.

Their Peruvian business partner had a small black tattoo on the inside of his left wrist in a shape of the sun or maybe a cross. It looked a little familiar and I needed to find out what it meant. Joe told us that after he moved to Eugene, Oregon, about fifty miles from our hometown, he met the founder of a beer manufacturer. Very impressed with the beer he sampled and sharing the same passion and values, he was soon offered a position. Joe loved creating new things and he discovered that Peru wasn't overrun by breweries and the environmental and climate conditions were perfect. He'd gone to school at George Washington University where he earned a B.S. in Environmental Science. He furthered his education with the American Brewer's Guide with a focus on Intensive Brewing Science and Engineering. Then he brought it to the Sacred Valley.

He showed us the tanks used for brewing and explained the procedures he'd instigated. They use only local ingredients like coffee, elderberry and prickly pear in some of their beers. He was a craft beer maker with a large selection of beers, ales, IPAs and stouts. My compatriots swigged down sample tastes of Chica Pils, Saco Sour, Roja, Coffee Stout and Belgian wit beer and I think one more to round it out to an even six generous tastings. A few of us non-beer tasters had the potent, not smooth ginger ale. Cookies made with oatmeal, sesame seeds and fruit were dense and tasty. We had a beer snob in the group who thought this place should be broadcast from the mountaintops having some of the best beers he'd ever tasted. I got so caught up in the total experience, I forgot to ask the meaning of the tattoo.

This couple have done what thousands of people would love to do—move to a foreign and picturesque country and open their own award-winning brewery along a river surrounded by nature. Later I read online that Joe and Louisa and son Gavin had returned to Oregon.

A little farther along we drove by several residences and small businesses before I asked Beth what the colored cloth tied on the edge of a long pole indicated. She said these poles with the cloth pieces or sometimes colored plastic shopping bags mean that the Chichería (a corn beer brewery) has chicha ready to sell; they are open for business. If they have two pieces of cloth, they also have food to sell, like choclo con queso (ears of steamed corn and a piece of cheese).

Our next stop was at El Descanso, del Valley Sagrado de los Inkas, a family-run information center; it was time for some cultural fun and more beverages going from beer tasting to fermented corn liquor. While part of the group went elsewhere, we played a game where we lobbed coins into the wooden box, one even went into the frog's mouth. Our coins disappeared forever.

We switched places with the other group, sat on picnic benches with flat baskets of colored corn on the cob, like our Indian corn, and learned from the owner that chicha does not really refer to one specific drink but rather a family of drinks comprised of corn maize and a few popular favorites along with numerous variations. We learned that during the Inca Empire women were taught the techniques of brewing chicha. In recent years, the traditionally prepared chicha is becoming increasingly rare. Only a small number of towns and villages around South America still make it. But it is still popular throughout Southern Peru, sold in every small town and in the residential neighborhoods.

Chicherias, consisting of an unused room or a corner of a patio of a home, are generally unlicensed businesses that can provide a significant boost to a family's income. Just like Beth said, they are generally identified by a bamboo pole adorned with flags, flowers, ribbons or colored plastic bags and sticking out the open door.

Normally sold in half-liter glasses to be drunk on location, or by liter if it's taken home, chicha is generally sold straight from the earthenware "chomboa" where it was brewed. For medicinal purposes, it is said to reduce blood pressure and it is being tested as an anti-inflammatory.

It was our turn to taste chicha, one pink and another one yellow, called jora, made from yellow maize. Always careful, I sipped it first and found it not terrible so politely drank a few more gulps before leaving the rest. We munched on large salted kernels of roasted corn that tasted delicious.

Then there were pens of guinea pigs. Who knew there were so many types of these cute rodents? Abisinio, Baldwin, Californiano, Coronet, Merino, Peruano, Rex, Sheltie, ending with Texel. The Sheltie breed had the same hair colors of our friend's Sheltie dogs named Cozmo and Brinkley. Baldwin and Rex types, I have no answer for. These creatures used to be eaten on a regular basis but now are more for a special Sunday dinner.

I discovered as I meandered under low hanging flowers through an archway that the family lived on the other side of the restaurant. Draped laundry hung over the second-story railing. Drying in the sunshine was a child's blue blanket, with a smiling bear's head at the top, moving slightly in the gentle breeze. Children's toys were scattered around the yard.

We had lunch at a nearby restaurant with a strikingly high ceiling made of natural wood and beams. It felt open and airy with bright yellow tablecloths and napkins with festive decorations on the walls. Instead of individual placemats they used soft green cloths the width and length of a table runner stretched across to service two people. What a smart idea and it looked pretty. Laid out for us was a buffet lunch of meats, corn, salads, a bowl of kumquats, fruits, and cakes for dessert. One colorful grain salad had a ring of unpeeled sliced cucumbers around it. Another quinoa salad had sliced round carrot circles surrounding it.

For those of us with a sweet tooth, there were many unique desserts such as flavored ice creams (lucuma is a Peruvian flavor), suspire a la limena (lemon meringue), alfajores (shortbread cookies with dulce de leche), arroz con leche (rice pudding, not for me), and mazamorra morada (spiced purple-corn jelly with fruit).

After lunch we walked back to the bus and I spotted a tree with unique long, smooth-skin pods. The smallest ones were red, the medium-size were orange, and the largest ones were about the size of a football and all brown.

Beth explained we were heading higher in elevation to a village where products and food were very hard to obtain and even harder to deliver. We would stop at a market where we could shop to take gifts to the people who lived at our next stop.

Standing on the street looking down at an open-air market, some stalls shaded by their own canopy, there were at least seven rows of twenty to thirty individual tables or plots. The market was huge, packed with all kinds of goods. Some tables were covered with blue plastic. Some ladies sat on stools and some on colorful blankets on the ground. Most older women wore dresses or skirts while younger women wore jeans.

Meat tables were lined against the cooler wall under an awning. I wanted to wander and soak it all in. The smells, colors, ambiance, and culture, all in one place. Often baskets three feet high had coca leaves, gently stacked as the leaves are fairly fragile. Common were one- to five-gallon plastic bags of beans and grains. One table displayed red, yellow, orange and green peppers much like our bell peppers but smaller and I suspected spicier.

One woman sat on a short stool, her burgundy dress touched the ground and her black braided hair hung down the middle of her back reaching her waist. She wore a top hat that reminded me of an Abraham Lincoln hat but hers was white with a three-inch wide burgundy ribbon around the base. I wondered if she changed it to match her dress each day. She sat with a knife cutting a carrot into julienne strips; don't ask me how, I thought machines did that.

Then there were the potatoes. I counted fourteen varieties in large plastic bags, like our black leaf-size bags, covering two booth spaces. One lady handed me a recipe for a dish:

Potatoes in Huancaina Sauce

5 aji Amarillo fresco/fresh yellow aji chili, 4 ripe Spanish olives pitted and cut in half, 2.2 lbs. yellow flesh potatoes, boiled, lettuce, salt and pepper. Remove seeds and veins from the aji or chili peppers and wash well with water rubbing against each other. Cut into pieces, in a medium skillet with oil, stir fry the aji, whole garlic cloves until tender. Season to taste with salt and pepper. To serve, arrange sliced potatoes on a bed of lettuce, pour sauce to cover. Garnish with sliced hard-boiled eggs and olives. Serves six.

Another stall had beans and grains in gallon clear plastic bags. There were six types of dried beans: white like a pearl, albino lima bean-shaped, white navy beans, brown ones like beans in chili sauce, two kinds of lighter tan ones, seven bags of grains, and one sack of corn kernels.

One woman wore a lilac-colored skirt that had an intricate white embroidered floral pattern, and a plain peach blouse. Two lengthy black braids on her back were linked at her waist by a soft purple ribbon.

Various shapes, sizes and colors of chilies were displayed on a table: red, purple, yellow and green ones, some as long and pointed as carrots, or as small and round as a cherry. People who don't know or aren't warned about some types and eat one for the first time usually think their mouth is on fire. A lady pointed to one called rocoto that is a lot like our bell pepper but with thicker skin. She cut one in half and it looked like a tomato with black seeds and handed me a nibble. I sniffed it first and the scent reminded me of a pine tree which immediately took me to a place in central Oregon called the Metolius River where my husband and I spent much of our lives together. Funny how a taste or smell could transport one immediately to a time and location. I had similar conceptional teleportations to a time gone by while listening to certain songs. The lady told me that this is a particularly popular pepper and is commonly diced and cooked with other ingredients or could be stuffed with rice and beans. Ground and dried options of vegetables and spices were also available which would have been fun to try at home but I doubted it would make it through the drug-sniffing dogs at customs.

Fruit bins overflowed with pomegranates as well as a round yellow unknown fruit, a dark green-skinned fruit and a lighter green fruit. I recognized mini-bananas and large avocados, about the size of a Nerf football, that they were happy to cut in half for you to eat on the spot.

We selected bags of practical oats and nuts as our share of the bounty we were about to deliver. I slipped in a bag of hard fruit-flavored candies.

Everyone generously and happily purchased items for our new Peruvian friends we were about to meet.

When we had dinner at Café Café in Lima, the owner mentioned that Peru is considered one of the finest in the world for delicious food with its diverse blend of native ingredients and traditional indigenous dishes, heavily influenced by Asian, African, Italian and other European culinary styles. Corn, maize, potatoes and beans are the main staples, along with rice, chili peppers and quinoa, and other Andean super grains. I had some interest in quinoa because our area in Oregon had been experimenting and growing it more and using it in a variety of ways. I had even seen lotion, shampoo and conditioners using quinoa. A woman at a booth selling quinoa products handed me a recipe card:

Quinoa Pilar/Pilaf

1 ½ c quinoa
1 ½ tsp vegetable oil
½ c green peppers, deveined and cut in small cubes
½ c red pepper, deveined and cut in small cubes
2 celery stacks, chopped in small cubes
2-3 T grated parmesan cheese
Dash of pepper
3 c chicken broth
1 ½ tsp olive oil
2 c carrots, peeled and cut in small cubes
3 green onions, chopped, using white and green parts
Salt

Rinse quinoa in a bowl at least five minutes, rubbing grains and letting them settle before pouring off water, until water runs clear. Drain in a fine sieve. Reserve liquid.

Pour chicken broth in a saucepan and bring to boil. Gradually add quinoa and cook 15 minutes. Reserve. Heat vegetables and olive oil in a large skillet and sauté red and green peppers, green onion, carrots, celery and parsley over high heat for 8 minutes. Add garlic and cook 1 more minute. Season to taste. Add vegetables to quinoa and stir. Season with salt pepper and parmesan cheese. Transfer to serving dish, 8 servings.

We drove farther and higher through the terraced mountains and had to slow down because of an orange Peru Department of Transportation truck hauling rocks, giving me plenty of time to look back at the gorgeous valley we'd just gone through and around several mountainous S curves. The terrain flattened into a massive plateau of green fields, blue sky and puffy white clouds, and a few mountaintops appearing about even with us. It reminded me so much of the Karen Carpenter song, "Top of the World," that I started humming and singing to myself, certainly not out loud: "Such a feeling is coming over me, there is wonder in most everything I see, not a cloud in the sky, got the sun in my eyes and I won't be surprised if it's a dream….I'm on the top of the world, looking down on creation…" The rest of the song didn't really apply to this moment in this magnificent setting. We passed a deep blue lake dotted with black shadow patches from the clouds above. Holber said Lake

Piura had been the water supply for Cusco. Miles away and barely visible, a colossal mountain was covered in snow.

As we drove down a narrow dirt road we squeezed between a young girl strolling on the right, and on the left I assumed were her herd of four smallish cows and two calves, all walking single file. The small Quecha community village of Chinchero would be the highest elevation for us on this trip, a whopping twelve thousand three hundred thirty-four feet. This Andean Indian village located high on the windswept plains of Anta is eighteen miles from Cusco, with the Cordillera Vilcabamba and the snow-capped peak of Salkantay in the western horizon. Chinchero is believed to be the mythical birthplace of the rainbow.

The village is mainly comprised of mud brick (adobe) houses and where the locals still go about their business in traditional dress. This village had been important in Inca times. The most striking remnant of this period is the massive stone wall in the main plaza which has ten trapezoidal niches. The construction of the wall and many other ruins and agriculture terraces, all of which are still in use, are attributed to Inca Yupanqui, who possibly enjoyed the town as a kind of country resort. In the main plaza, an adobe colonial church, dating from the early 17th century, was built upon the foundations of an Inca temple or palace.

We walked down a dirt road with dwellings lining each side, dogs barking and some sleeping in the warm sunshine. We were welcomed with lovely smiles at Balcon del Inka, a cooperative of hard-working women. Six ladies in full black skirts, each skirt trimmed with red ribbon about two inches wide, wore white blouses with embroidered royal blue designs and long-sleeve red coats and matching red hats. They accepted our gifts and were appreciative and thrilled with the items we'd brought from the market.

We sat on wooden benches as two men brought us coca leaf hot tea in earthenware cups that made me even hotter sitting in the direct sun in the thin air. They explained, via our translator Holber, the process of the upcoming presentation but I had a hard time concentrating because of the incredible sights. I looked back to Chinchero and the views of the town, ruins, church, llamas, mountains and more. Holber explained the meaning of the dances, and several danced and sang and persuaded a few from our group to join them. One woman had a baby, maybe six months old, safely stowed away in a woven pack on her back. He wore a bright red cap that covered his tiny ears. His mother's hat looked like our chip and dip serving bowl set, with her head sticking through the middle. Behind the entertainers were terraced green hills sharply going up, like a fjord. Dried grasses were used on an umbrella-shaped contraption for shade. For some reason, the dried grass on the roof of their building reminded me of a toupee placed on a head. After the dancing ended, two ladies then sat about six feet apart with a loom in each lap. Some strings had already been pulled, one tossed a ball of yarn to the next, then they'd weave and then the other would toss the yarn back. Back and forth and back and forth.

Two demure young girls, maybe five or six years old, helped but mostly watched and looked especially cute with their deep brown eyes and big smiles. Getting a closer look at the darling baby, I saw that he or she wore a yellow sweater with two gray stripes on the arms, a gray vest over that, wrapped in a blanket then tucked into mama's pack. The little one looked toasty and secure and I remembered even though the weather felt perfect to me, it was fall and close to winter for them. Another demonstrator showed how they color yarn with containers of crushed flowers, soil, or grain and then combine it with whatever else they have to make the hues. Purple- , red- , and burgundy-colored yarns for a blanket were being woven on a narrow loom about ten feet long.

After our demonstration finished each lady went and stood by their handmade products. We found them to be excellent quality and reasonably priced. I had to show my appreciation by purchasing a sunglasses case and a small bag that I knew would be perfect for carrying a few things when going to a neighbor's party or a dinner where I didn't need more than reading glasses and lip gloss. I wasn't too picky as everything was high quality, plus I wanted to support them.

Andean villages we visited had modest assorted handicrafts and some had larger offerings. Buying direct in the villages probably does the people who created the objects the most good. The kind people lined up on the dusty road waving farewell to us as we departed, and we waved back. At 3:40 p.m. the sun dropped, now hidden by fifteen thousand-foot peaks.

Altitudes can affect people in different ways. There's a whole slew of remedies, cures, preventive measures and therapies for altitude sickness and lots of advice from those who had traveled before us. All the hotels and buses have oxygen tanks and masks if needed. We did not hesitate to do anything we could to prevent pounding headaches, nausea and shortness of breath.

Since we'd had a generous late lunch, we deemed two bowls of thick chicken quinoa soup adequate enough, hoping to prevent waking up hungry at 2 a.m. We skipped a big dinner.

Some went to bottle-feed baby llamas. Instead we hiked to the far end of the property looking for a two-story planetarium that a local man who loved astronomy had built. He opened for our group on a full-moon clear night when we hoped to see planets, craters on the moon and stars through a large telescope mounted for viewing the southern night sky.

The planetarium took up the entire ground floor. Up one set of stairs, mounted on a platform stood the biggest telescope I'd ever seen. Our very own scientist of the stars told us some common terms associated with telescopes: concave, lens or mirror that causes light to spread out; convex, lens or mirror that causes light to come together to a focal point; field of view, the area of the sky that can be seen through the telescope with a given eyepiece. He had a special adapter that fit over the eyepiece for use in high-power lunar, solar and planetary photography displayed downstairs. This was already totally cool.

Each one of us politely took turns as we each squeezed one eye closed while gazing with the other through the large round eyepiece at planets as he moved the telescope ever so slightly. We viewed the rings of Saturn, planets Jupiter and Mars, and the bright full moon plus some distant nebula spotted through the high-powered telescope. With no light pollution everything appeared crystal clear. Several constellations, including the Southern Cross and Scorpio, were prominent in the black, clear sky decorated with gazillions of little dots of light, some brighter than others and some twinkled with colors. Layers upon layers, the stars appeared brighter or dimmer depending on distance.

He explained that we were also able to see The Crane above the Southern Fish, and the Ship's Keel that was below the Ship's Sails just to the right of the Ship's Stern. In my methodical, administrative left-brain, I just couldn't see those creative, artsy right-brain stars patterns. I saw only mind-blowing, phenomenal, wondrous, hard-to-articulate, zillions of luminaries. Even showing us a cheat-sheet chart on the wall, I was unable to see the figures.

We'd seen Northern Lights before so I wondered aloud about the Southern Lights or the Aurora Australis and he said it is highly unlikely, requiring us to go farther south like to the tip of South America, Australia, New Zealand or Antarctica.

Going back downstairs, we sat on cement benches surrounding the room and reclined against the wall with heads tilted up, looking at the white convex ceiling while watching a presentation on astronomy during a short and well-done movie that he produced.

Back in the hotel lobby, two local artists had set up a display of their handmade items. I struck up a conversation with Angelica, and bought a woven clutch purse after she showed me the process she used in making it. It took her hours to make and I paid so little overall even with giving a bit more than the asking price. She gave me a turquoise stone-carved piece on a thin black cord. It was the same design I'd seen on fabrics and tattoos on a couple of men. She explained that traditionally the Chakana (or "Cruz cuadrada" means four-sided cross in Spanish) represents the constellation of the Southern Cross. According to the opinion of the Old Andean population, this, as the center of the universe, was easy to find when they looked up at the sky at night. There are twelve points on the Inca Cross: #1) Love, Trust, Connections, Acknowledgment, Protection, Awareness, and #7 at the bottom, Happiness, then Passion, Expression, Responsibility, Productivity and ending at #12, Present. These are the points of the Inca Cross, authentically with the N in Inca printed backwards.

The Inca Cross is a strong symbol of the old cultures of the Andes and is considered the most complete, holy, geometrical design of the Incas. This symbol is often found in old palaces and holy centers in the Andes in Peru and Bolivia. The Chakana has had, and still has, a considerable meaning to the Incas and also represents many meanings in its design.

This unique experience and the observatory made this hotel stay even more enjoyable. I wish we could have stayed a few extra days here. But I could hardly contain myself because of everything I'd learned and experienced today but also for what lay ahead—Machu Picchu. I soaked in the extra-large tub not knowing if we'd have another one this impressive on this trip.

Today, April 27, 2016, we would be in Machu Picchu. It was also a special day because it is the birthday of one of my brothers and also his second daughter, and of my great grandmother. This would be a significant day forever.

We boarded our motorcoach early for an easy ride with spectacular views through the mountainous countryside past the brewery, and looking straight up I spotted those three hanging pods glued to the mountainside and could see how they were attached by three steel poles anchored to the rocks. There was still no way I'd stay there. At the train station, we all took pictures by the sign for Machu Picchu.

At 7:38 a.m. we boarded the Machu Picchu Vista Dome train, which meant large windows on the side and on the top of the train car. We slid into Coach D, seats 39 and 41 on PERURAIL in luxury class with woven table coverings, surrounded by open windows, complete with reclining seats. As we pulled away from the station and chugged slowly across the glistening rushing river, the sun popped up over the mountaintops.

The Urubamba Gorge running from the Sacred Valley to Machu Picchu is so treacherous and serpentine that the Incas built a paved stone highway up the mountain. This route, known as the Inca Trail, rises and falls through ecosystems and high passes before making a dramatic entry to Machu Picchu's legendary Sun Gate. As we rode by the Inca Trail and the famous bridge, we could see hikers and their Sherpa guides embarking on the hike of a lifetime. I was grateful to be sitting in first class in the vista dome car. We rumbled by terraces, old structures, more modern facilities mostly for hikers, through valleys that flattened temporarily for plots of crops, farms and trees, then back to squeezing through mountains. Once when the river flattened I could see some ducks floating on the river and Holber said they are Torrent Ducks, black with white chest and head and orange bill and feet. Evidently they prefer fast-flowing rivers.

We ate a lunch consisting of a small banana, crunchy corn, half of a pomegranate, a small sandwich and a dense cake with chocolate swirls complemented by silverware and napkins and beverages. Meanwhile, we passed hamlets, people hiking, mountaintops with scattered glaciers, cows grazing and more and more mountains with more and more snow but just toward to the top. We followed the river then went inland. llamas were common and a man walking in a field of tall crops wouldn't have been noticeable except for his bright red vest. He reminded me of a red ladybug in our backyard. A hydroelectric plant created a low waterfall. Big boulders were partially hidden in greenish-brown water.

We got off the train in the small town of Aguas Calientes, the town before reaching Machu Picchu. This little town is basically an island, separated from all roads, surrounded by mountains, cliffs and rivers. Vendors weren't far away and after Beth's recommendation to prevent sunstroke, I purchased a bright pink hat with, of course, Machu Picchu embroidered in the front.

Our luggage would be taken to the hotel for us and would be in our rooms when we returned from our mountain exploration. Hotel Sumaq is located across the street from the Vilcanota River at the edge of the Hiram Bingham Highway, which I laughed about when I read the sign. Basically, this highway is a dirt road full of potholes and large rocks and wasn't like any highway we'd been on but conveniently only ten minutes of an uneven walk from the train station.

As we walked through a maze of handicrafts in an outdoor market, we were told to keep blinders on because this wasn't the time for shopping. We were on a mission to get to Machu Picchu. We crossed one of three footbridges over the Rio Aguas Calientes, a roaring river coming down the mountain, then continued walking below another bridge, to wait in line for a shuttle bus which would take us up to the Inca sanctuary.

A four-mile zigzag road trip in a bus that was one grade up from a jalopy took about twenty-five minutes to the site. In one area, PDOT workers dressed in neon orange vests and pants were installing a rock wall on the outer edge of one section in a curve of the road. I wondered how many people drove off the curve before it had been deemed prudent to install the wall. This was one time in my life I shouldn't have taken the window seat.

This drive is not for the faint of heart. It's a good thing that our driver has probably driven this narrow, bumpy road full of hairpin turns thousands of times, and could probably do it with his eyes closed, or so I hoped, because he could hardly see through the dirt-encrusted windshield.

There are no guardrails. Beyond the edge, it dropped straight down thousands of feet and was a shoulder-less dirt road where the driver had to pull over to the edge to allow oncoming traffic past or to back up. It scared the bejeebers out of me. I closed my eyes and prayed, really hard, and muttered to myself that if I'm dying here in the Peruvian Andes, at least I was already that much closer to heaven.

Mark suggested I open my eyes and I snapped a quick photo of a large sign, "Parque Argueológico Nacional de Machupicchua Patrimonio Culteral de la Humanidad, Bienvenido Welcome Bienvenue." We were officially in the national park!

Now keeping my eyes wide open I saw several people in small groups walking on the dusty, narrow, winding road which supposedly would take them around ninety minutes to the top. Peeking through trees I could see even more terraces, and a glimpse of the familiar shapes of the famous Machu Picchu mountains. Far below, the river followed the base of the mountains. This was unbelievably better than watching it on National Geographic.

Getting off the bus I exhaled a big sigh of relief and almost kissed the ground. I was dressed in a purple, aqua and teal medium-weight, long-sleeve cotton blouse (my tribute to colorful Peruvian clothing), cotton pants and heavy-duty walking shoes, along with my crossbody Baggalinni bag containing a bottle of water, sunscreen, lip gloss and cell phone for a backup camera. And, of course, wearing my fashionista bright pink totally touristy hat, I felt ready to embark. Draped across the front of me in the other direction hung my new water bottle holder with sixteen ounces of water. In my left hand was another spur-of-moment purchase, a bright blue walking stick; my camera was secured in my right hand. I felt totally prepared. It would turn out, however, that I would need both hands free for grasping anything possible while climbing up and down knee-high blocks of stone.

We smeared on #40 sunscreen and the oddly satisfying smell reminded me of when my mom slathered me head to toe at the beach or in arid central Oregon or when playing at home. I have a fair complexion and she always took care of me. It's odd how our minds can play tricks on us through smells, tastes and music.

Mistake #1: Hauling too much stuff and not bringing enough water. We had been told to double our normal intake; double should have been quadruple. My faulty thought process included knowing there were no toilets in the ruins, not even an outdoor privy. So how is one to drink all that water with nowhere to dispose of it except to walk back out at least of a quarter mile to the entrance, down a flight of stairs, then return, all in high altitude?

Mistake #2: Not knowing that in high altitudes, somehow water is absorbed into your system and very little comes out. An added plus is that it is putting oxygen into your body.

Holber got our tickets and we had one final bathroom stop before about three hours hiking around the ruins. As is commonplace around the globe, we knew to have coins for entry and tissues with us when using the public toilets. Now we were really ready. Tanks on empty, I drank my first bottle of water that was tucked away in my purse.

My husband channeling Indiana Jones, and me, Marion, were complete with proper mountain climbing attire with hats, but minus Indy's whip and gun. My Indy wore cotton pants and a sensible, breathable long-sleeve cotton shirt, in case of bugs but there were none this time of year. He brought the video camera in a square bag and draped it over one shoulder keeping his right hand available to help his Marion.

Mistake #3: It was now evident; we brought too much stuff. My head wasn't throbbing but instead sort of tingling with a random piercing stab in my left ear. I felt slightly assured that people lived at these elevations and had for thousands of years, so I certainly could for a few hours.

Off we went walking on a dirt path, about two people wide, actually one of the hundreds of terraces. When we came to the first structure, we entered through an archway with stone walls about ten feet tall, then threaded our way on a narrow rock path with more high walls. We went around a corner, ducking under the rock ledge then shinnying through more skinny spaces and around sharp corners. We weren't even there yet! Several people had to remove their backpacks to squeeze through the tight openings.

Flabbergasted, my mouth dropped open about three inches when I first laid eyes on the mysterious 15th century Inca city, Machu Picchu. I glanced from side-to-side and saw hundreds of abandoned buildings resting on a slope beneath stark peaks surrounded by puffy clouds, almost eight thousand feet above sea level. It doesn't take much imagination to understand why Inca royalty would choose to build a hideaway or retreat for nobility high in the middle of nowhere. Now this is only a theory as no one knows for sure, but that's the latest Yale University researcher's take on it.

Holber said that generally Machu Picchu can be divided into two parts, the agricultural sector and the urban sector. The agricultural sector consists of an impressive network of terraced fields and steps where people were milling around, sitting and soaking in the views. This area gets a lot of rain so the terraces, along with a sophisticated water and drainage system, also help prevent the city from sliding off of the mountain.

The urban section has about a hundred fifty structures, including important temples and buildings, many with astronomical alignments. Looking at the rock complex commonly referred to as the citadel, it was hard to believe this entire place had been built without iron tools, mortar, or anything with wheels to move the heavy rocks. Many of the rocks weigh more than fifty tons and were either chiseled from the mountainside or pushed up to the site by hundreds of men. The Incas are renowned for their sophisticated masonry and used a technique called ashlar where rocks were perfectly cut and then fused together. These people were so darn impressive.

Machu Picchu has three primary structures: The Intihuatana, the Temple of the Sun, and the Room of the Three Windows. Most of the outlying buildings have been reconstructed in order to give tourists a better idea how they originally appeared. Holber explained that the sun, moon, water and weather were revered by the Incas—they drive the city's efficient layout. Of course, adding to the intrigue and mystery is that archaeologists still do not know when or why it was built. Or what actually happened to the Incas.

Getting to one of the New Seventh Wonders of the World isn't easy but it is worth it. At first sighting, I thought of the undoubtedly gobsmacked explorer Hiram Bingham in 1911, who stumbled across this site only one hundred years ago while looking for the Lost City of the Incas. What a shocker he had.

There is no mention of it in any of the colonial chronicles and it lay forgotten for centuries until Hiram Bingham discovered it. He was a thirty-six-year-old adventurer who ended up being both a United States Senator and the inspiration for the character Indiana Jones, who came to Peru to find Vilcabamba, the legendary Lost City of the Incas. This had been the jungle hideaway, well-described by Spanish soldiers, to which Mano Inca and his followers retreated following their unsuccessful rebellion against the Spanish in 1537. Bingham began his search walking down the newly built road along the Rio Urubamba (now the train line) and asking locals if they knew of any ruins along the way.

Local resident Melchor Arteaga led Bingham to the vine-covered site, which Bingham would return to in 1912 and 1915 to excavate. He was convinced, to the end of this life, that Machu Picchu was the Lost City of the Incas. But historians are now certain he wasn't correct at all. A wealth of supporting evidence indicates the real Vilcabamba to be hidden farther into the jungle, which Bingham also visited but dismissed at the time as too insignificant. He discovered more than one hundred human skeletons in cemeteries around Machu Picchu and subsequent research on the remains proved that half were men and half were women.

The latest theory which appears to be gaining widespread agreement is that Machu Picchu really was a winter retreat built by Inca Pachacutec in the mid-15th century.

My second thought was of my father who, in 1943 in World War II, was one of the first soldiers in the Army's 10th Mountain Division training for the Italian Alps conflict with the Germans. He'd told me stories about training at Camp Hale, high in the Colorado Rockies, at nine thousand two hundred feet elevation. If that wasn't hard enough, they had to carry ninety-pound rucksacks while on snow skis carrying a rifle. If my dad could do it, so could I.

Already breathing heavily carrying just my water bottle and lightweight purse and camera, I quickly discovered Mistake #4: Not bringing another bottle of water. Mistake #5: Not bringing a fourth bottle of water.

We all took photos of each other with the famous scenery in the background. I had made a sign before we left home honoring special California friends who'd come a few months earlier and showed us photos and shared some tips. We held up a "Chuy & Deanna, We Love You," and texted them fond memories when we were back in civilization. We stood where millions of photos have been taken except these had us in the frame.

A worker painstakingly plucked lichen from in between rocks that eventually would be tested to find out what he'd found. Natural plants grew and a

Christmas-red and green one stood about five feet tall.

Then we saw a space under an A-frame-shaped rock ledge with a short staircase that had probably been used for storage. It was dark inside but I could faintly see three doors. It was the Temple of Mother Earth or the mausoleum. We went through rooms of a building in which one room had two water catchers each carved in stone on the floor, or maybe the stones came that way. It would be a perfect birdbath on our patio at home. It was the Mirrors of Waters. Streams of water flowed down a rock wall and it is called The Fountains. Narrow paths separated rock walls and buildings, and glancing through windows I could see alpacas grazing on hardy grasses in the higher plateaus.

We toured the site with guide Holber escorting us around because you must enter with a certified guide. You can't just wander in on your own and the number of people who can enter at one time is regulated.

I took pictures of famous mountains with green grasses and one terrace after another. A brunette llama stood among boulders on the side of the mountain that dropped off sharply. One llama had a brown body with an all-white neck and three white legs, yet its fourth leg was the same brown color as its body with an even darker brown head.

In the bright sunshine was a transparent moth or butterfly shimmering in iridescent green, blue and pink hues flying toward some flowery bushes. It fluttered rapidly around the flowers. It was trimmed entirely in black with transparent wings and black veins with red at the base of its body. Then it flitted away. I didn't even get a photo, instead marveling at its craftsmanship for just a few seconds. I checked my guidebook later and it is called a Sylphina Angel.

The delicate pink and purple feathery flowers framed a lot of my pictures including The Temple of the Sun, all its walls standing without a roof. Many delicate pink and purple wild orchids drooped from stems and popped out of gaps in rock walls. Holber told me that there are over thirty-five hundred types of orchids in the world with three hundred fifty in this area alone. At the entrance of The Temple of the Condor, a two-inch beetle of some kind had a bright yellow tail matching its shoulders, a black head with antennae and legs and a bright purple shell on its back. I did not crunch it as I might have done at home.

Taking more pictures of colorful blazing flora, I felt like something was looking at me and indeed, a camouflaged green and white hummingbird, the color of celery with a dark tail, stared right at me. It didn't seem to care that I had been taking its picture.

Up ahead were dozens and dozens of uneven steps and hundreds of feet to the House of the Guardian that we didn't climb. At the Temple of the

Three Windows, I peered through a square window seeing more terraces and dwellings on green mountains. Closer to the rock wall that made a terrace, a llama stood against a rock scratching its back. This gave me a terrific reference for how tall the terrace walls really are, probably eight to ten feet high.

Gawking wide-eyed in amazement standing on a terrace looking down into a grassy area, I saw the Funerary Stone, a huge chiseled rock at the base of a row of terraces. It looked like a baby carriage without wheels. Some motion caught my eye and I noticed a large black bird soaring in the wind currents, then lost it when it hugged the rock cliffs, but as it flew back into the open I pointed it out to Holber. He confirmed our first condor. Then a second one came into view. Holber told me it is the largest flying bird in the world, some having a wingspan almost eleven feet. This bird is really a large black vulture with white feathers around the base of its neck and large white patches on the wings. These were way too high to determine male or female but he suspected they were a pair as they mate for life. These birds are the clean-up crew as they prefer carcasses of meat; they are not vegetarians. Some have lived over fifty years, he added.

I sat on a rock wall drinking the last several drops of water, watching the two condors soaring higher and higher on the heat thermals, soaking it all in and basically zoning out. I had a feeling like this once before in the Galápagos Islands, being one bazillion times better than a National Geographic program. Below me stood a structure of collapsing walls with some window frames still intact. It stood roofless like other structures but I could see the rock ruins that had previously been complete walls. A lone tree valiantly grew out from the top of one corner.

By now we knew we should have been drinking not just twice the recommended amount of water but really four to five times as much. According to a Peruvian doctor, the altitude pills, which we'd both taken, depleted water causing no retention.

It had become a habit started some years ago as my dear friend Heather introduced us to a way to create a special memory by taking a selfie, turning our backs to the sun and taking a picture of our shadows on the ground. We took one here, too, then sadly bid farewell to one of the most unique places on planet Earth.

We drove down the narrow, frightening road, this time on the inside against the mountain brushing by ferns and branches, taking out anything else in our way, which we almost did coming around a corner as a rickety bus was making its way up. Both drivers slammed on the brakes and we ended stopping about a foot from the front of the other vehicle. He backed down and moved over so we could inch by.

Sumaq Hotel, a beautiful modern hotel on the river and a few blocks from the downtown, welcomed us with a cold drink and a snack on white china trays as we sat on a tan sofa with hand-crafted pillows in orange, red, yellow and tan stripes with a matching rug and cloth napkins. We nibbled on rolled corn chip strips, swirls of green avocado purée, something yellow, and a square inch of a cold vegetable appetizer. We drank iced tea, the first of the trip.

Our spacious room had two queen beds and three doors onto the balcony overlooking the dirt road, a row of trees then the roaring river. Goldish-tan square tiles made up the cool floor. The bathroom was done in warm goldstones with a shower in the tub, bowl-sink on the countertop with an excellent selection of toiletries in bottles shaped like a guitar, and plush towels. Some of these bottles of goodies disappeared into the gallon Ziplock baggy joining others I had taken earlier in the trip. When exceptional local products are presented, it is my habit to take them and use them at home as a nice remembrance of our foreign travels. But they had to be extraordinary and these were. A tray of edible goodies decorated with a purple orchid welcomed us in the room. Octagonal chocolates, kumquats, five nuts, three large white raisins or maybe dried apricots, a round truffle ball and something like a chocolate orange stick about three inches long were consumed quickly.

Knowing we had limited time here and with Indy wanting a rest, I totally acknowledged the hike had been exhilarating but exhausting, yet I only had several hours to see the town and buy a few things such as the must-have fridge magnet. I lost Indy as soon as he lay down on the bed plus he wasn't feeling terrific.

Maybe I'd encounter some colorful doors, my obsession, and hoping something might happen around one. This illness started with our first trip to Scotland in 1997, searching for my roots and visiting friends Joyce and Andy. I call this regular travel occurrence my made-up word, "graviosity" (curiosity and gravity). My husband had seen me in action before on many adventures where I simply HAD to discover what might lay behind or through that colorful door. That's why I'd learned it was best that I discover these revelations on my own.

Leaving the hotel walking toward town, I veered off the dirt road or Bingham Highway, where eight chickens were napping on a pedestrian bridge that consisted of two planks of wood. I heard a familiar fast rapping on wood and saw a woodpecker on a tree by a house. It had a Grey Poupon mustard body with a small red patch on the top of its head. It was a Golden-Olive Woodpecker. I love looking for birds and hoped to see many more the following morning as we'd signed for a bird and butterfly tour at 7:00 a.m.

An elderly woman seated on her sagging front step greeted me in broken English. I raised my hand, smiled and said, "Hola." I felt a little proud of myself that I could speak at least one word in Peruvian. All of the houses were well-worn with flaking paint and one had a partially open red door, about the size for a hobbit to enter. I dared not. Another house's bottom half was painted a soft green with the top portion a goldish-yellow with a wood front door and faded red step. Another house was painted vivid green with a burgundy door, only half of the door showing above the sidewalk. Apparently, one would have to turn the doorknob to open it, push it wide, then step down into the house.

Two years earlier, my parents and I did Ancestry DNA tests. I knew we didn't have one drop of South American blood in us. But on this trip sometimes my roots tingled just a bit yet not as strongly as when I explored Scotland, Ireland, Norway and Germany, stepping through countries of my forefathers and mothers. My best guess is the feelings were tied to the closeness of nature...hopefully not altitude sickness.

In no time at all, I was standing at a remarkable statue that seemed to command me to stop and look at him, anchoring a plaza called Manco Cápac in the center of this small town. He is the Inca warrior Pachacutec with arms out, and in his right hand is a rod or spear with a weathervane-looking thing at the top proudly protecting his land. The founder and first emperor of the Inca empire, he stands on a round rock pedestal that is a fountain where spouts of water burst forth rising around his waist, somewhat like Old Faithful on cue. On the ground below stand two Inca women statues and one is Mama Ocllo. In Inca mythology she was deified as a mother and fertility goddess. According to popular folklore, Manco and Mama began teaching the Inca people how to construct homes and Mama taught women the art of spinning thread, sewing, and household duties.

I walked across a bridge past bars and restaurants to the market for a bit of shopping and got a fridge magnet and postcards. By the train station were more Inca statues of men and women. One statue is an Inca king named Atahualpa, carved in stone. He looked different because he wore a long robe trailing to his feet and dropping around the three-foot tall pedestal. His spear at the top was gold matching the round medallion around his neck resting on his chest, and three gold leaves crowned the top of his head. Another king, Tupac Yupanqui, was similarly dressed but looked younger and his left foot was a step higher than the right. King after king was identically attired. King Huir Acochia, crossed-legged with his robe gathered at his knees and wearing sandals, obviously wasn't as prestigious since the only thing gold on him was the round medallion. There is a small chapel called Virgen Del Carmen with a gold altar in the front window. A stone cross stands to the right of a bell tower that is several stories tall and looms over the chapel.

I noticed some swallows overhead that were blue and white, not dark like ours. Other birds that I could easily identify were finches, sparrows and wrens, all different colors than ours at home. I was hoping a Cock-of-the-Rock would show itself in the morning.

Some boys were playing soccer in a field as I walked by an opened wooden door showing orange and black square tile flooring. A wooden door at the front of an orange house was next to a bright blue house. A tall flower with a single thick red stem had green circular pencil-thin cone leaves.

There is an iron artwork map on the ground and a fountain with a snake surrounding it with a condor on top, and the first set of three recycling bins I'd seen complete with Inca designs. There is also an Inca statue with a mountain lion at the base. Two vehicles waited as construction on the bridge had them temporarily stopped but first across was a person pulling a hand-cart with five huge colorful plastic bags full of whatever, walking toward our four-story hotel.

I returned to find my explorer feeling rested but he decided to pass on the Peruvian cooking class and possibly dinner. The menu didn't sound appealing to him so he requested some pasta if I could bring it to him. I felt okay, drank a bottle of water and said I'd take care of his request and be back later.

A cooking demonstration making ceviche and the famous, now appreciated and refreshing Pisco Sours, was entertaining but I took just one small bite of the ceviche only to be polite because the smell didn't sit well with me. We were all given a brown hotel apron as a memento of our unique time. They shared their popular recipe for the drink of Peru.

Pisco Sours
3 ounces Pisco, 1 oz. lime juice, 1 oz sweet sugar syrup, 1 egg white, 5-8 ice cubes. Place ingredients in a shaker or blender and shake for ten seconds. Then using a strainer, pour the contents into a glass. Finally, add two drops of Angostura bitters on top of the foam. Yummmmm.

Ceviche is Peru's flagship dish and comes from fresh fish marinated in salted lime juice. I'm not providing this recipe because it makes me queasy just thinking about it and what came next.

Dinner at the hotel restaurant according to the menu would be an "exquisite trip of entrées, cappuccino of olluco with duxelles of vegetables, ceviche of trout marinated with passion fruit and tabbouleh of quinoa with thin slices of avocado." I had "Trigoto of the Valley, with vegetable kebabs on rice and Andean chimichurri."

It all tasted ok but I wasn't quite feeling up to par. Too much sun and elevation, I presumed. One travel-mate asked, "How did you get so sunburned wearing sunscreen and a hat?" Good question, I thought, as my stomach started making gurgling sounds. I knew I had put on plenty of sunscreen as

Beth and Holber had repeatedly warned us that even though maybe not hot, those of us with west coast pale skin would burn easily and rapidly. I hadn't taken any chances plus I wore my newly purchased wide-brim pink hat embroidered with "Machu Picchu." I'd certainly wear it again, maybe picking strawberries or weeding the garden at home. We were prepared for wind, rain and sunshine and were blessed to have the sunshine with poufy white clouds most of the trip. We could tell by the standing water in puddles that it had poured the day before our arrival.

I tasted a couple bites of the trio of desserts: small chocolate doughnuts on pear cream, chicha ice cream with tangerine, and lastly cherimoya, a delicacy about the size of an apple without the smooth skin and had a creamy texture like custard. But I wasn't that hungry, again undoubtedly from the altitude. I ordered some takeout for my husband, who now reported he felt hungry when I returned to our room around 8:30 p.m. He ate pasta on the balcony overlooking the sights.

I stood there also overlooking the loudest, most violent river I had ever seen, with boulders about the size of a car. Standing side by side, we couldn't hear each other talk; we could only point to show something of interest. They must have used quadruple-pane glass at the hotel because the sound was barely noticeable inside.

We signed up for the 7 a.m. bird and butterfly walk the next morning, as we enjoyed both species and expected to see dozens of different types and hopefully the infamous Cock-of-the-Rock. Maybe we'd even see some one-of-a-kind hummingbirds that only live in the Andes, or some colorful butterflies, a few about the size of my hand, judging by the pictures in the guidebook.

We were both sound asleep until about ten o'clock when a déjá vu moment happened to me. I awoke suddenly as it started in my toes and worked upward to the top of my head in a few seconds. Not a typical mid-life hot flash but a blazing, sizzling skin-pricking heat-flash. If this was anything like before, I knew I had about twenty seconds to get to the bathroom. I had likely contracted a norovirus or maybe food poisoning, but I knew this wasn't just the plain old stomach flu. This virus causes inflammation of the stomach or intestines and unfortunately I'd had past dealings with this nasty, horrible bug.

Taking a seat and grabbing the trash bin, fortunately plastic, this began round after round of vomiting and diarrhea. Parched and burning, to frosty and shivering back to scalding in seconds, head pounding, body aching, could there be anything else? There would be.

From several past experiences and information I'd read before from the CDC, I knew it usually developed twelve to forty-eight hours after being exposed and recovery was usually one to three days, not including gaining back strength and stamina. This nasty bug is spread through contaminated food. It can also be spread on contaminated surfaces or through air from an infected person. Prevention involves proper hand washing, and disinfection of contaminated surfaces and not touching your face. I knew I hadn't been washing my hands enough.

It is common with millions of cases a year and usually two hundred thousand deaths a year worldwide. I knew all this because I'd had it several times before over the past thirty years, twice while traveling, now three, and other times in my own hometown, so luckily had been at home to recover. This is the nasty bacteria that has locked down hotels, retirement facilities, hospitals, and most commonly reported on cruise ships. We had been on over thirty cruises over the years and fortunately I'd never gotten it then.

After a miserable night and completely exhausted, at 6:30 a.m. my husband went to the lobby where he met up with Beth who called for a doctor. This doctor had already been at the hotel around 3 a.m., as another traveler had been ill, hers from altitude sickness.

Dr. Molero Tegiera didn't speak any English but his assistant Dr. Gar Raul did, and along with patience, sympathy and meds, they promised I would be better soon. And it wasn't altitude sickness.

Doctor T. injected a needle into the only vein he could find in my left hand, slowly dripping hydration through the I.V. back into my queasy system, then gave me white tablets (Cipro) to take twice a day for five days in case it might be bacterial instead of viral. This meant four yellow tablets together at one time to try to kill any parasite if that might be the case, one brown tablet every eight hours for two days taken twenty minutes before meals, for what I didn't ask, and their version of Imodium, that magic orange tablet, a maximum of eight in a day. I swallowed all eight over two days.

I tried to look at the bright side. I mean, who gets to have two handsome Peruvian doctors with them in their hotel room for close to three hours of undivided attention? Even though hooked up to an I.V. of an elixir of who knows what good stuff, I appreciated their attention through my bouts of napping. I could hear muffled talking in the background but didn't understand a thing. Indy stayed in the room with me the entire time not even going for breakfast.

Two hundred sixty US cash dollars later for their medical attention in our hotel room converted to an observation room and treatment center, I felt a bit better. At least the worst of the symptoms had stopped. Then I stood up.

Extremely weak, I could hardly stand for any amount of time. Beth took care of late hotel checkout at noon instead of 11 a.m. We needed to be at the train station before 2 o'clock for the 2:50 p.m., two-hour train ride, then another two-hour bus ride back to Cusco. It would be a long day. This did give plenty of time for those who wanted to buy trinkets and explore the area for the last time. I just wanted to sleep.

In spite of this blip in our adventure, I felt extremely grateful it happened now and not one day earlier because I would have missed Machu Picchu. I kept telling myself: I saw Machu Picchu, I walked around Machu Picchu, I did Machu Picchu.

Doctor T. insisted I couldn't walk the half mile, normally a breeze, to the train so they called for a wheelchair and escort. Now, I am not a small person and Peruvians are. I walked gingerly down several steps and sat in the wheelchair when a nice petite man, to whom I apologized many times, pushed me on a gradual incline, not a convenient decline, and serpentined through a rock and pothole obstacle course. About thirty minutes later I gingerly walked onto the train.

My husband shook his hand and placed a large wad of cash into his palm thanking him very much. I went directly into my first-class seat, this time not at the window but on the aisle just in case I needed a quick departure. Mark slid into the window seat. This was the first time I'd ever given up a window seat, but sitting on the aisle made more sense. I put my bag down on the tabletop, placed my right hand on my bag, lowered my head and fell asleep.

I woke once, confused seeing something in bright clothing sauntering down the aisle with a scary animal mask. All the colors fused together, and in my delusional state thought it might be a clown but why would there be a creepy clown on board? I missed all the incredible scenery, the Andes and the river, but fortunately I'd seen it all on the way up. I didn't eat or drink anything. I didn't want to take any chances and knew the I.V. fluids had hydrated me enough for a few hours.

Here's what I missed on the ride down the mountain that I saw photos of later: Indeed, there had been a sort of clown. Well, a man in a tiger mask, dressed in wildly bright garb with a crab on his jacket, portraying some historical figure while walking back and forth down the aisle. So, I did see something weird and wasn't hallucinating. Whew.

Staff and guides put on a fashion show of high-quality, handmade garments that we were welcome to purchase. One woman wore a black coat trimmed in white; a guide wore a tan wool sweater; a woman was in a blue and white cloak that was royal blue underneath.

My kind husband played photographer chronicling peaks and greenery, the river, the Inca Trail and bridge, while another woman displayed a stunning red and black dress, the top decorated in Peruvian designs of zigzags, and solid red from the waist down.

When we got off the train I knew we had another two-hour bus ride to the hotel so hopefully if nothing went in, nothing would come out. I slept most of the ride slouched against the window and my philosophy worked, I made it.

Two bottles of orange Gatorade were handed to me as we waited for our room at our final hotel. Someone said to drink them both and I did. We checked into what would be the smallest room of the entire trip—two double beds and a TV on the wall, but a window that opened for fresh air and overlooked colorful flowers and a bubbling fountain in the courtyard. My knight in shining armor went to a small market close by and returned with bottled water of San Luis sin gas, meaning no bubbles, and Gatorade to replenish my weakened body with electrolytes. My husband drank more fluids, too.

That day is a blur but that night my dear protector thought I should try to eat something or I'd not have the strength to fly back to Lima, let alone the long flight home in a few days. To appease him, we went to the hotel restaurant and they had chicken soup on the menu. Evidently it's popular for those with altitude sickness, too. The combination of sodium, protein and soothing broth tasted like comfort food and the four spoonfuls hit the spot.

I slept well and didn't move all night, resulting in about twelve hours of sleep which meant I missed out on the tour around Cusco and my husband stayed in the room with me, sleeping also and watching nothing in particular on the TV. I kept the shades drawn but the window open so I could hear the bubbling water from the large fountain. At some point, we needed to pack to fly from Cusco back to Lima then home. Nothing fit back into the luggage as nicely as when we left and I didn't even care. We crammed everything in and I put delicate items in my canvas bag, secure in cushy bubble wrap.

I decided to give breakfast a try and although a plentiful spread, I didn't eat much. This day turned out to be pretty boring and I didn't have the energy or interest in a full day of exploration riding on a bus. Beth checked in with us several times offering help and letting us know what was going on. About half of our group had some type of affliction from the altitude.

That afternoon my husband decided fresh air would be good so we ventured out around the neighborhood seeing colorful buildings with tile rooftops. We dilly-dallied on cobblestone streets, peeked in a church, saw lush ferns, cactus, rock arches and a baby blue Volkswagen bug from the sixties. A large double bright blue door with round Inca designs on each panel caught my attention and I hoped somebody could come out so I could peer in but it didn't happen, and if I loitered too much longer it might make someone nervous and call the police. The home had a matching blue second story balcony. Late afternoon we returned to our hotel restaurant for more chicken soup and I ate most of it. I felt that I might be returning to normal as all the fluids were now flowing through on a regular basis and I felt rehydrated, only tired.

The next morning standing on the front steps of our hotel, low and behold, out of nowhere appeared the same man who had taken our pictures when we got off the plane days earlier. He knew right where to find us and of course we bought the photos of us superimposed on Machu Picchu scenery and other attractions. I bought a watercolor of Machu Picchu city and mountains with two condors overhead and a llama in the foreground. The artist is a local Picasso named Sondori who packed it in a tube that I would hand-carry home.

We boarded LAN and said farewell to the Sacred Valley and Cusco and flew back over the majestic Andes into Lima. We bussed to the Larco Museum, a former mansion built on the site of a pre-Columbian temple. The museum offers a collection of over three thousand years of ceramics, textiles and precious metal artifacts from pottery, masks of faces, jewelry and items made of silver or copper, most engraved. All I could think of was how exciting it would have been to come across one of these gems on a dig. Maybe a new line of work for me?

We shared a farewell dinner at the museum's lush outdoor garden restaurant with lanterns hanging from vertical ladders suspended about twelve feet from the floor. I had the Solterito Salad made of corn, olives, rocoto peppers, onions, tomatoes and fresh cheese in olive oil and lime juice that tasted light and yummy. The main course was Lomo Saltado, or beef tenderloin strips, stir-fried onions, peppers and tomatoes with fried potatoes, finishing with Lucuma Mousse, a fruity mousse. But I just ate a few bites of each thing. I wasn't risking anything.

Mark selected the fish of the day, a grilled white fish with sautéed vegetables and mashed potatoes. He wasn't too hungry so skipped dessert and I thought uh oh, since this was totally unlike him.

Outside meandering around the expansive grounds, we walked through meticulously groomed flowerbeds that lined the cobblestones where there were dozens of different kinds of tall flowering plants and flowers such as sweet-smelling orchids of various colors and types. Bougainvillea slid down the wall, bromeliads were everywhere, as were crimson tropical Heliconias, sort of like Bird of Paradise, and sweet little purple flowers that looked like mini-petunias but weren't. Then there were five dramatic palms silhouetted against the scarlet sunset. I stood under a gigantic fern, about the size of a tree, looking up to see the darkening sky through its gaps. Vines flowed down and created a floral hedge and the gentle breeze causing a slight movement of the flora. I never had such a wordless appreciation for something as simple as flowers—maybe paradise might be similar to this.

We re-boarded the bus, said thank you and farewell to Holber, and returned to the airport for our late-night, five-and-a-half-hour flight from Lima to Miami. As I watched a movie and read a book, my husband felt a bit queasy and slept on this leg of the trip.

From Miami to Dallas/Fort Worth I had been assigned the middle seat with him at the window and somebody else had the aisle. Feeling a little warm as with a temperature, and at six-foot two inches tall, he thought it would be best if he had easier access to the aisle so took the middle seat. Then the man assigned to the aisle seat flopped down and within ten minutes of taking off ripped open a crackling cellophane bag and began stuffing himself and chewing, smacking loudly with mouth gaping open, cramming in stinky nacho cheese-flavored Doritos on the long flight from Miami to Dallas/Fort Worth. The bag seemed bottomless. My husband had to step over the man repeatedly to go to the small airplane toilet, but the man never offered to move to the middle for easier access for my poor husband. Now I felt really bad; he had it, too. He started popping Imodium. It wasn't a highlight of our trip.

I was so glad to see our familiar Mt. Hood and the lineup of the Cascade mountain range with snow-covered Mt. Saint Helens, our famous volcano. We made it home with no emergency stops. My husband provided a sample to his doctor which confirmed he too had contracted the norovirus with different symptoms than mine, fortunately for him and me. This was his first experience with this bug. Episodes like this are part of life, and made the trip even more distinctive and certainly not perfect.

As I look at my photos, glossy postcards and the watercolor painting I purchased from Pablo Picasso of Cusco, nothing can really capture the sweeping majesty of the Sacred Valley and Machu Picchu. Terraces, gardens, temples, staircases, aqueducts, windows with ancient instruments that track the sun, all have a purpose.

Because of the unexpected illness, I was unable to purchase my usual souvenirs, normally waiting until the end of a trip to do so, and missed out on purchasing Christmas ornaments. I was thrilled when friends Greg and Linda explored this region two years later and brought me a hand-painted red gourd with poinsettias and a miniature wooden pan flute. She also found a woven yarn red ball with yellow dots around the top and bottom, with carefully embroidered green and yellow designs.

I am completely flummoxed as to how the Incas built structures and terraces without using a crane, electricity and modern-day assistance. And where did they go? My guess is they were abducted after aliens helped them set up this haven. Since the outer space visitors were able to foresee the future, they knew the Spanish would kill off the Incas, so took them from this world because the Incas were brilliant and much more advanced than other humans around the world. They even might be the same aliens that constructed Stonehenge in England.

Trip Tips:

Don't forget to study up on the country you are visiting. There are many inventors and artists who had their start in Peru. You may wish to use this information when striking up a conversation with a local.

-Pedro Paulet designed, built and tested the first liquid fuel rocket engine.

-NASA astronauts regularly take freeze-dried food with them on their explorations but the process wasn't hatched in a lab. The Incas developed it in the highest altitudes of the Andes where freezing temperatures are pretty much guaranteed at night. The Incas worked this to their advantage by bringing potatoes to these chilly regions and letting them freeze beneath a cloth, then would walk on the cloths in the morning to squeeze out the moisture. This repeated process would result in freeze-dried potatoes known as chuño.

-Musical instruments were developed in Peru long before the Spanish arrived. Many are wind and percussion, including a type of pan pipe made of five or more bamboo pipes notched together, charangos or small guitars with bodies commonly made from armadillo shells, and harps and drums. Another instrument is the cajon, a wooden box with a round hole in the front. Players slap the front face as you would a drum.

-Environmentalists invented a response to the pollution in Lima by erecting a five-meter high metal structure that works like a tree to remove pollutants and carbon dioxide from the air. The environmental impact of the mining in the Amazon rainforest is a modern-day problem for Peru.

-Peruvian engineer Villachica invented a simple machine to isolate gold from sand without using dangerous toxic mercury. The small machine uses water and biodegradable chemicals to isolate the gold.

-Paolo Guerrero, Claudio Pizarro, Nolberto Solano, and Juan Manuel Vargas, all football (soccer to us) players.

-Gabriela (Gaby) Pérez del Solar is a retired Olympic volleyball player, then was elected to congress.

-Cecilia Tait is a retired Olympic volleyball player, then was elected to congress.

-Henry Ivan Cusick, actor, played on the TV series "Lost," "24," "Scandal," and the movie "Hitman."

-Pastuso/Paddington Bear arrived in London from his home in darkest Peru. Pastuso's story is that he was sent to London from Peru by his Aunt Lucy who could no longer look after him as she had to live in a Home for Retired Bears in Lima. The Brown family found him at Paddington railway station, and because his Peruvian name was too difficult to pronounce, they named him after the train station where they found him. Paddington Bear is based on the Spectacled Bear that, according to the famous story in *Deepest Darkest Peru*, came more specifically from the northern part of the country, close to the border with Ecuador.

-The Peanut was thought to originate from the foothills of the Andes. Anthropologists have found evidence of peanut cultivation here dating back at least seven thousand years. Once the Spanish invaders discovered it in the 1500s, it quickly spread in popularity across the world. Now I wondered if this is how Spanish peanuts got named, taking credit for Peruvian peanuts.

-Kings of Quinoa (Kin-wa), an Andean plant and staple food across the country, has become a fashionable superfood due to its immense health benefits: protein, fiber, iron, copper, thiamine, vitamin B6, magnesium, phosphorus, manganese and folate. Good grief, we should be eating this by the gallon. We saw it everywhere on eggs, in salads, pancakes and soups.

Some words that might help:

Hola/Buenos Días	Hello/GoodMorning
Buenos tardes, noches	Good afternoon /Good evening
Hablo usted ingles?	Do you speak English?
No hablo español	I do not speak Spanish
Cómo estás?	How are you?
Bueno	Good
Por favor	Please
Gracias	Thank you
Hola, dónde está el baño?	Where is the restroom?
Agua	Water
Café	Coffee
Postre	Dessert
Helado	Ice cream
Pastel	Cake

Don't forget items in your carry-on for your long flight like earplugs or noise cancelling headphones, inflatable pillow, a shawl or large scarf that works well as a blanket or to block out light, eye mask, sanitizing wipes, compression socks, sleep aids, food and water, pen, paper and notepad or journal, chewing gum and one set of extra clothing. And don't forget your prescription medications.

Don't take a photo of someone unless you ask first. Have some coins handy to thank them.

Don't be disrespectful. Address locals as Señora (Mrs.) or Señorita (Miss) or Señor (Mr.) Use your

Spanish-speaking skills; people will be impressed. And they all know some English.

Don't worry if a Peruvian gets too close. For the most part, people will greet each other on arrival and departure. It is common to shake hands when you greet someone. Personal space can have different boundaries than ours. This means when you are speaking with locals they might lean in closer or stand rather close to you, and when they do it can feel a bit weird. Try to go with the flow because they might feel offended if you move away from them. If you are confused, observe and let them take the lead.

Don't ask them to repeat themselves if you don't understand them. And don't speak slowly or loudly when talking with them, they are not deaf.

Don't be paranoid, just be friendly. Occasionally foreigners that refuse to make friendly eye contact and say a greeting can be perceived as scared. This highlights the fact that they are not from here and are out of their element. This can potentially put a target on them for theft.

Don't use the wrong hand gestures. Don't beckon someone with a single finger and a fist. Using your fist and moving one finger is considered a rude gesture. Instead, place your open hand in front of you with your palm down and make a sweeping gesture down towards yourself. Before going anywhere in the world, go online and check out hand gestures used in different countries.

Don't be grossed out by the cute Cuy, Guinea Pig. Our childhood pet for some but not me, is a delicacy and it is served in a number of unique ways. I avoided it but many don't. It is reportedly similar to chicken. Eat well in Peru and try the Inca Kola. One friend said it tastes as if bubblegum and Sprite had a baby. I still think of it as carbonated Nyquil. Do try the local foods; it's part of your journey of experiencing other cultures. Don't burp or wipe your nose at the dinner table; excuse yourself.

Don't forget your passport and make a copy to put somewhere else in your luggage or give to your travel companion. Make a copy to leave at home with a trusted friend, relative or travel agent.

Don't avoid people, be polite and greet everyone with a hello. Always say "please" and "thank you" as Peruvians are polite. If you bump into someone, say "sorry." Try saying these in Spanish.

Don't avoid trying to say some words in Spanish even though they speak English. Get a list of commonly used words and practice before you go so you don't say them incorrectly. Review on YouTube.

Don't ever snap your fingers or wave your hand at a waiter in a restaurant.

Don't forget to take some postcards from home to write thank you notes for staff, tour guides or bus drivers, or anyone else you'd like to show your appreciation. If you've made it, even better. Are you a writer or an artist? Taking something personal is even more meaningful.

Don't forget that the metric system is used almost everywhere in the world, so weight and volume are calculated in metric. A kilogram is 2.2 pounds and one liter is about a quart. Temperatures are generally given in Celsius. Twenty-eight Celsius is a perfect eighty-two degrees to us.

Don't wear revealing clothes. Peru is a modest country, religious beliefs and traditions mean that people mostly cover their bodies when they are out and about in public. Not only is dressing conservatively respectful, it will help you avoid attracting unwanted attention and make you blend in so you are not targeted by scams aimed at gullible tourists.

Don't freak out about the coca leaves. Yes, these leaves are used to make an illegal drug, but you do not have to think that you're a drug dealer if you drink coca tea. This magic leaf is used in teas, candies and gums to help people adjust to altitude sickness.

Don't even think about bringing home any coca leaves. You might have some explaining to do with the customs agents and their drug-sniffing dogs.

Don't think Peru is just about Machu Picchu. This country has a ton of sights to see and one could easily spend a month exploring.

Don't throw toilet paper down the toilet. The systems are outdated and downright old and the pipes can't handle the paper, so you place paper and other products into the trash bin next to the toilet. This is extremely common in most countries.

Don't be afraid to haggle in the markets. Price tags are not always on products. So it is OK to haggle for a better price except in the cities at traditional stores. However, this is not my philosophy. If I think it's a good value and I appreciate and love the item, I pay the cost and sometimes round it up. If something was 9/S, I would leave ten. It's just my way of trying to be a nice American, never dubbed an ugly American.

Don't forget to have cash. Cash is still king in many countries. Credit cards are accepted at tourist destinations, restaurants, and stores, but if you are out and about and seeing sights and meeting locals, cash is still the preferred method of payment. And you'll need small bills and change for tipping guides or porters as well as grabbing a snack on the side of the road.

Some things I would add to my sparse packing list are: Water purifications tablets, hydration mix packets for water, remembering the water in Peru is not safe to drink and you should only drink bottled water. If hiking, bring water purification tablets or a pump. Don't mess with your health as many sights are at high elevations and sunburn and altitude sickness affect a large number of travelers. Bring your own strong sunblock and when you visit places like Cusco, make sure you take extra time to adjust to the high altitude or else you may end up with headaches, shortness of breath, or nausea, all part of altitude sickness.

A 10% tip suffices in most restaurants unless the service is exceptional. Porters in hotels and airports expect S/2 per bag. There is no need to tip taxi drivers, although people round up the fare. At bars, the tip is S/1 per drink. Tour guides should get S/20 and bus drivers S/10 each.

Before visiting, please purchase a vocabulary guide. And please, please, please buy a well-respected travel authority's book or two and read every word.

"Travel opens your eyes and your heart."
Deleen Wills